Maximizing Tableau Server

A beginner's guide to accessing, sharing, and managing content on Tableau Server

Patrick Sarsfield

Brandi Locker

BIRMINGHAM—MUMBAI

Maximizing Tableau Server

Publishing Product Manager: Sunith Shetty
Senior Editor: Mohammed Yusuf Imaratwale
Content Development Editor: Nazia Shaikh
Technical Editor: Devanshi Ayare
Copy Editor: Safis Editing
Project Coordinator: Aparna Ravikumar Nair
Proofreader: Safis Editing
Indexer: Subalakshmi Govindhan
Production Designer: Shyam Sundar Korumilli

First published: October 2021

Production reference: 1240921

Published by Packt Publishing Ltd.
Livery Place
35 Livery Street
Birmingham
B3 2PB, UK.

ISBN 978-1-80107-113-0

www.packt.com

Foreword

I was working as an unemployment insurance law trainer. Although known as the *tech guy* in the office, I worked primarily with Excel until Tableau was introduced as a demo at a conference in 2014. It was mind-blowing, the ways you can work with extensive data and create visuals and reports in neat dashboards; but sometimes moments take hold, and it's the beginning of a life-altering event. So, I knew I had to get my hands on Tableau.

I did get access to the tool, but only as a web author via our server without access to Tableau Desktop. Tableau Server now is so robust with extensive AI tools like Ask and Explain Data (much enhanced for users of 2021.2 Server versions and later), powerful web authoring functionality, and so much more. Back in 2014, there was none of that, and web authoring was only suitable for making basic charts and crosstabs. It didn't matter; it offered so many possibilities and was easy enough to pick up without a ton of assistance.

Since that introduction, my career changed almost as extensively as the Tableau Server environment. I used Tableau over the next couple of years. I became a data analyst in 2017, responsible for delivering visualizations and metrics to hundreds of people, working on both the Tableau Desktop and Server environments. In 2021, my career transformed to leave an employer after 22 years and work as a Tableau Evangelist for Keyrus US (a Tableau Gold Partner).

I knew those resources were very limited to assist those learning Tableau Server. Fortunately, I grew up with it, so the enhancements came as quarterly morsels of goodness, raising the excitement for each release. However, if you are new to Tableau Server or even Tableau, it must be overwhelming.

Where to start?

Where to access resources?

Maximizing Tableau Server, written by experienced and proven Tableau practitioners, is a must-have for any employer looking to help onboard staff because there are few resources and no free sandbox server accessible to the general public. The purpose is not to give an extensive coding lesson to Tableau Server Administrators but as an essential asset to those that want to know where to start, where to go, and how to extend it and their capabilities. It's in plain language with abundant context suitable for anyone.

Acknowledgements

Thank you to our families. We would not have made it this far without your continued love and support.

We are immensely grateful to **Adam Mico** for taking the time to write a thoughtful foreword to this book.

A very special thank you to **Mark Bradbourne**, **Chimdi Nwosu**, and **Luther Flagstad** for allowing us to feature your incredible **#RWFD (Real World Fake Data)** dashboards as examples throughout the book. Thank you, Mark, for your work in creating and hosting the #RWFD initiative.

Thank you, too, **Kevin Flerlage** and **Autumn Battani** for allowing us to highlight your Tableau Public profiles at the end of our book. Also, thanks to Andrew Pick for allowing us to reference your work on –– *Tableau Desktop vs Tableau Web Editor*.

A massive thank you to **Scott Love**, **Chantilly Jaggernauth**, and everyone at **Lovelytics** for their help, support, and enabling us to utilize a demo Tableau Server site for many of the images in this book.

Thank you to our co-workers and friends at Allstate Insurance, particularly **Shawn Hester**, **Ryan Broussard, Kyle Lanigan, Eric Gallo, Ryan Thompson, Lisa Nilsen Neary, Scott Dickinson**, and **Manoj Panchagnula** for helping to support our Tableau development.

To our friendly neighborhood Tableau consultant, **Ahson Jalali**, thank you for the excellent training, for the continued encouragement, and for laughing at our jokes more than we deserve.

To our friends in the **North Texas Tableau User Group**, **Joey Ramos** and **Tim Cady**, thank you for welcoming and supporting us.

We would like to thank the **Tableau Community** for fostering such a positive and supportive environment of sharing, creativity, collaboration, help, and encouragement. The dedication of community members to welcome others and continuously grow together make this such a unique and genuine experience. Thank you to all who host Tableau User Groups or webinars, write blogs, facilitate data initiatives, create videos, and share your work on Tableau Public. Your work is so valuable and does not go unnoticed.

Thank you to the kind team at **Packt** who patiently walked us through each step of the writing process and who made this book possible.

Lastly, thank you, **Rick Lamond**, for being the best boss, mentor, and friend we could ask for. We appreciate all the support and encouragement, while keeping us laughing the whole time.

About the reviewer

Ashwin Govindaraj is a data visualization designer who works to provide coherent reporting and analytic solutions to organizational challenges. He has worked in roles such as business intelligence developer, data analyst, and web analyst at Citi, Nationwide, University of Arizona, and Cognizant. Ashwin enjoys using Tableau to experiment with data, artistic styles, and colors. He was introduced to Tableau in 2015 and has worked with marketing analytics and banking teams to transform their reporting systems. His approach to reporting is to provide insights that are easy to understand and stand out. Some of his hobbies are traveling, watching sports, reading, running, and designing.

Table of Contents

Section 2: Navigating and Customizing the Tableau Server Interface

3

The Tableau Server Navigation Pane

4

Tableau Server Top Toolbar

5

Filtering and Sorting Content

Section 3: Managing Content on Tableau Server

6

Navigating Content Pages in Tableau Server

7

What is in the More Actions (...) Menu

8

Interacting with Views on Tableau Server

Section 4: Final Thoughts

9

Tableau Server Best Practices

10

Conclusion

Other Books You May Enjoy

Index

Preface

Tableau Server provides a centralized location to store, edit, share, and collaborate on content such as dashboards and curated data sources. This book gets you up and running with Tableau Server to help you increase end user engagement for your published work, as well as reducing or eliminating redundant tasks.

You'll explore Tableau Server's structure and understand how to get started by connecting, publishing content, and navigating the software interface. Next, you'll learn when and how to update the settings of your content at various levels to best utilize Tableau Server's features. You'll explore how to interact with the Tableau Server interface to efficiently locate, sort, filter, manage, and customize content. After that, the book shows you how to leverage other valuable features that enable you and your audience to share, download, and interact with content on Tableau Server. As you progress, you'll discover ways to increase the performance of your published content. All along, the book shows you how to navigate, interact with, and best utilize Tableau Server with the help of engaging examples and best practices shared by recognized Tableau professionals.

By the end of this Tableau book, you'll have a comprehensive understanding of how to use Tableau Server to manage content, automate tasks, and increase end user engagement.

Who this book is for

This book is for BI developers, data analysts, and everyday users who have access to Tableau Server and possess basic web navigation skills. No prior experience with Tableau Server is required.

What this book covers

Chapter 1, What is Tableau Server?, introduces Tableau Server, Tableau Online, and Tableau Public, with a focus on the Server version. You will learn about each available platform and the license and role types used to access the platform. You will gain a broad understanding of the tools at your disposal and how these tools are maintained by your organization.

Chapter 2, How to Connect and Publish to Tableau Server, teaches you how to get connected to Tableau Server so that you will be able to publish your own content and interact with your company's content. You will also learn how to connect and publish to Tableau Public so that you can learn from the Tableau community and enhance your skills.

Chapter 3, Tableau Server Navigation Pane, teaches you how to navigate the Tableau Server sidebar options and the uses for each option. This toolbar is a main feature of Tableau Server navigation that is always available, regardless of what you are viewing in the main server window. Proper utilization of these available options will increase your efficiency in navigating Tableau Server.

Chapter 4, Tableau Server Top Toolbar, teaches you how to utilize the features available in the top toolbar, including searching for content on the server, accessing Tableau Help, reviewing notifications and troubleshooting, and changing your view and account settings. Understanding how to use the top toolbar enhances your experience with Tableau Server and helps identify crucial notifications to manage your content.

Chapter 5, Filtering and Sorting Content, teaches you how to search, sort, and filter through available content by utilizing the content toolbar. This is useful when you have a large volume of published content and need to locate specific information or a particular item. The available options will change based on the content type you are currently viewing.

Chapter 6, Navigating Content Pages in Tableau Server, teaches you how to locate and interpret additional details for workbooks, data sources, and metrics by exploring the information found within their individual content pages. Understanding where to find this information will help you manage content and troubleshoot common issues.

Chapter 7, What is in the More Actions (…) Menu, covers the more actions (…) menu on Tableau Server, which is a primary location to manage many of the important components of your published content. This is where you can set and review access privileges, view and edit data connection details, view and manage data extract refresh information, monitor usage of your content, and more.

Chapter 8, Interacting with Views on Tableau Server, teaches you how to customize various preferences for yourself and those using your published content. You can also use Tableau Server to increase customer utilization of your work by creating subscriptions for your audience. You will then learn how to leverage other valuable features that enable you and your audience to share, download, and interact with content on Tableau Server.

Chapter 9, Tableau Server Best Practices, teaches you about best practices when publishing content to the server, refreshing the data, and ways you can optimize the performance of your data and workbooks. Understanding these principles will help reduce the space used on the server, improve the refresh speed of your data, and increase the efficiency and performance of your published content. Following these guidelines will help you in discussions with your company's Tableau Server administrators and will help improve the user experience of those interacting with your published content.

Chapter 10, Conclusion, provides a brief recap/wrap-up of the principles learned throughout the book. It will encourage you to practice working with data and to develop a personal portfolio on Tableau Public. This chapter will also provide a brief overview of the Tableau Community and how to get involved. Doing so will enhance your analytic and technical skills and will serve you well by having a professional portfolio available and a network of Tableau professionals to provide help when needed, as well as encouragement, collaboration, and possibly even opening the door for future career opportunities. The chapter will end with suggested resources for furthering a developer or analyst's skills in Tableau and Tableau Server.

To get the most out of this book

You will need access to Tableau Server version 2020.1 or later. Examples in this book were provided using the 2021.1 and 2021.2 versions of Tableau Server. Depending on which version you have access to, your interface may vary slightly from the example images used throughout the book. These minor variations should not impact the concepts presented in this book.

Software/hardware covered in the book	Operating system requirements
Tableau Server 2021.1 and later	Chrome, Microsoft Edge, Mozilla Firefox and Firefox ESR, or Apple Safari

Because this book is written for developers and not for administrators, the installation and deployment of Tableau Server are not covered in this book. It is assumed that you have web access to an established Tableau Server environment.

While there are some references to Tableau Desktop features and concepts, particularly in *Chapter 9, Tableau Server Best Practices*, no prior knowledge of Tableau Desktop is required to apply the Tableau Server concepts presented in this book.

Download the color images

We also provide a PDF file that has color images of the screenshots and diagrams used in this book. You can download it here: `https://static.packt-cdn.com/downloads/9781801071130_ColorImages.pdf`.

Conventions used

There are a number of text conventions used throughout this book.

`Code in text`: Indicates code words in text, database table names, folder names, filenames, file extensions, pathnames, dummy URLs, user input, and Twitter handles. Here is an example: "These refer to a subset, or snapshot, of data that is stored in Tableau file format, that is, `.hyper` or `.tde`."

Bold: Indicates a new term, an important word, or words that you see onscreen. For instance, words in menus or dialog boxes appear in **bold**. Here is an example: "Click on the **Server** menu from the top menu bar in Tableau Desktop."

> **Tips or important notes**
> Appear like this.

Get in touch

Feedback from our readers is always welcome.

General feedback: If you have questions about any aspect of this book, email us at `customercare@packtpub.com` and mention the book title in the subject of your message.

Errata: Although we have taken every care to ensure the accuracy of our content, mistakes do happen. If you have found a mistake in this book, we would be grateful if you would report this to us. Please visit `www.packtpub.com/support/errata` and fill in the form.

Piracy: If you come across any illegal copies of our works in any form on the internet, we would be grateful if you would provide us with the location address or website name. Please contact us at copyright@packt.com with a link to the material.

If you are interested in becoming an author: If there is a topic that you have expertise in and you are interested in either writing or contributing to a book, please visit authors.packtpub.com.

Share Your Thoughts

Once you've read *Maximizing Tableau Server*, we'd love to hear your thoughts! Scan the QR code below to go straight to the Amazon review page for this book and share your feedback.

https://packt.link/r/1801071136

Your review is important to us and the tech community and will help us make sure we're delivering excellent quality content.

Section 1: Getting Started with Tableau Server

In this section, you will be introduced to Tableau Server and its structure, licenses, and permissions. You will gain an understanding of the difference between Tableau Public and Tableau Server, how to quickly get connected, and how to start publishing content.

This section comprises the following chapters:

- *Chapter 1, What is Tableau Server?*
- *Chapter 2, How to Connect and Publish to Tableau Server*

1
What is Tableau Server?

Tableau Server is part of the Tableau business intelligence platform that provides
a centralized location to store content, including dashboards, data sources, and much
more. It can be used as a collaboration tool for product development and as
a communication tool to distribute information to end users. It facilitates the interactive
exploration of shared data visualizations and connections and automates tasks so that
your content is up to date and convenient to access. In this context, **content** simply refers
to reports and data sources that have been published to Tableau Server.

After completing this chapter, you should have a keen understanding of the basic structure
of Tableau Server and how it interacts with other Tableau products. Additionally,
you will learn about the various Tableau Server licenses, site roles, and permissions that
are available and how they impact each other to dictate the user experience.

In this chapter, the following main topics will be covered:

- What is Tableau Server and why should I care?
- Examining Tableau's basic structure
- Understanding what a site is on Tableau Server
- Understanding licenses, site roles, and permissions

What is Tableau Server and why should I care?

Tableau Server is a web-based application that provides Tableau Desktop users with the ability to upload and store interactive dashboards and data sources within a centralized location. Once content has been published to Tableau Server, the owner has the ability to determine the individual users or groups who have access to it and to what extent. Content such as dashboards, worksheets, and stories can be easily shared by providing a hyperlink. This platform fosters and enhances collaboration, knowledge sharing, data exploration, and data communication.

This book has been written to benefit Tableau Server end users and content creators first and foremost. Learning how to navigate and leverage Tableau Server is the primary focus of this book. This book will help you to understand the tools that are used to drive the engagement and utilization of this amazing platform within your group or organization.

If you are reading this book, you might already be familiar with a Tableau product such as Tableau Desktop, Tableau Public, Tableau Prep, or one of the many other products the company offers. Conversely, you might have no experience with Tableau or any other data analytics or data visualization software at all and were just granted access. Whichever camp you fall into, this book can help you. Why? Well, this book is written for the majority of users: the people who create and publish content and the end users with whom this content is shared. It is not an expectation that the reader of this book is or plans to become a Tableau Server Administrator or possess the knowledge of a Tableau Zen Master.

This book is written for regular analysts and developers who just want to gain a better understanding of this product to increase their productivity, drive engagement, and increase the utilization of their data-driven products. The reasons for wanting to explore this topic can be multifaceted and varied: for self-growth, for the better dissemination of information, or to gain a competitive advantage. Whatever your goal with Tableau Server, this book will help.

Tableau Desktop is where data analysis and visualization take place. But then what? Next, you need to share this information with consumers. Historically, this has been done by sharing unsecured reports with static data in the form of a spreadsheet or slide. Tableau Server provides information to consumers via a more secure, interactive, and automatable process to accomplish a task.

There are several major benefits of Tableau Server, including the following:

- *Automation*: Instead of using a static report that needs to be updated every week, month, or quarter, you can connect to a report that has a live connection to your data or that updates at scheduled intervals selected by the creator of the report or Tableau Administrator.

- *Customization*: You can tweak an existing piece of content to your own specifications (for example, you can filter a report you use by default to only show a particular region when you log on) or edit a piece of content right on the server using the Web Edit feature.

- *Data security*: When your company hosts its own server, it allows itself to set up and alter the specifications based on the data privacy policies determined by your organization.

- *Organization*: You can have all of your data stored within a single location. This can help you to create a single source of truth for your data and reporting.

- *Subscriptions*: You can send an automated email to be delivered to selected users or groups who are interested in receiving a report. You even can schedule when the email is delivered so that it is sent after an extract refresh occurs to ensure email recipients are only being notified when a report contains the most recent data.

After completing this chapter, you should have a broader understanding of Tableau Server and how it relates to other Tableau products. You will also have a clear understanding of the different licenses, site roles, and permissions available and how they interact with one another. Let's begin by looking at Tableau's basic structure and where Tableau Server falls within it.

Examining Tableau's basic structure

The Tableau platform has a multitude of products and features to choose from to help you and your organization best utilize data to make informed decisions. These products can be integrated for an optimal experience and are flexible enough to adapt to your organization's needs. Because each product can be customized and utilized in so many ways, no two Tableau Server environments are exactly the same. Every organization has its own practices regarding data collection, storage, management, and access. Likewise, every organization will deploy the use of Tableau products and services to fit their data needs and culture. No matter the differences, there are some basic processes that apply to all who use Tableau Desktop and Tableau Server. This process is illustrated in *Figure 1.1*:

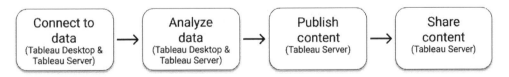

Figure 1.1 – The process of developing and sharing analytic insights with Tableau

In this section, we will examine each of these steps and the application of their corresponding Tableau products. Let's begin by gaining an understanding of data sources.

Data sources

Before any analysis takes place, first, you must connect to your data. You can do this from Tableau Desktop by connecting directly to your database or by connecting to a published data source on Tableau Server. The various types of Tableau data connections include the following:

- **Data extracts**: These refer to a subset, or snapshot, of data that is stored in Tableau file format, that is, `.hyper` or `.tde`. (Note that you will only encounter a `.tde` file format if you use a version of Tableau Desktop prior to 10.5.) These files are optimized for performance within Tableau. Extracts can be embedded in a workbook when publishing to Tableau Server and can be scheduled to refresh on a regular basis so that the data stays up to date.

- **Live connections**: These allow you to query the database to update with real-time data. Every action performed in Tableau Desktop or Web Edit from Tableau Server initiates a query to the database.

> **Tip**
>
> While "real-time" data might sound ideal, in reality, your data source is rarely optimized to provide real-time performance. In fact, if the underlying data tables that you are connected to only update once a day, then real-time queries with a live connection from Tableau will not provide any new data until that initial data table has been updated. In this case, it would be best to use an extract. Likewise, if you have a slow live connection, you will benefit from creating an extract.

- **Published data sources**: These refer to a data source that has already been established using either a live connection or a data extract and then published to Tableau Server. Once on the server, a single published data source can be used by multiple workbooks to provide consistency, reliability, and efficiency.

You might find that the raw data available to you is not formatted in an optimal way nor is it clean enough to perform an accurate analysis. For example, there might be inconsistencies with the spelling or number formatting. When this occurs, your data should be cleaned before you begin your analysis using tools such as Tableau Prep or Alteryx. Once you have cleaned and prepared the data, you can establish a data connection in Tableau Desktop using one of the methods described earlier.

Tableau Desktop

Once you have established your data connection, you are ready to begin analyzing the data. This is where Tableau Desktop comes in. Tableau Desktop is a tool that allows users to explore and visualize their data for analysis, operational reporting, and more. *Figure 1.2* shows the Tableau Desktop interface when it is connected to the included *Sample – Superstore* dataset that comes with Tableau:

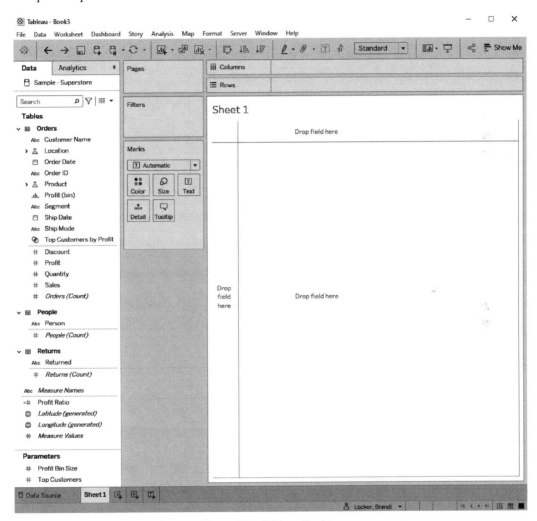

Figure 1.2 – Tableau Desktop

Using this interface, analysts using Tableau can create reports and data visualizations, known as dashboards, to share with others. An example of a dashboard is shown in *Figure 1.3*:

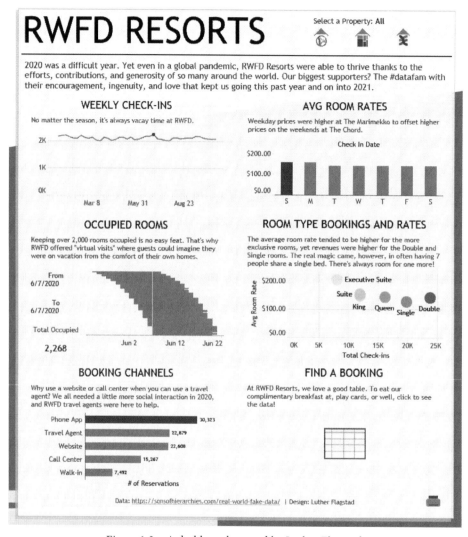

Figure 1.3 – A dashboard created by Luther Flagstad

Throughout this book, there are examples of dashboards created by individuals within the Tableau community. These examples highlight some of the community initiatives and resources that are available to anyone wishing to develop their data analysis and visualization skills further. You can learn more about the Tableau community by visiting `https://www.tableau.com/community`. We will also discuss these resources in more detail in *Chapter 10, Conclusion*.

> **Tip**
> To find inspiration and discover what Tableau can do, you can visit
> `https://public.tableau.com` and browse the gallery to see the
> **Viz of the Day**. Additionally, you can use the search feature to search for
> "superstore." This will allow you to browse Tableau Public to view some of
> the amazing data visualizations created by individuals within the Tableau
> community using the *Sample – Superstore* dataset.

There are a few terms used within this book that are commonly used on the Tableau
platform that you need to be familiar with. Some of these are as follows:

- **Worksheet**: This refers to a single page within Tableau Desktop where
  a visualization (such as a chart, graph, or table) is created.

- **Dashboard**: This refers to a collection of worksheets containing charts, graphs,
  or tables that are arranged in a single view.

- **Story**: This refers to a sequence of worksheets or dashboards that are arranged to
  explain an analysis or to tell an informative story.

- **Workbook**: This is a Tableau file containing worksheets, dashboards, and stories.
  Files can be saved as a `.twb` or `.twbx`:

  - `.twb`: This is the default Tableau Desktop file type. The data source will not be
    embedded (available to other users who are sent a copy of the file).

  - `.twbx`: This is a packaged workbook that has the data embedded within the file.
    This file type can easily be shared with others since they will be able to view and
    interact with the included data.

- **View**: This is normally used in a more general context as something that is *viewed*
  on the screen, such as a worksheet, dashboard, story, or metric.

Once your analysis is complete, these data creations can be shared with others within your
organization using Tableau Server.

Tableau Server

As outlined in the previous section, Tableau Server provides a place to store and share
data visualizations created in Tableau Desktop. It can be used as a communication tool
to provide users with up-to-date information and alerts. There is also a feature known
as Web Edit that allows you to make changes to the content on the server from your web
browser. Your capabilities within the Web Edit feature will depend on your permissions.

You might encounter similar Tableau products that allow you to share data visualizations, such as Tableau Online and Tableau Public. Here is a quick overview of the Tableau products that enable you to publish and share your content:

- **Tableau Server**: This is a self-governed and self-hosted server that gives an organization full control and responsibility for managing its content and processes.

- **Tableau Online**: This provides the same functionality as Tableau Server but is fully hosted by Tableau for a hassle-free experience.

- **Tableau Public**: This is a free, public server that allows individuals within the Tableau community to practice and develop their data visualization skills and share that information with the world. Tableau Public can also be an excellent resource for non-profit organizations.

The purpose of this book is to examine the Tableau Server experience, but most of the principles learned here will also apply to Tableau Online. Tableau Public is a unique service that is simpler, free to use, and available to anyone. We will discuss how to connect and publish content to Tableau Server and Tableau Public in the next chapter, *Chapter 2, How to Connect and Publish to Tableau Server*.

Once content has been published to Tableau Server, it is ready to be shared with the end users.

End users

The end users are those users who use the data to make business decisions. This can include analysts, front-line management, business executives, and everyone in between. They require access to the insights provided by the data products. When a dashboard is created and published to Tableau Server, it is the end user who views the dashboard and determines what to do with the information and how it can impact the organization.

As an analyst, developer, or business partner, you can share content on Tableau Server with other users by sharing a URL or using the **Share** feature discussed in *Chapter 8, Interacting with Views on Tableau Server*. Throughout this book, you will learn how to best utilize Tableau Server in a way that optimizes your own efficiency and maximizes the value of your organization's server content for the business. End users can access the data through a web browser using their computer, tablet, or smartphone. Tableau Server is flexible enough to facilitate these needs and can be optimized for a variety of viewing methods.

So, you now have a basic understanding of the structure of the Tableau platform and how various content creators, and users interact with each component. The varying needs of these users will impact the way the server is used and managed. Understanding how other users interact with the server will help you to find ways to improve the end user experience and drive engagement with the content available on the server.

In the next section, we will review licenses, site roles, and permissions along with the impact they each have on the user experience.

Understanding what a site is on Tableau Server

To begin, what is a **site** on Tableau Server? Is it like a "website?" Nope. When it comes to Tableau, a site refers to a grouping of content and users that are blocked from other content and users using that same Tableau Server. Put simply, your company can have many sites on its Tableau Server, but you might only have access to a limited number of them. This is because Tableau Server has a multitenant software architecture. This just means that a single instance of software (Tableau Server) can support multiple tenants (sites) on a server. Ultimately, this means that the content you publish to one site is separated from the content on other sites within the same instance of Tableau Server.

> **Note**
>
> The content on Tableau Server is accessed, managed, and published at the site level. In addition to this, every site on Tableau Server receives its own web address (or URL).

In this brief section, you learned what a site is on Tableau Server. Having a solid understanding of what a site is will be useful in later sections of this chapter. Next, we'll get a broad overview of licenses, site roles, and permissions.

Understanding licenses, site roles, and permissions

The combination of all your permissions determines your capabilities on Tableau Server. Your license is the maximum level of permission, and every user on Tableau Server requires one. As a user, you receive a single site role for each site that you belong to. This site role restricts what you can do with the content. Finally, content permissions are the lowest level of permissions. These permissions are applied at an individual user or group level to different object types (such as a project, workbook, view, or data source) on a site, but they are constrained by your license and site role. This means that when changes are made to your content permissions, it is possible that they might not impact any of your existing capabilities if your license or site role already restricts them.

Figure 1.4 provides a high-level overview of the three levels of permissions in a descending hierarchy:

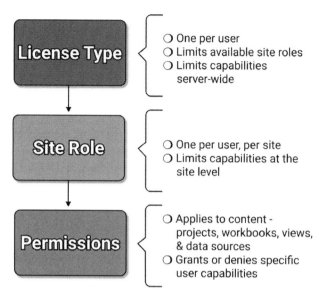

Figure 1.4 – An overview of the License, Site Role, and Permissions hierarchy

All users on Tableau Server require a **license**. As a user, you will receive a single license. Your license type is at the top of your capability's hierarchy, as it determines the limits of your abilities across the server, which, in turn, determines the limits of your capabilities on every site within that server. Put simply, the license you are assigned represents the *maximum* number of site role capabilities you can have on that server. There are three license types: **Creator**, **Explorer**, and **Viewer**. In the next section, we will go over each of these licenses in detail.

For each site that you belong to as a user, you will have a single **site role**. Your site role is restricted by your license type. This just means that the license you receive will place constraints on your capabilities at a site level. You can't have any capabilities at a site level that exceed the abilities provided by your license. There are eight types of site roles: **Server Administrator**, **Site Administrator Creator**, **Site Administrator Explorer**, **Creator**, **Explorer (can publish)**, **Explorer**, **Viewer**, and **Unlicensed**. We will go over each of these site roles, in detail, later in this chapter. Just remember that your site role will limit your capabilities at a site level.

You have **permissions** to the content (such as projects, workbooks, views, or data sources) on a site that is restricted by what your site role allows. The permission rules assigned to you as a user, or to a group that you are a part of, determine your capabilities in terms of what you can do with a piece of content.

> **Note**
>
> It is important to remember that licenses and site roles apply to users, whereas permissions apply to content.

We understand that this can be a little abstract and confusing to follow at first. Don't worry. We'll go over licenses, site roles, and permissions separately, and in greater detail, before we tie everything back together at the end of the chapter.

License types

In the previous section, we briefly touched on license types. As a reminder, licenses apply to users, not content. You will receive a single license on a server, regardless of how many sites exist on that server. The license you are assigned represents the maximum site role level a user can have on that server.

Figure 1.5 provides an example of the dynamics of each license type:

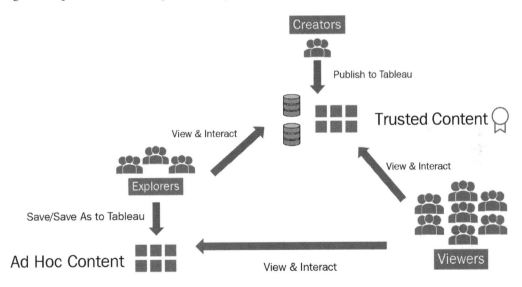

Figure 1.5 – An overview of the license types

Next, we'll review each of the three Tableau Server license types from the highest level of access to the lowest level of access:

Creator license: This is the highest license type available and is intended for people who make content. Making content includes everything from designing dashboards to developing data sources. As the name of the license suggests, individuals who receive this license will be responsible for the creation of most of the data sources and any other content utilized by your organization.

Explorer license: This license type is primarily intended for people who analyze content. Individuals who receive this license are able to access and examine content published to Tableau Server. Users with an Explorer license are likely to be accustomed to working with data and developing ad hoc reports to ask and answer questions.

As a user with an Explorer license, you *can* create, manage, and share your new workbooks and dashboards using data sources published to Tableau Server. Additionally, you can edit existing dashboards or make your visualizations via the Web Edit feature on Tableau Server using data sources created by other users for which you have been granted access. From a Tableau Server perspective, the only difference between an Explorer license and a Creator license is that with an Explorer license, you *cannot* create data sources.

Viewer license: This license type is primarily intended for individuals who want to view and interact with published content. Users with this license have the ability to interact and engage with dashboards and workbooks but not create them. In addition to this, users with a Viewer license can subscribe to dashboards to receive regular updates and set data-driven alerts.

Figure 1.6 provides a breakdown of the capabilities of each license type:

PERMISSIONS/ CAPABILITIES	LICENSE		
	CREATOR	EXPLORER	VIEWER
View	✔	✔	✔
Download image/PDF	✔	✔	✔
Download summary data	✔	✔	✔
View comments	✔	✔	✔
Add comments	✔	✔	✔
Subscriptions and alerts	✔	✔	✔
Filter	✔	✔	
Download full data	✔	✔	
Share customised	✔	✔	
Web edit	✔	✔	
Overwrite	✔	✔	
Download a copy	✔	✔	
Move	✔	✔	
Delete	✔	✔	
Set permissions	✔	✔	
Publish views	✔	✔	
Download data source	✔	✔	
Connect data source	✔	✔	
Download flow	✔	✔	
Run flow	✔	✔	
Create data sources	✔		

Figure 1.6 – Tableau license capabilities

> **Tip**
>
> Your license is at the top of the permissions hierarchy in Tableau Server, so make sure that the license you receive provides you with the permissions you will need. It's likely that your company has a limited number of Tableau licenses, so talk to your manager or Tableau Server Administrator if you believe that you should have a different one.

Site roles

Earlier in this chapter, we briefly discussed site roles. As a reminder, site roles apply to users, not content. You will have a single site role for each site to which you are a member, and your site role will be restricted based on the type of license you are assigned by your Server Administrator.

Let's review each of the eight Tableau Server site roles from the highest level of access to the lowest level of access:

- **Server Administrator**: This is the highest site role available and uses a Creator license. It allows complete access to Tableau Server, including access to all content. Server Administrators can add users and set their site roles. They have the ability to create projects and set permissions for all users. They also have full editing and saving rights to all workbooks. Additionally, they can create sites, add users to those sites, and assign Site Administrator site roles to users.

- **Site Administrator Creator**: This site role is assigned by a Server Administrator to a user with a Creator license to help delegate creating and managing the user and content framework of an individual site. These users can add server users to their site. Within their site, they can create groups, projects, assign permissions, schedule extract refreshes, and have full editing and saving rights to all workbooks on their site. Finally, this site role *can* also publish content to the server.

- **Site Administrator Explorer**: This site role is assigned by a Server Administrator to a user with an Explorer license to help delegate creating and managing the user and content framework of an individual site. These users can add server users to their site. Within their site, they can create groups, projects, assign permissions, schedule extract refreshes, and have full editing and saving rights to all workbooks on their site. Unlike the Site Administrator Creator site role, this site role *cannot* publish content to the server.

- **Creator**: This site role is assigned to users with a Creator license. The default permissions for these users *can* publish content to Tableau Server and edit, download, and save content on the server. These abilities represent the maximum level of access for Creators' permissions and can be changed by a Site Administrator.

- **Explorer (can publish)**: Users with this site role possess, at the very least, an Explorer license. The default permissions for these users allow them to save changes made to content via the Web Edit feature; however, they *cannot* publish new data sources to Tableau Server from Web Edit. Again, these abilities can be restricted by a Site Administrator.

- **Explorer**: Users with this site role possess, at the very least, an Explorer license. This site role can open dashboards on Tableau Server using Web Edit. Users can analyze and explore the data by making edits and building new views; however, users *cannot* save these changes. Again, these abilities can be restricted by a Site Administrator.

- **Viewer**: Users with this site role possess, at the very least, a Viewer license. This site role allows users to view content in the format it was published. They can interact with dashboards, but they *cannot* access the Web Edit function.

- **Unlicensed**: Users with this site role *cannot* edit or view any content on Tableau Server. The purpose of the Unlicensed site role is largely for users who have left a company or changed departments. The user owns the content that they create and publish to a server. As a result, any content associated with a user will be removed when they are deleted from the server. This role type allows the accounts of ex-coworkers to still exist and for their content to continue to be accessed by other users.

In this section, you learned about site roles. We examined each available site role in detail. Next, we'll take a look at the different combinations of licenses and site roles that are available.

Take a look at the following link to view all license and site role combinations: `https://help.tableau.com/current/server/en-us/users_site_roles.htm#tableau-site-roles-as-of-version-20181`.

Figure 1.7 shows the capabilities of each license and site role combination:

Permissions / SITES ROLES	EXPLORER OR CREATOR — Server Administrator	CREATOR — Creator	CREATOR — Site Administrator Explorer	EXPLORER — Explorer	EXPLORER — Explorer (can publish)	EXPLORER — Site Administrator Explorer	VIEWER — Viewer
View	✔	✔	✔	✔	✔	✔	✔
Download image/PDF	✔	✔	✔	✔	✔	✔	✔
Download summary data	✔	✔	✔	✔	✔	✔	✔
View comments	✔	✔	✔	✔	✔	✔	✔
Add comments	✔	✔	✔	✔	✔	✔	✔
Subscriptions and alerts	✔	✔	✔	✔	✔	✔	✔
Filter	✔	✔	✔	✔	✔	✔	
Download full data	✔	✔	✔	✔	✔	✔	
Share customised	✔	✔	✔	✔	✔	✔	
Web edit	✔	✔	✔	✔	✔	✔	
Overwrite	✔	✔	✔	✔	✔	✔	
Download a copy	✔	✔	✔	✔	✔	✔	
Move	✔	✔	✔	✔	✔	✔	
Delete	✔	✔	✔	✔	✔	✔	
Set permissions	✔	✔	✔	✔	✔	✔	
Publish views	✔	✔	✔	✔	✔	✔	
Download data source	✔	✔	✔	✔	✔	✔	
Connect data source	✔	✔	✔	✔	✔	✔	
Download flow	✔	✔	✔	✔	✔	✔	
Run flow	✔	✔	✔	✔	✔	✔	
Create data sources	If on Creator license	✔	✔				
Manage site	✔		✔			✔	
Create site	✔						
Manage server	✔						

Figure 1.7 – License and site role capabilities

Permissions

Permissions determine how users can interact with content (such as projects, workbooks, views, and data sources). The capability to filter, utilize Web Edits, delete, and download full data is granted to users or groups on a specific piece of content.

To make applying permissions rules quicker and easier, Tableau Server provides the ability to select several predefined permission templates. You can select permission templates for **Administrator**, **Publish**, **Explore**, and **View**. An example of the permissions provided by these predefined templates is shown in *Figure 1.8*:

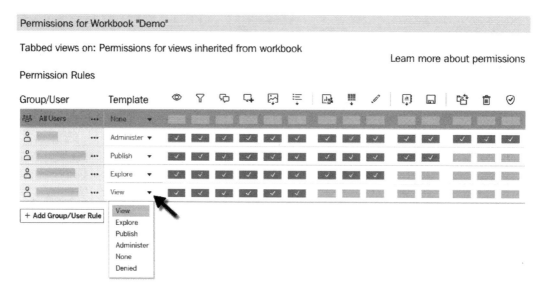

Figure 1.8 – Predefined permissions templates

Permission rules determine the capabilities that you as a user or group member are allowed or denied access to on a piece of content. The predefined permissions templates have set permission rules. If you make and save any changes to a predefined permission template, it will change into a "Custom" role. In addition, you can create your own "Custom" roles from scratch. This is because there is always the option to manually assign specific capabilities to users or groups instead of using one of the predefined options. You can accomplish this by selecting each capability you want to grant or deny an individual or group on the **Permission Rules** page. In *Chapter 7, What is in the More Actions (…) Menu*, we dedicate an entire section to reviewing the fundamentals of permission settings.

> **Tip**
>
> Whenever it is possible, we recommend that you set permissions at the project level and use groups when assigning permissions. Managing permissions rules at a project level is much easier than at the content level. Additionally, setting permissions to all users within a group is much quicker and more efficient than assigning them per user. Also, when new users receive access to Tableau, you can easily add them to the group(s) that provide them with the proper access.

Finally, it's helpful to understand that individual permissions rank higher than groups in the hierarchy of permissions. This means that it is more important to have a capability granted or denied at an individual user level than at a group level. Finally, a user can be a member of many groups. If a user is a member of two or more groups being granted permissions on a piece of content and any of those groups are denied a capability, this user will be denied that capability.

In this section, you learned about permissions. We touched on predefined permissions, manually assigned permissions, and the dynamics of individual versus group permissions. Next, let's take a look at how licenses, site roles, and permissions tie together.

How licenses, site roles, and permissions tie together

To recap what we've discussed regarding licenses, site roles, and permissions, let's organize what we've learned in a hierarchy from the highest user capabilities to the lowest user capabilities:

1. **User license**: Your license type is at the top of the hierarchy when determining your capabilities across the entire server.

2. **Site role**: Your site role is below your license in the user capabilities hierarchy. You receive one site role per site. The site role that you receive will be restricted by your license type.

3. **Content owner/project leader**: Owning a piece of content or project is next in the hierarchy below the license and role type. You become a **Content Owner** by publishing a piece of content to the server, having ownership transferred to you, or by being assigned a content owner role by a Server Administrator, Site Administrator, or Project Owner. As a content owner, you have full access to the content you publish to the server. If the Project Owner allows for content permissions to be customizable, then a content owner will have the ability to modify content permissions. A content owner becomes **Project Leader** the moment they publish an object to Tableau Server, but not every project leader is a content owner. This is because content published to the server can have many project leaders, but only one content owner.

4. **Content permissions locked or customizable**: The content permissions setting can be set in two ways, either locked or customizable. To configure content permissions, you need to be logged into a site as an administrator, project owner, or project leader. **Locked Content Permissions** means that a content owner cannot modify the permission rules on their content. As a result, the content will reflect the permission rules of the project, and the content-level permissions cannot be modified. The project owner has control over the permissions for the project and all its underlying objects. **Customizable Content Permissions** means that a content owner can modify content permissions for users or groups.

5. **Individual permissions**: These permissions are applied to a specific user, and they determine how that user can interact with the content (such as projects, workbooks, views, and data sources). Permissions assigned to an individual rank higher in the hierarchy of permissions than permissions assigned to a group.

6. **Group permissions**: These permissions are applied to a group of users, and they determine how they can interact with the content (such as projects, workbooks, views, and data sources). A user can be a member of many groups. If a user is a member of two or more groups that are being granted permissions on a piece of content and any of those groups are denied a capability, it will result in that user being denied that capability.

Figure 1.9 visually presents the hierarchy of user object capabilities from the highest to the lowest, as we just discussed:

Figure 1.9 – Hierarchy of the user's object capability

In this section, you learned how licenses, site roles, and permissions interact with and impact one another on Tableau Server. We examined the different license types and site roles that are available and their possible combinations. Additionally, we examined permissions, their rules, predefined roles, and custom roles. Lastly, we looked at how all of these varying levels of permissions tie together.

Summary

In this chapter, you learned about the Tableau platform, its most popular products, and how they work together. You also learned what a site is and how a single instance of Tableau Server can have multiple sites to help your organization manage its content. Finally, you learned about the available Tableau product license types and which type is required for your role within an organization, the difference between site roles and permissions settings for server content, and how all of these things work together to determine what you can do within your Tableau Server environment. The principles learned in this chapter set the foundation for the remainder of this book, as well as how you interact with Tableau Server and its content.

In the next chapter, you will learn how to connect to Tableau Server and Tableau Public, how to publish content to each platform, and how to determine at which level to manage various settings.

2
How to Connect and Publish to Tableau Server

In this chapter, you will learn how to connect to **Tableau Server** to publish your own content and interact with your company's content. You will also learn how to connect and publish to **Tableau Public** so that you can learn from the Tableau community and practice your skills.

When you complete this chapter, you will understand the following:

- How to connect and publish to Tableau Server
- How to connect and publish to Tableau Public

How to connect and publish to Tableau Server?

Tableau Server is where you can create, store, and share data sources, views, dashboards, and metrics for your company. You will begin by learning how to access this content by connecting to your Tableau Server environment in a web browser. Then, you will learn how to sign in to the server from **Tableau Desktop** and publish content directly to the server to be shared with others.

Learning these skills will establish the foundation for many concepts learned throughout the remainder of this book. This chapter will also quickly get you started with the basic knowledge of how to get your newly created content out there for end users to see and interact with.

Let's begin by getting connected to Tableau Server using your web browser.

Connecting to Tableau Server using a web browser

Before attempting to connect to Tableau Server, you will need to contact your Tableau Server administrator to obtain your organization's server URL and confirm your login credentials.

The process to connect to your Tableau Server environment may vary slightly, as each organization has its own configuration. Generally speaking, the URL will be similar to `tableau.<company name>.com`.

Once you open a web browser and enter your company's Tableau Server URL, you will need to log in using the credentials provided to you. An example of a login page is shown in *Figure 2.1*. Your login screen may look different from what is shown in this screenshot:

Figure 2.1 – Tableau Server login window

Your organization may have configured **single sign-on (SSO)** credentials that allow you to use the same login credentials that are used to access other programs in your company.

> **Note**
> When signing into Tableau Server from a web browser, first-party cookies must be allowed. This is how Tableau Server confirms that the user has been authenticated and is allowed to access the server.

Once you have logged into your Tableau Server environment, you may have the option to choose your server site. Recall from *Chapter 1, What is Tableau Server?,* that a site is a selection of content, users, and groups that is separated from another selection of content, users, and groups. Both use the same instance of Tableau Server, without having access to each other's site. An example of the site selection window is shown in *Figure 2.2:*

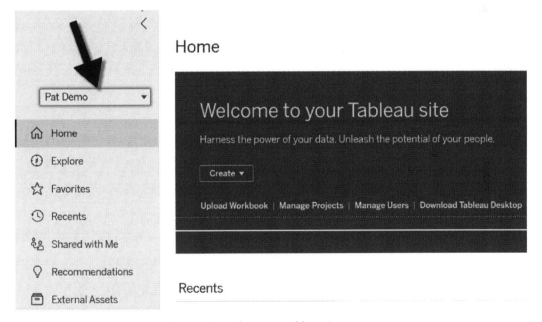

Figure 2.2 – Selecting a Tableau Server site

You will only see this window if you have access to multiple sites within the Tableau Server environment. If you do not see this window, then you will see your Tableau Server home page immediately after logging in.

If you had to select a server site when logging in, you can see the site name on your server window, as illustrated in *Figure 2.3*:

Figure 2.3 – Tableau Server site indicator

Dashboard images created by Chimdi Nwosu and Luther Flagstad

At this point, you are ready to browse and interact with the server's content. Next, you will learn how to connect to the server from Tableau Desktop and how to publish content to the server.

Connecting to Tableau Server from Tableau Desktop and publishing content

Your first creation using Tableau Desktop is a very exciting thing! The first question many content developers ask themselves after creating their first dashboard is *Now what?* or *How do I share this with others?* This is where connecting and publishing to Tableau Server comes into play.

Connecting to Tableau Server

The following steps will help you connect to the server from Tableau Desktop:

1. Click on the **Server** menu from the top menu bar in Tableau Desktop. From the drop-down menu that appears, select **Sign In...**, as shown in *Figure 2.4*:

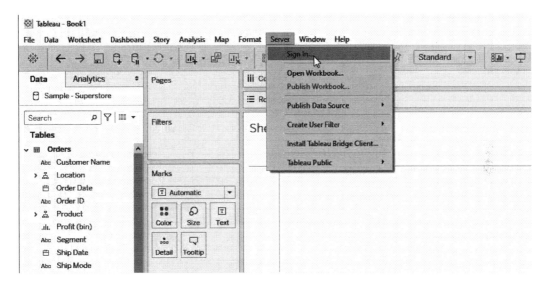

Figure 2.4 – Signing in from Tableau Desktop

This will open the **Tableau Server Sign In** window shown in *Figure 2.5*:

Figure 2.5 – Tableau Server Sign In window

2. In this window, enter your organization's Tableau Server name or URL in the textbox or select it from the drop-down menu and click **Connect**. Depending on the settings of your organization, this may open an additional sign-in window for you to enter your server login credentials, as shown in *Figure 2.6*:

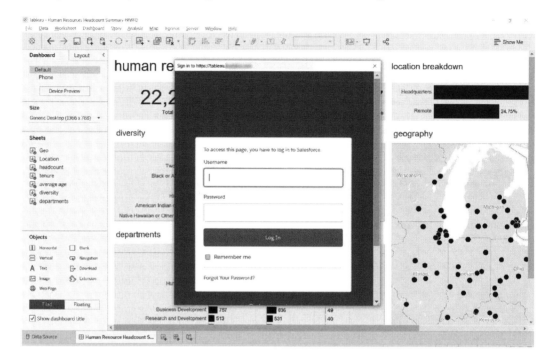

Figure 2.6 – Tableau Server login

Dashboard image created by Mark Bradbourne

3. Enter your **username and password** and click **Log In**.

4. You may see a window similar to the one shown in *Figure 2.7*, where you are required to enter a verification code and then select the site that you want to log in to:

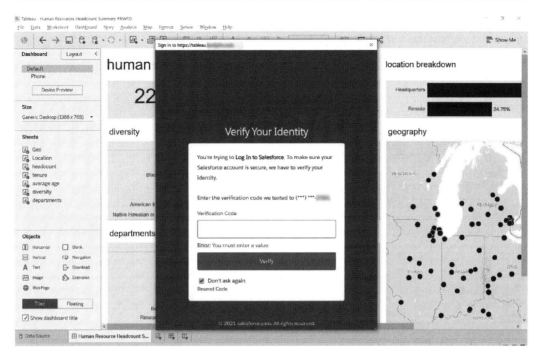

Figure 2.7 – Tableau Server Verify Your Identity window

Dashboard image created by Mark Bradbourne

Once you are logged in, the pop-up windows will disappear, and you will be returned to your Tableau Desktop window.

> **Note**
> Unless you log out of Tableau Desktop, you will remain logged in from session to session.

If you would like to confirm that your login was successful, you can open the same **Server** menu from the menu bar. Instead of seeing a **Sign In…** button, you should now see **Signed In to [server name]**, as shown in *Figure 2.8*:

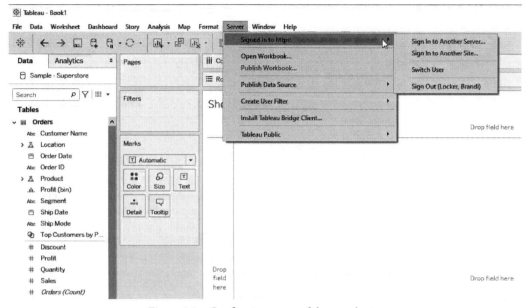

Figure 2.8 – Confirming successful server login

If you are logged in to a particular site, this information will be displayed in parentheses next to the server name. In the previous screenshot, the site is the user's **Default** site. The **Sign Out** option, shown in the additional menu, indicates which user is currently logged in by including the user's name in parentheses.

You can also verify all of this same information in the status bar **tooltip** at the bottom of the Tableau Desktop window, as shown in *Figure 2.9*. A tooltip is a window containing additional information that appears when hovering the cursor over an item on the screen. In this case, when you hover over the username, a tooltip appears to provide the server and site information:

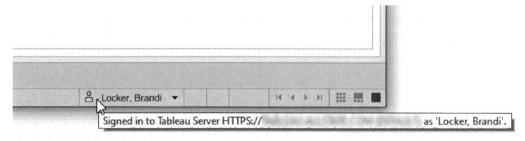

Figure 2.9 – Status bar within Tableau Desktop

As shown in *Figure 2.8*, hovering over the **Signed in to [server name]** detail will open a secondary menu to the right that allows you to **sign in to another server, sign in to another site, switch users, or sign out**.

Now that you are signed in, you are ready to publish content to Tableau Server.

Publishing content to Tableau Server

Publishing content to Tableau Server allows you to share it with others so that they can interact with and glean insights from the data. To do this, you first need to create a visual on a worksheet or dashboard that you want to publish. The final chapter of this book, *Chapter 10, Conclusion*, will contain recommendations of resources for further development of your skills to create content.

If you are brand new to Tableau and have no experience using Tableau Desktop, then you can create a simple chart on a worksheet to use for practice as you learn how to publish content in this section.

To create a simple visual, or *viz*, complete the following steps. If you already have a view created that is ready to be published, you can skip the following steps:

1. Open Tableau Desktop.

2. Connect to the **Sample – Superstore** dataset by left-clicking on the **Sample – Superstore** dataset label in the lower-left corner of your Tableau Desktop window, under **Saved Data Sources**. This sample dataset is available with all Tableau Desktop applications and is a great way to practice using the software.

3. On **Sheet 1**, find the **Segment** field in the data pane on the left side of your Tableau Desktop window. Left-click on **Segment** and drag it into the **Rows** shelf at the top of the Tableau Desktop window.

4. Left-click on the **Sales** field and drag it into the **Columns** shelf at the top of the Tableau Desktop window. The label, or **pill**, will read as **SUM (Sales)**.

5. Double-click on the worksheet tab at the bottom of the Tableau Desktop window where it is labeled **Sheet 1** and rename the worksheet Sales by Segment.

After following these five steps, you should have a chart like the one shown in *Figure 2.10*:

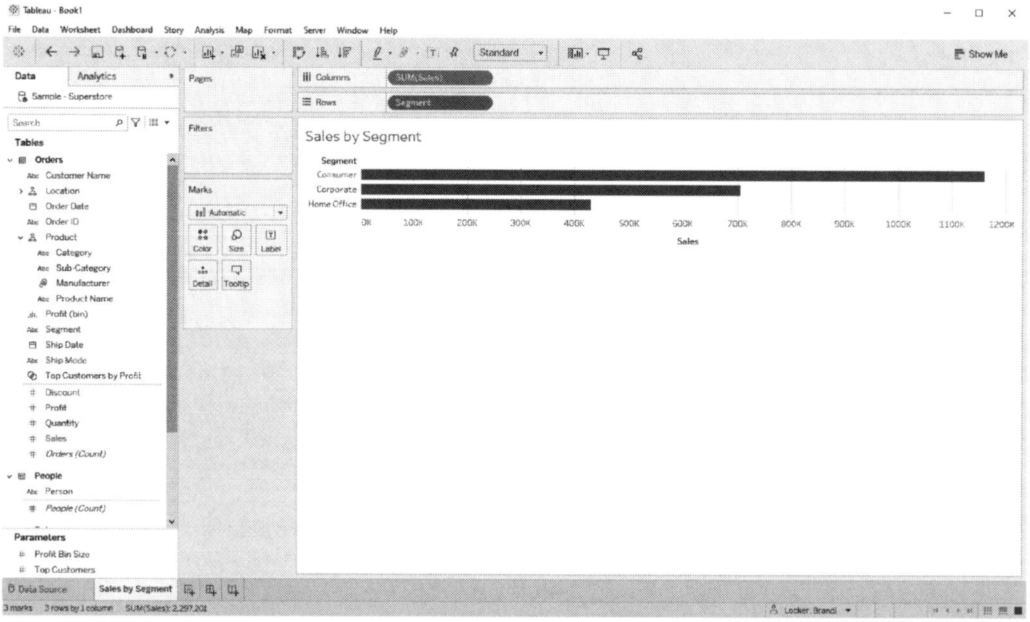

Figure 2.10 – Sales by Segment chart

You can use this simple bar chart worksheet to follow along with the rest of this section in learning how to publish content to Tableau Server.

Note

For our examples in this book, we will use images of dashboards created by members of the Tableau Community as part of various community initiatives that encourage learning data visualization skills. These community initiatives will also be discussed in the last chapter of this book.

Publishing workbooks

You can publish your viz by following these steps:

1. Click on the **Server** menu in Tableau Desktop and select **Publish Workbook…**, as shown in *Figure 2.11*:

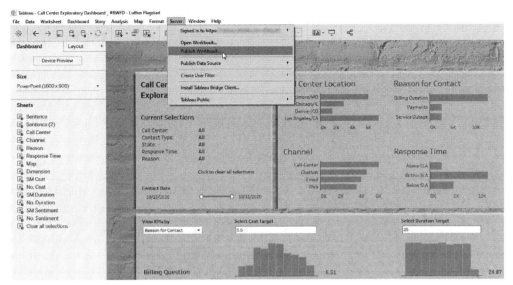

Figure 2.11 – Publish Workbook... option from the Server menu

Dashboard image created by Luther Flagstad

Clicking **Publish Workbook…** will open the **Publish Workbook to Tableau Server** window, as shown in *Figure 2.12*:

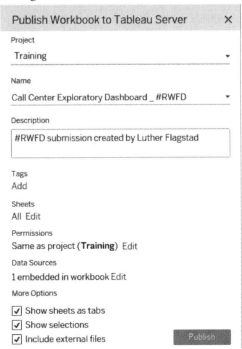

Figure 2.12 – Publish Workbook to Tableau Server window

2. The **Publish Workbook to Tableau Server** window contains the following options for you to review and adjust as needed:

- **Project**: Opens a drop-down menu that allows you to select which **project** to publish the workbook to. A project is like a folder within Tableau Server where content is stored. If you have the appropriate permissions, a workbook can be moved to another project directly on Tableau Server after it is published. Projects will be discussed in the next chapter. Moving content will be discussed in *Chapter 7, What is in the More Actions (…) Menu*.

- **Name**: A textbox where you can name the workbook for Tableau Server. The name you provide here will only affect how the workbook is labeled on Tableau Server and will not affect the name of the workbook file itself. If you have the appropriate permissions, workbook names can be adjusted directly on Tableau Server after the workbook is published.

- **Description**: A textbox where you can provide a brief description or explanation about the workbook and its contents. You can leave this box blank, but a thoughtful description can be very helpful to other users. If you have the appropriate permissions, descriptions can be adjusted directly on Tableau Server after publishing the workbook.

- **Tags**: A **tag** is a keyword that can be attached to workbooks, views, metrics, and data sources to help you filter and categorize content on Tableau Server. If you have the appropriate permissions, tags can be adjusted directly on Tableau Server after publishing the workbook. You can read more about tags in *Chapter 7, What is in the More Actions (…) Menu*.

- **Sheets**: By default, *all* worksheets within a workbook will be published to Tableau Server. You can adjust this by clicking **Edit** and selecting which specific sheets you would like to publish. If you publish the workbook and need to make changes to which items were published to Tableau Server, you will have to republish the workbook and overwrite the original.

> Tip
> If you are publishing a dashboard, you are *not* required to select every worksheet contained within that dashboard in the **Sheets** section for them to appear in the dashboard once published to Tableau Server.

- **Permissions**: These determine which content Tableau Server users can access, interact with, edit, and manage. Most of the time, you can leave this set to the default of **Same as project**, which means that permissions will be inherited from its server location. If you need to adjust these settings, you can use the **Edit** button to **add, edit, or remove** individual users or groups and adjust their permissions **template** and individual capabilities for the workbook. Once you are finished adjusting permissions settings, you can click off of the pop-up window and onto the **Publish Workbook to Tableau Server** window to continue with the publishing process. Permissions can be a complex topic. They are introduced in *Chapter 1, What is Tableau Server?,* and explained again in *Chapter 7, What is in the More Actions (...) Menu.* Permissions can be adjusted directly on Tableau Server after publishing content. Some projects may have permissions settings locked by your server administrator.

- **Data Sources**: This section indicates whether data sources will be embedded in the workbook, which is the default selection, or published separately. You can adjust this by clicking **Edit**, which will open the **Manage Data Sources** pop-up window. In this window, you can choose whether to embed or separately publish each data source in the workbook and adjust their authentication settings. Embedded passwords are generally recommended and are required if you need to create an extract refresh schedule so that the data automatically updates. If your data source is a Tableau data source, prompting users for credentials requires them to have additional permissions for that data source.

- **More Options**: Additional options that are relevant to workbooks being published:

    - a. **Show sheets as tabs**: Checking this box allows users to use tabbed navigation for workbooks that have multiple sheets or dashboards published. Unchecking this box only allows users to open one view at a time.

    > **Note**
    >
    > Whether or not you show tabs has an impact on permissions. If tabs *are* shown, workbook-level permission rules apply to all of the sheets within the workbook. If tabs *are not* shown, permission rules must be set at a view level. In this case, changes made at a workbook level will not apply to the views.

    - b. **Show selections**: Selecting this option will allow users to see a highlighted portion of the view that you selected in Tableau Desktop prior to publishing.

    - c. **Include external files**: Includes relevant files that are used in the workbook but are not available to others or to the server, including Excel, CSV, or data source files that are local to your computer.

> **Note**
>
> The options available to you in the **Publish Workbook to Tableau Server** window may vary slightly depending on which version of Tableau you are using.
>
> If you are using **Tableau Online** instead of Tableau Server, you will need to take additional steps to include external files. You can read more about how to do this on the Tableau Help pages at `https://help.tableau.com/ current/pro/desktop/en-gb/publish_workbooks_howto. htm#include-external-files`.

3. After you have finished reviewing all of the publish settings in the **Publish Workbook to Tableau Server** window, you are ready to click **Publish**. Once the publishing process is complete, a new web browser tab or window will open to that workbook's content page and will display a **Publishing Complete** confirmation. This window includes shortcuts to **Preview different device layouts** and to **Share** the workbook, as shown in *Figure 2.13*:

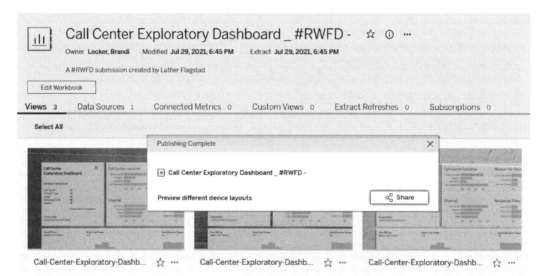

Figure 2.13 – Publishing Complete confirmation

Dashboard image created by Luther Flagstad

Device layout previews are a way to test your view to see how it would look from another device. This is discussed further in *Chapter 8, Interacting with Views on Tableau Server*. If you preview a device layout and need to make adjustments, you can republish the workbook after making the necessary changes in Tableau Desktop.

Clicking the **Share** button opens a window that enables you to specify other Tableau Server users that you would like to share the workbook with directly. You can also copy a link to the workbook location on Tableau Server and paste it in an email, chat, or any other location of your choice. You need to ensure that whomever you share your content with on Tableau Server has been granted permission to see it. Sharing content with others is discussed in *Chapter 7, What is in the More Actions (…) Menu.*

Publishing data sources

The process of publishing a data source is very similar to the process of publishing a workbook that you learned in the previous section.

To publish a data source from Tableau Desktop to Tableau Server, follow these steps:

1. Click on the same **Server** menu, hover over the **Publish Data Source** option until another menu opens, and select the data source that you wish to publish from that menu. In *Figure 2.14*, the data source to be published is named `Call Center`:

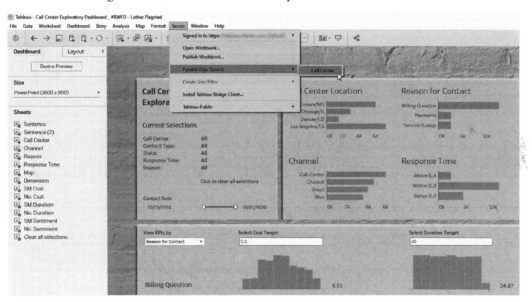

Figure 2.14 – Publish Data Source menu

Dashboard image created by Luther Flagstad

Clicking on the name of the data source that you wish to publish will open the **Publish Data Source to Tableau Server** window shown in *Figure 2.15*:

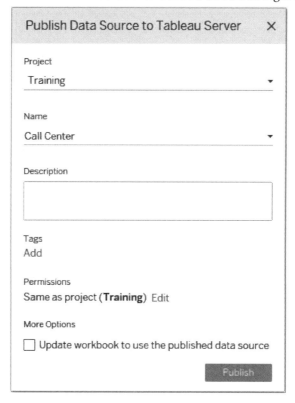

Figure 2.15 – Publish Data Source to Tableau Server window

2.   Complete the options in the **Publish Data Source to Tableau Server** window. The options in this window are almost identical to the options available in the window that appears when publishing a workbook. It allows you to select the **Project** location, choose a **name** for the data source as it will appear on Tableau Server, add a helpful **description**, add **tags** to act as keywords for finding the item on the server, and confirm or edit **permissions** for the data source. The options available to you in this window may vary slightly depending on which version of Tableau you are using.

> **Note**
>
> As with workbooks, the name that you provide in the publish window will only change the name of the data source on Tableau Server. It will not update the name of the data source in the Tableau Desktop workbook that you are publishing the data source from.

The biggest difference in publishing a data source is that the **More Options** section has changed to reflect the content type you are publishing. You may still have an option to **Include external files,** depending on your workbook connections. A new option that you have is **Update workbook to use the published data source**.

When you publish a data source to Tableau Server, it will be available to use in multiple workbooks. Selecting the **Update workbook to use the published data source** option replaces your existing live data connection or data extract with an updated connection to the newly published data source from Tableau Server. This option is selected by default.

> **Note**
>
> If your data source was created using custom SQL and you select the box to **Update workbook to use the published data source**, your SQL query will be replaced by a live connection to the newly published data source on Tableau Server. If you still need your custom SQL, then you should confirm it is saved elsewhere before selecting this option and clicking **Publish**.
>
> If you do this by mistake, you can click **Undo** in Tableau Desktop after the publishing process is complete to revert the workbook to use the local data source. You can also recover your custom SQL by downloading the data source from Tableau Server and opening the Data Source tab within Tableau Desktop.

3. After completing the information in the **Publish Data Source to Tableau Server** window, you are ready to click **Publish**. Once the publishing process is complete, a new web browser tab or window will open to that data source's content page. An example of a data source content page is shown in *Figure 2.16*:

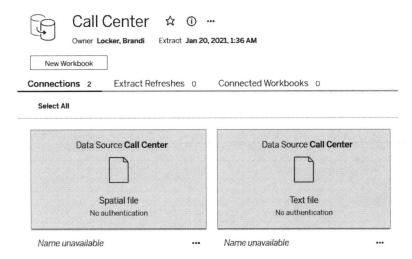

Figure 2.16 – Example of a data source content page

You will learn more about content pages in *Chapter 6, Navigating Content Pages in Tableau Server*. You will also learn how to create an extract refresh schedule in *Chapter 7, What is in the More Actions (…) Menu,* so that your data can be automatically refreshed for the most up-to-date information.

In this section, you learned how to connect to Tableau Server from a web browser and Tableau Desktop. You also learned how to publish workbooks and data sources to Tableau Server so that your data sources, data visualizations, and analytic insights can be distributed to the appropriate users. You now have the tools to store and distribute content on Tableau Server. As you continue reading through this book, you will learn how to maximize your efficiency and capability with Tableau Server in order to improve the utilization of your data products within your organization.

In the next section, you will learn about Tableau Public and how it can be a valuable tool for your personal development and to enhance your portfolio for future career opportunities.

How to connect and publish to Tableau Public?

To begin, what is **Tableau Public**? Tableau Public is a free online version of Tableau's visualization software. It's a cloud service that allows users to publicly share and explore data visualizations. Tableau Public provides you with many of the same functionalities of Tableau Desktop without the cost. If you or your organization are new to Tableau or considering implementing the software, the Tableau Public platform is a great place to start. The Tableau Public home page is shown in *Figure 2.17*:

Figure 2.17 – Tableau Public home page

This free version of Tableau allows you to begin exploring the platform, find inspiration, connect with community members, utilize learning resources, build your own personal portfolio, and so much more.

Figure 2.18 provides an example of Tableau Public's gallery. This is a place where you can go for inspiration by looking at highlighted work by community members:

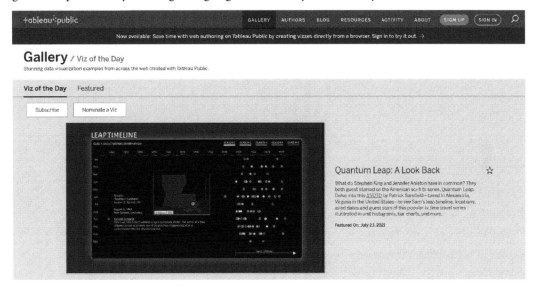

Figure 2.18 – Tableau Public Gallery/Viz of the Day

Figure 2.19 provides an example of how you can search for and find individual authors or vizzes. An **author** on Tableau Public refers to the person who developed and uploaded their dashboard or worksheet to Tableau. A **viz** in Tableau simply refers to a visualization created using Tableau:

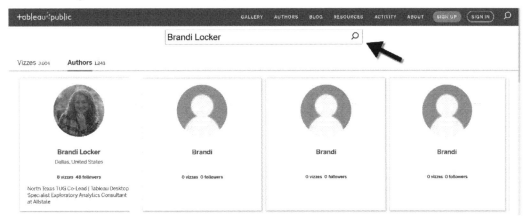

Figure 2.19 – Finding community members

Figure 2.20 provides an example of some **sample data**. This is one of the many free resources available on Tableau Public:

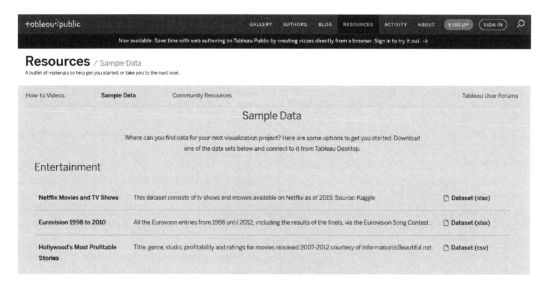

Figure 2.20 – Tableau Public Resources/Sample Data

Here, we presented a few of the benefits of using Tableau Public, however, there are many more.

How to create a Tableau Public profile?

We'll go over two ways in which you can quickly create a Tableau Public profile:

- From the web
- From Tableau Desktop

Creating a Tableau Public profile on the web

One way to create a Tableau Public profile is by signing up online.

To use this method, follow these steps:

1. First, navigate to the Tableau Public website using the following link: `https://public.tableau.com/`.

2. Next, you will see Tableau Public's home page. In the top right-hand corner, there is a list of button options laid out horizontally. Click the orange **SIGN UP** button shown in *Figure 2.21*:

Data Storytelling   Spark Conversation   Be Inspired

Figure 2.21 – SIGN UP button for creating a Tableau Public profile

After clicking the button, a **Create a Profile** window will open. A screenshot of this window is displayed in *Figure 2.22*:

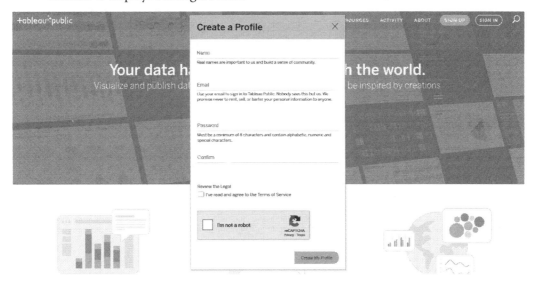

Figure 2.22 – Tableau Public Create a Profile window

3. Read and enter the required information within this window and click **Create My Profile** to complete the process.

Creating a Tableau Public profile from Tableau Desktop

You can also create your Tableau Public account directly from Tableau Desktop.

To create an account using this method, follow these steps:

1. In Tableau Desktop, go to your **Server** drop-down menu, select the **Tableau Public** option, and pick any of the options provided. An example of this is shown in *Figure 2.23*:

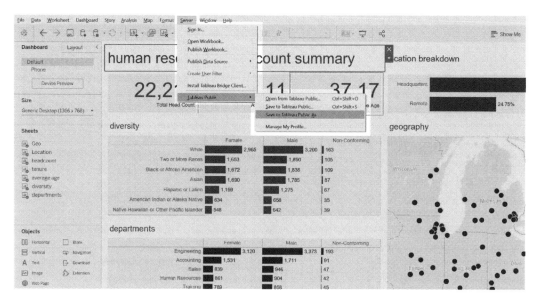

Figure 2.23 – Server drop-down menu to Tableau Public

Dashboard image created by Mark Bradbourne

2. After selecting a Tableau Public drop-down option, the **Tableau Public Sign In** window shown in *Figure 2.24* will open. To create a Tableau Public account, click the **Create one now for free** hyperlink at the bottom of the window:

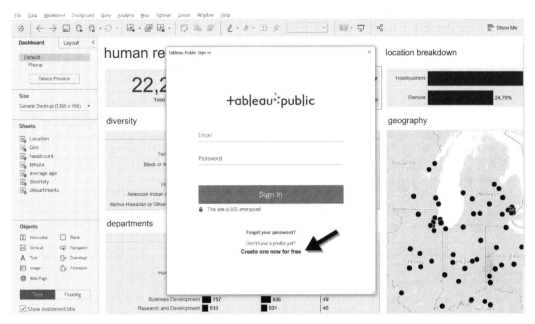

Figure 2.24 – Creating a Tableau Public profile from the Sign In window

Dashboard image created by Mark Bradbourne

3.   A **Create a Profile** window like the one shown in *Figure 2.25* will open:

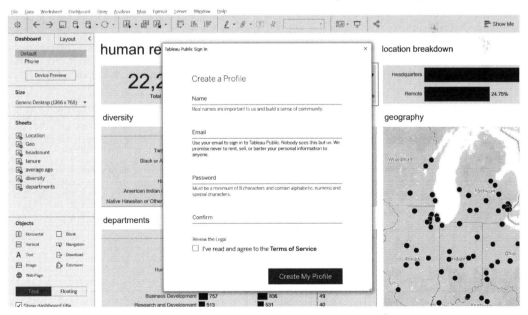

Figure 2.25 – Creating a Tableau Public profile from Tableau Desktop

Dashboard image created by Mark Bradbourne

4. Read and fill out the requirements of this window. To finish, click the **Create My Profile** in the bottom-right corner of the window.

    Whichever option you choose to create your Tableau Public profile, we just hope that you select one. This decision will help introduce you to one of the strongest, kindest, and most helpful business intelligence communities in the world today. We discuss the benefits of the Tableau Community in greater detail in *Chapter 10, Conclusion*.

How to connect and publish content from Tableau Desktop to Tableau Public?

After you have created a worksheet or dashboard in Tableau Desktop and are ready to share it publicly, you can follow these steps to publish your workbook to Tableau Public:

1. From Tableau Desktop, go to your **Server** drop-down menu, select the **Tableau Public** option, and click **Save to Tableau Public As**.... An example of this is shown in *Figure 2.26*:

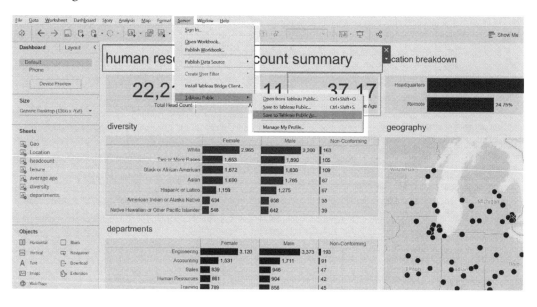

Figure 2.26 – Saving a workbook to Tableau Public

Dashboard image created by Mark Bradbourne

2. If this is your first time publishing a workbook, you will be prompted to log in to your Tableau Public profile. *Figure 2.27* provides an example of the **Tableau Public Sign In** window:

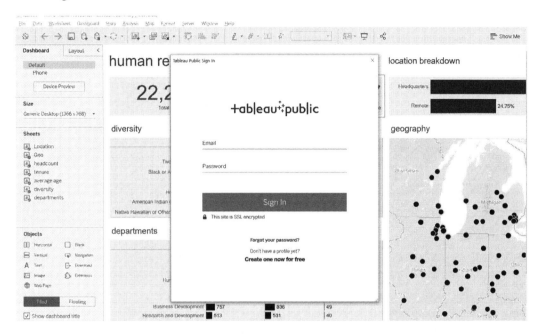

Figure 2.27 – Tableau Public Sign In window

Dashboard image created by Mark Bradbourne

3. Enter your **email and password**. Then click the **Sign In** button.

4. Next, you will be prompted with a **Save Workbook to Tableau Public** window. You are provided with a final reminder that you are saving your workbook to Tableau Public and to make sure it does not contain private or confidential information. *Figure 2.28* provides an example of this window:

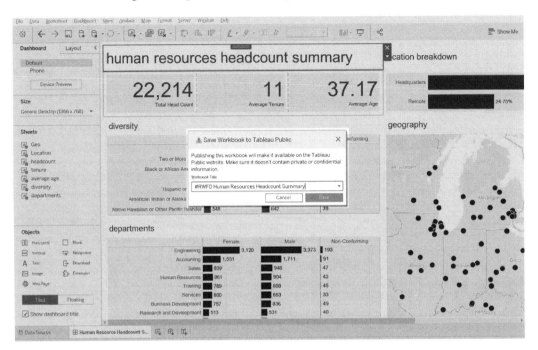

Figure 2.28 – Saving a workbook to Tableau Public

Dashboard image created by Mark Bradbourne

5. Click **Save** on this window to save your dashboard to Tableau Public or click **Cancel** to return to your workbook on Tableau Desktop without saving your dashboard to Tableau Public.

> **Note**
> Make sure that you convert all your data source connections to extracts as Tableau Public does not support live connections.

Once the publishing process is complete, your web browser will automatically open to the newly published view. *Figure 2.29* provides an example of a dashboard after it has been saved to Tableau Public:

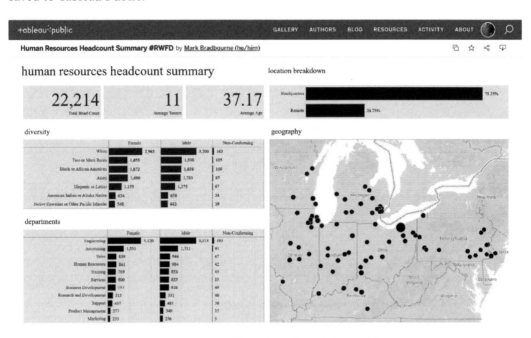

Figure 2.29 – Dashboard saved to Tableau Public

Dashboard image created by Mark Bradbourne

> **Note**
>
> Remember, when you share content on Tableau Public, the visualization and the underlying data can be seen by the world. Please remember to exercise caution when working on sensitive topics and avoid publishing any sensitive data.

Don't worry if you're not ready to share your dashboard with the world just yet. If you would like to review and change your dashboard before making it available for all to see, you can hide it so that others cannot see it. To do this from the view page, click on the gear icon on the top-right corner of the window and click the **Show Viz on Profile** toggle. You can also do this from your profile page that displays all of your content previews by clicking on the ellipses (**...**) at the bottom-right corner of the viz preview. This opens a menu called **More Actions**. From this menu, click on the **Show Viz on Profile** toggle switch shown in *Figure 2.30*:

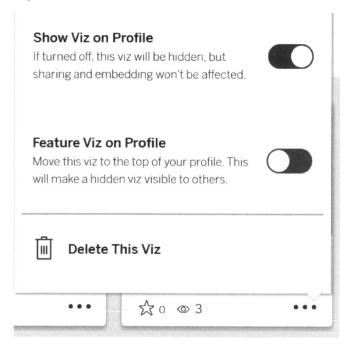

Figure 2.30 – Show or hide a viz on your public profile

When this toggle is blue, the viz is shown on your profile; when it is gray, the viz is hidden. *Figure 2.31* shows an example of a view that is hidden:

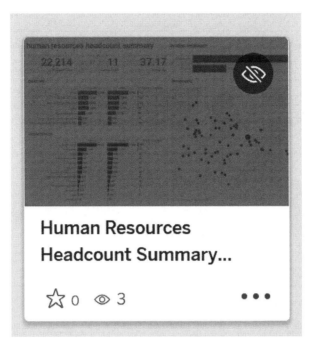

Figure 2.31 – Hidden viz on Tableau Public profile

Dashboard image created by Mark Bradbourne

Notice that a hidden view has a gray overlay on the image preview and an eye icon with a line through it. You can adjust the visibility of your content at any time.

> **Tip**
> You can set your Tableau Public profile to automatically hide views under your profile settings. This could be beneficial if you prefer to double-check the view after it is published to Tableau Public, but before anyone sees it. You would then manually choose when to make a published view visible to others.

As we end this section, we hope that you are excited to begin exploring and to create your own Tableau Public profile. You have learned the steps to take to create a Tableau Public profile and have been introduced to how you can leverage your Tableau Public portfolio to learn, practice, create a professional portfolio, or just explore data and have fun creating visualizations.

Summary

In this chapter, you learned how to connect to Tableau Server from a web browser and from Tableau Desktop. You also learned how to publish workbooks and data sources and were introduced to how Tableau Server can be utilized to store and share content. These skills are the first step in maximizing your Tableau Server experience and optimizing this tool within your organization. Finally, you learned what Tableau Public is, how to create your own free profile, and how to start leveraging Tableau Public for your own personal development.

In the next chapter, you will learn how to navigate the Tableau Server interface, starting with one of the most prominent and helpful features that is available to you – the Navigation Pane.

Section 2: Navigating and Customizing the Tableau Server Interface

In this section, you will learn how to navigate the Tableau Server interface to efficiently locate, sort, and filter content, as well as adjust basic settings. This will build a foundation to further customize and manage content in *Section 3*.

This section comprises the following chapters:

- *Chapter 3, Tableau Server Navigation Pane*
- *Chapter 4, Tableau Server Top Toolbar*
- *Chapter 5, Filtering and Sorting Content*

3
The Tableau Server Navigation Pane

You can think of the Tableau Server Navigation Pane as your constant companion, there to assist you as you navigate through the Tableau Server interface, quickly helping you find what you need.

In this chapter, you will learn how to access your **Home** page, explore all the content available to you, save your favorite or most frequented items, find your most recently visited content, and view items that have been shared with you. Content on Tableau Server comes in the form of projects, workbooks, views, and data sources. In Tableau Server, projects are created by a server administrator to help organize and contain related content when it is uploaded. A workbook is a view or collection of views. A view can be a dashboard, worksheet, or story. A data source is a data connection that has been published to Tableau Server.

By the end of this chapter, you will know how to utilize the most common options on your Navigation Pane:

- Introducing the Tableau Server Navigation Pane
- Examining the **Home** page
- Examining the **Explore** page
- Examining the **Favorites** page

- Examining the **Recents** page

- Examining the **Shared with Me** page

- Examining the **Recommendations** page

Introducing the Tableau Server Navigation Pane

The **Navigation Pane** appears on the left-hand side of your Tableau Server window and provides a convenient list of options that are linked to your most frequently sought-after content. The Navigation Pane, or **sidebar**, will stay with you as you explore Tableau Server. It will only disappear when you choose to open a view, dashboard, or story so that your screen space is maximized for the content that you want to see. The following screenshot shows an example of the Navigation Pane within the Tableau Server window and identifies the available shortcuts:

Figure 3.1 – The Tableau Server Navigation Pane

> **Important Note**
> Please note that you may see additional options, depending on the settings that have been established by your server administrators or company.

In this book, we will review the most common options available in the Navigation Pane:

- **Collapse/Expand Arrow**: Appears as a directional arrow at the top of your Navigation Pane. Depending on which way the arrow is pointing, clicking it will either collapse or expand your sidebar.

- **Home**: Appears as a house icon on the Navigation Pane. Clicking this will open your Tableau Server **Home** page.

- **Explore**: Appears as a compass icon on the Navigation Pane. Clicking this will open a page that allows you to see all the content you have access to on Tableau Server.

- **Favorites**: Appears as a star icon on the Navigation Pane. Clicking this will provide you with a page showing content that you have selected as a favorite.

- **Recents**: Appears as an analog clock icon on the Navigation Pane. Clicking this will open a page that displays your most recently viewed content.

- **Shared with Me**: Appears as an icon of two people connected by an arrow on the Navigation Pane. Clicking this will reveal any content that has been directly shared with you by other users on Tableau Server.

The Navigation Pane can be collapsed or expanded simply by clicking on the directional arrow near the top of the pane. The following screenshot shows an example of the collapse and expand arrows on this sidebar:

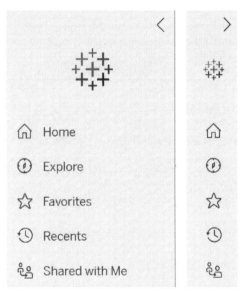

Figure 3.2 – Navigation Pane – collapse and expand arrows

Clicking the arrow icon pointing to the left is an easy way to condense your Navigation Pane and return some valuable screen real estate. Clicking the arrow icon pointing to the right will expand your Navigation Pane.

> **Note**
>
> Depending on the decisions of your Tableau Server Administrators, a custom logo may appear in the top left corner of your sidebar.

After completing this chapter, you will have a strong understanding of how and when to use the Navigation Pane. Many of the things you will learn here will continue to pop up in the same or similar ways as you explore Tableau Server. Now, let's look at the first item on your sidebar: your **Home** page.

Examining the Home page

The **Home** page is the first thing you see when you open Tableau Server. It is designed to assist users by providing quick access to their most valuable content, which it does by prominently displaying much of what they may need in a single location. To return to this page from another server location, simply click the link identified by the house icon and the word **Home**, which can be found on the Navigation Pane on the left-hand side of your Tableau Server window.

Clicking the house icon will open your **Home** page, where you will see a welcome banner at the top of your screen with the available page content displayed below it. Your content appears in the form of thumbnail images with labels directly below. Selecting a thumbnail will immediately open that item and transport you to its location on Tableau Server. We will learn more about this in the next section when we discuss the **Explore** page.

If you have never used Tableau Server before, you will not have any content previews available. As you begin to use and browse the server, the **Home** page items discussed in this section will begin to populate with thumbnail images of the content you have viewed.

Let's begin by scrolling through the **Home** page to see what is available. First, let's look at the options that are available on the welcome banner.

The welcome banner

The first item that you will notice at the top of your **Home** page is the **welcome banner** shown here:

Figure 3.3 – Welcome banner shown on the Tableau Server Home page

The welcome banner is designed to help new users quickly get started. The actions available to you will vary based on your assigned role within the Tableau Server environment. In this book, we will focus on reviewing the most common options available to Tableau developers and analysts using Tableau Server. Recall that roles were discussed in *Chapter 1, What is Tableau Server?*

The first option available in the welcome banner is the **Start Exploring** button. This is a shortcut to the **Explore** page, which can be found in the Navigation Pane on the left-hand side of the server window.

Below the **Start Exploring** button is a shortcut that reads **Create Workbook**. This option will open another web browser tab or window with a new workbook using Tableau Server's **Web Authoring** feature. The Web Authoring/Edit feature is a convenient way to quickly explore your data and build data visualizations without having to open the Tableau Desktop application. This feature will be discussed in depth in *Chapter 8, Interacting with Views on Tableau Server*. Note that with web authoring on Tableau Server without the **Data Management** add-on, you can only connect to data sources that have already been published separately to the server, referred to in this book as Tableau Server published data sources. You cannot connect to a data extract that is embedded in another workbook or to an external data source. If the data you need has not been published as a separate data source yet, you will need to connect to the data through Tableau Desktop. If your organization has the **Data Management** add-on, then you will have additional options to connect to data from external assets. For more information about data connection types, please refer to *Chapter 1, What is Tableau Server?*

Next to the **Create Workbook** option is a shortcut that reads **Upload Workbook**. Clicking on this option will open the window shown here:

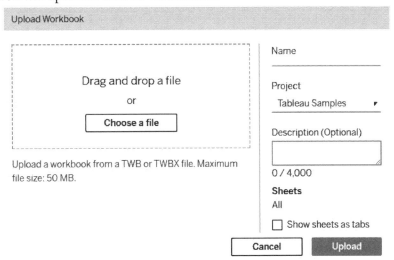

Figure 3.4 – Upload Workbook window

If you look on the left-hand side of this window, you will see the option to either drag and drop a file directly to this window or choose one from a saved location. You can upload either a Tableau Workbook (`.twb`) or Packaged Workbook (`.twbx`) with a file size that's up to 50 MB. On the right-hand side of this window, you can type the name of your item. This will serve as its title. It is best to choose a name that is simple and clear, as this will be shown on the server under the item's thumbnail or icon. You have the option to include additional or clarifying details about the workbook in the **Description** section if needed. This description will be visible to others using the server. The following screenshot provides an example of a filled out **Upload Workbook** window:

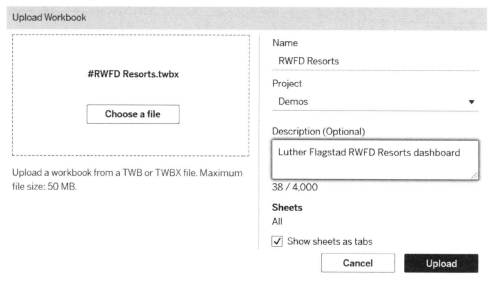

Figure 3.5 – Upload Workbook window filled out

To finished uploading your workbook, click the **Upload** button in the bottom right corner of the window. Click the **Cancel** button to close the window without uploading a workbook.

> **Tip**
>
> It is a best practice to use clear and consistent naming conventions for your titles and descriptions. This will help you and others quickly and easily find the content you/they are looking for, since the titles and descriptions are utilized in searches when filtering content. In addition, this small amount of additional effort can greatly aid the estimated 1 in 7 people who fall within the neurodivergent population.
>
> (Figures via `https://www.bbc.com/worklife/article/20190719-neurodiversity`).

Once you've identified the item's name, you can designate the project location that the file will be published to on the server.

> **Tip**
> You can move items to different projects once they have been published. We will discuss how to move content in *Chapter 7, What is in the More Actions (...) Menu.*

After identifying the project's location, you have the option to **Show sheets as tabs**. If you select this option, Tableau Server will include navigation tabs at the top of the screen for workbooks that contain multiple views, dashboards, or stories, as shown in the following screenshot:

Figure 3.6 – Worksheets shown as tabs in a published workbook

These tabs allow users to browse through the content within that workbook, similar to how you can have multiple tabs open in a single web browser window.

Please note that this **Upload Workbook** shortcut defaults to publishing all sheets within the workbook. If you wish to only publish select items, such as publishing only dashboards, then you must publish the workbook from Tableau Desktop. Once you have completed all the fields in the **Upload Workbook** window, simply click **Upload** for your content to be published to Tableau Server. Once the upload process has been completed and your content is ready to be viewed, a web browser tab or window will open directly to the new content on the server.

The welcome banner may also have additional options set by your Tableau Server administrator, such as contact information or other useful details that may be relevant to your organization.

Now that you have learned how to take advantage of the conveniences found in the welcome banner, let's continue scrolling through the rest of the **Home** page's content.

Home page content

Below the welcome banner on the **Home** page, you will find a compilation of various content. Included on this page is a preview of your latest favorited items (**Favorites**), recently viewed content (**Recents**), and shared content (**Shared with Me**). Each of these Navigation Pane options and others will be discussed in depth later in this chapter. Your **Home** page will show you a condensed version of the available content on the actual pages being referenced on your Navigation Pane. Your **Home** page intentionally limits the amount of content shown on the page as it is only intended to serve as a high-level view.

The following figure shows the **See All** hyperlinks that will appear to the right of your page for each Navigation Pane item listed on your **Home** page. Clicking the **See All** hyperlink will transport you from the limited display of content on your **Home** page to the actual full page associated with the content you want to explore further. The **See All** shortcut allows you to never lose your focus as you scroll through a limited number of content preview images on your **Home** page. The **See All** option also allows you to transition to another page on your sidebar, once you have had the chance to review a portion of its content:

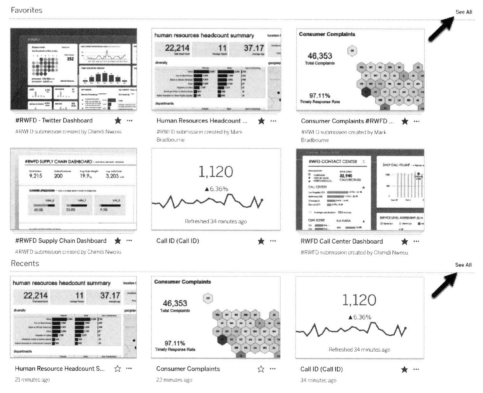

Figure 3.7 – See All shortcut

Dashboard images created by Chimdi Nwosu and Mark Bradbourne

At the bottom of the **Home** page is a link that conveniently directs you to resources for additional learning on Tableau's website. This can be seen in the following screenshot:

Learn Tableau. **Free training videos** →

Figure 3.8 – Link to Tableau training videos, found at the bottom of the Tableau Server Home page

Clicking this link will open a new web browser tab or window that contains free training videos directly from Tableau, as shown here:

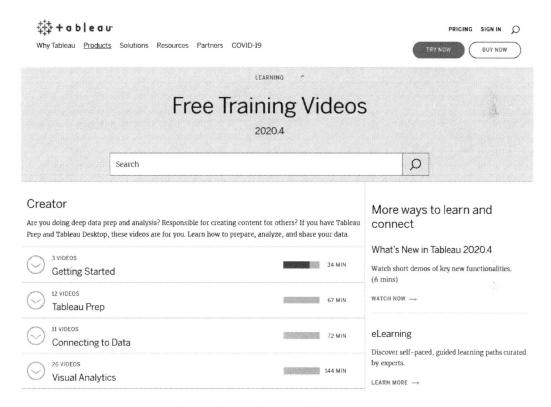

Figure 3.9 –Free Training Videos window

As we conclude this section, you are now acquainted with your **Home** page. You understand that this page provides you with a broad picture of much of the content available to you on the rest of the Navigation Pane. You should feel confident in using the welcome banner to create or upload a workbook, have a clear understanding of the way content is organized on this page, and know where you can find a link to access free Tableau training videos. In the next section, we will discuss how to explore and review all the content that you have access to.

Examining the Explore page

The **Explore** page allows you to browse all the content that you have been granted access to on Tableau Server, including content that's been published by other users. This page contains several unique filtering and sorting options to help you browse and understand how things are organized. Let's start by looking at the content type menu.

The content type menu

The **Explore** page features a filter at the top left-hand side of the page that allows you to select what type of content you would like to see. This filter is referred to as the **content type menu**. The following screenshot shows the commonly available options that you can choose from when you click this filter:

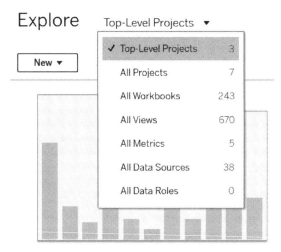

Figure 3.10 – Content filter on the Explore page

This filter allows you to see and browse everything available to you on Tableau Server, broken out by type. It will also indicate the quantity of each type of content available to the right of its menu name. This menu is unique to the primary **Explore** page and will disappear when you navigate to another project or page. You may have additional options based on your company's server specifications. Let's review the most common options available in this menu.

Top-Level Projects

The default selection for the content type menu is **Top-Level Projects**. All content that's published to Tableau Server is stored in a project. You can think of projects as being similar to folders on your computer. Folders store content but also allow nesting so that you can have a primary folder and subfolders within it, as shown in the following diagram:

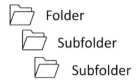

Figure 3.11 – Illustration of nested folders

"open folder" icon by Nancy, from thenounproject.com

Tableau Server projects function similarly. They allow you to create a project within a project so that you can organize your content effectively. A Top-Level Project is like a primary folder that contains additional items and projects.

> **Note**
>
> A Top-Level Project may also be referred to as a parent project. A project that is located within a parent project may be referred to as a child project.

Another way to illustrate nested content is by exploring the project hierarchy that appears as you view an item on Tableau Server. An example of this is shown in the following screenshot:

Explore / **Tableau Samples** / **Sandbox** / Sample Workbook

Figure 3.12 – Project hierarchy within Tableau Server

As you click through the nested projects, you will see a nesting hierarchy at the top of your server window. In the preceding screenshot, **Explore** is the Top-Level Project, and the **Tableau Samples** and **Sandbox** projects are nested projects that contain the Sample Workbook.

> **Tip**
>
> You can use the links within the project hierarchy as an easy way to navigate back to a certain project location, without having to click the back arrow on your web browser or starting over from the **Explore** page.

When **Top-Level Projects** is selected in the content type menu, you will be able to see all the primary projects available to you on the server. Clicking on any Top-Level Project icon will open that project so that you can see its contents, which may include workbooks, data sources, and additional projects.

All Projects

The next option available in the content type menu is **All Projects**. Selecting this option allows you to view all the projects available to you on the server, regardless of how they may be organized within other projects. In other words, you will see all the Top-Level Projects, as well as any project within them, on the same page. This can be helpful to you if you are trying to locate a specific project but cannot recall where it is located, or to get an idea of what is available on the server in general. An example of this is shown in the following screenshot:

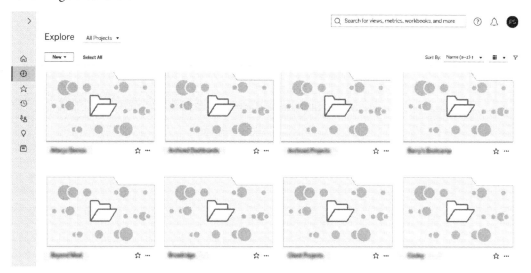

Figure 3.13 – All Projects on the Explore page

Clicking on a project will open it so that you can see all the content within. It will also take you to that project's nested location on the server, if applicable. You can see this in the project hierarchy at the top of your Tableau Server window.

All Workbooks

Next is the option to see **All Workbooks**. This selection allows you to see all the workbooks available to you on Tableau Server, regardless of which project the content was published to. In other words, you do not have to click through any projects to locate a certain workbook. A single workbook can contain multiple dashboards, views, stories, and data sources. Clicking on a workbook will open it so that you can see all the content within. It will also take you to that workbook's location on the server. You can see this in the project hierarchy at the top of your Tableau Server window.

To return to the **Explore** page, you can click on the back arrow in your web browser, use the Navigation Pane shortcut, or use the folder hierarchy links shown at the top of your Tableau Server window.

> **Tip**
> Returning to the **Explore** page will take you back to the top of the page. If your server has a large volume of content, it may be more convenient to open this content in a new tab within your web browser. You can do this by right-clicking on the content and selecting *Open link in new tab* or holding down *Ctrl* while you left click.

All Views

All Views is the next option available in the content type menu, and it functions similarly to the **All Workbooks** option. This selection allows you to see all the views available to you on Tableau Server, regardless of which project or workbook the content was published to. Notice that when you click on this menu, the count for views are likely to be much higher than the count for workbooks. This is because you can have many views within a workbook, as we just learned. A view in this context is any worksheet, dashboard, or story within a workbook. This does not include data sources.

All Metrics

The next option you will see on the content type menu is **All Metrics**. This selection allows you to see all the metrics that are available to you on Tableau Server. Metrics can be viewed by anyone who has been granted access to the metric, but they can only be created by someone who has a site role with the ability to publish (Creator or Explorer). You will learn how to create a metric in *Chapter 8, Interacting with Views on Tableau Server*. Metrics are created to monitor important numbers at a glance, and filtering by **All Metrics** via the content type menu is one way you can monitor them all in one place. Alternatively, you can quickly track them by creating them within the same project or by adding them to your favorites.

All Data Sources

All Data Sources is the next available filter in the content type menu. This option allows you to see all the Tableau Server data sources available to you. This does not include data sources that have been embedded in a workbook.

If you open a Tableau Server data source, you can use web authoring to create a new workbook that already has the data connection established directly from the data source page. To do this, simply navigate to the data source and click the **New Workbook** button, as shown in the following screenshot:

Figure 3.14 – Creating a new workbook with an established data connection

The **Data Source** page has another unique menu option, labeled **Show As**. The default selection for this menu is **Data Sources**. You can also select **Data Connections**, as shown in the following screenshot:

Figure 3.15 – Show As menu available when viewing All Data Sources

A single data source can have multiple data connections, so you will likely have more data connections than data sources. For example, when you join two tables from a database in Tableau Desktop, you will have two data connections within a single data source.

> **Tip**
> You can use the **Show As** connections feature to quickly update the connection details for a data source that you own directly from Tableau Server. This is convenient if a username or password has changed, for example. Simply click on the corresponding ellipses button (…) in the **Actions** column and select **Edit Connection**.

With that, you have learned how to utilize the content type menu to efficiently filter through content on the Tableau Server **Explore** page. Next, let's learn how content is displayed on the server.

Contents Toolbar

Below the content type menu is the Contents Toolbar menu, as shown in the following screenshot. We will briefly introduce the toolbar here and discuss it in more depth in *Chapter 5, Filtering and Sorting Content*:

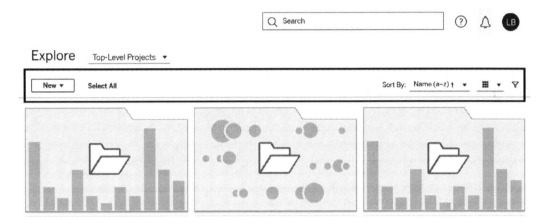

Figure 3.16 – Contents Toolbar

Here's a quick overview of the **Explore** page's Contents Toolbar options:

- **New**: Clicking this option will provide you with a drop-down list of options that allow you to create a new project or workbook, or even upload a workbook directly to the server without opening Tableau Desktop.

- **Select All** : Clicking this option allows you to quickly select all content on the page. Once selected, a list of actions will be available via a drop-down menu on the toolbar. The actions available to you will vary based on what you have selected in the content type menu, which we discussed previously in this section, and your permissions for that content.

- **Sort by**: Clicking this option will provide you with a drop-down list of options that allow you to organize the page by a single option. The list of sort options will also vary based on what you have selected in the content type menu. The interactivity of this drop-down filter closely resembles a **Single Value (Drop-down)** dimension filter on Tableau Desktop.

- **View Modes**: Clicking this option will provide you with a drop-down list of two view options, a grid view or a list view. The grid view icon appears as a 3 x 3 grid of nine squares, while the list view icon appears as three rows. A grid view provides a series of thumbnail images or icons representing your content, while a list view presents your content and some of the data surrounding it in a tabular format.

- **Filtered Search**: This option appears as a funnel icon and clicking it will open a sidebar on the right-hand side of your screen containing filter options. The sidebar filter options will vary, depending on your content type menu selection.

This toolbar is a valuable resource that helps you navigate Tableau Server quickly and efficiently. Let's continue learning about some of the helpful features that are available on the server by examining how content is organized and displayed.

How is content organized?

Content that's been published on the server is organized into folders called **projects**. These projects may contain workbooks, data sources, and additional projects. If your organization has the Data Management add-on available, you may also see flows and data roles.

> **Note**
>
> Recall from *Chapter 2, How to Connect and Publish to Tableau Server*, that you must select a project when publishing a workbook to the server. If a project is not selected, it will publish to a default project, determined by your administrator settings.

Projects can be nested so that they contain additional child projects to allow you or your server administrator to organize content as needed. We learned about nested projects in the previous section, when we learned about the content type menu.

We will discuss some project organization best practice ideas later in this book. Depending on your company's settings, you may not have the ability to manage projects on the server yourself. If you need assistance organizing and managing projects, please see your Tableau Server administrator.

When browsing content on the server in the **grid view**, you will see a preview, also referred to as a thumbnail, of the content or an icon representing the content type, the title of the item, and a description, if one is available. Next to the title, you will see a star icon and an ellipsis button, as shown in the following screenshot:

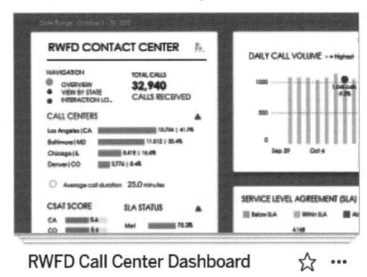

RWFD Call Center Dashboard   ☆ ⋯

#RWFD submission created by Chimdi Nwosu

Figure 3.17 – Preview of a dashboard on Tableau Server

Dashboard image created by Chimdi Nwosu

The star icon is a quick way to add an item to your favorites list. This will be discussed in more detail in the next section of this chapter, when we learn about the **Favorites** page. The **More Actions Ellipses** button opens a list of content management options that will vary based on the type of item you have selected. **More Actions Ellipses** and its options will be discussed in depth in *Chapter 7, What is in the More Actions (…) Menu.*

Tooltips aren't isolated to only the views you create on Tableau Desktop or online. You can also hover over the content on the server to see a tooltip that provides additional details about that item. Please see the following screenshot to review an example of a tooltip you may see:

Figure 3.18 – Example of a tooltip you may see on Tableau Server

Tooltips will contain different details based on the type of content you are looking at. Hovering over a project will show you a tooltip that contains the project's name, the owner, and the date it was last modified. When you hover over a workbook, dashboard, or view, the tooltip will show you the content's name, description, tags, number of published sheets or items, data connection names, the project's name, the owner's name, and the last modified date. Finally, hovering over a data source will reveal a tooltip that presents you with its name, tags, connection information (with an icon that indicates the connection type), the project's name, and the owner's information.

You can also browse content on the server in the **list view**, which allows you to see content and some of the data surrounding it in a tabular format. If you are viewing content on the **Explore** page using a list view, the columns available in the view will vary based on what you have selected in the content type menu, which we learned about previously in this section.

While in list view, each item has a record of information, including the item's name, its type, and various other details. Next to the content's name, you will see an icon that represents the type of content that item is. Some of the most common icons are shown in the following screenshot:

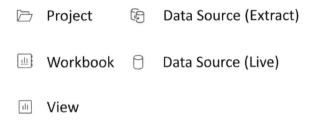

Figure 3.19 – Content types and their corresponding icons

The list view is useful for many reasons. You can use it to quickly review the size of content, the number of views, see the item owner, check the modified date, and much more. We will review both the grid view and list view options in detail in *Chapter 5*, *Filtering and Sorting Content*, and learn how to filter and sort your content effectively.

Let's reflect on everything that you have learned as we end the *Examining the Explore page* section. You should now have a better understanding of how to find different types of content and feel confident navigating the resulting items on the page. It is important to remember that the options you are presented with will vary in a filtered search, depending on the selection you make in the content type menu. This is also true for the columns you will be presented with when using a list view. In the next section, we will discuss how to mark, view, and organize your favorite content.

Examining the Favorites page

Your **Favorites** page enables you to create and maintain a list of shortcuts to your favorite or most frequently viewed content on Tableau Server. This page is located on the Navigation Pane on the left-hand side of your screen and can be identified by the star icon and the word **Favorites**. Your **Favorites** page starts empty and gradually fills in as you select and add content you find important or valuable.

Ways to favorite content

Any content on Tableau Server where you see a star icon can be added to a list of your personal favorites. To add your most frequently used or viewed content to your **Favorites** page, simply click the star icon where you see it available.

You can find a favorites star in three locations:

- In the header of an open view:

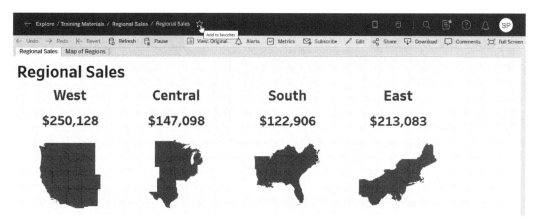

Figure 3.20 – Favorites page star in the header

- In a grid view:

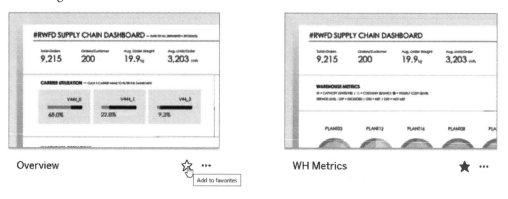

Figure 3.21 – Favorites page star in a grid view
Dashboard images created by Chimdi Nwosu

- In a list view:

Figure 3.22 – Favorites page star in a list view

Clicking on a star icon once, places that content on your **Favorites** page. Once selected, a filled star icon toggles on, signaling that this piece of content has been added as a favorite. To remove a favorite, simply click the filled star; the content will be removed from your **Favorites** page and the star icon will appear as an outline once more.

> **Note**
>
> You can mark any View, Workbook, or Published Data Source as a Favorite. The only type of content that cannot be marked as a Favorite is an Embedded Data Source. An Embedded Data Source is restricted to only the workbook that the data is contained in. A data source that is published separately, called a Published Data Source, can be utilized in multiple workbooks.
>
> While you may not be able to Favorite an Embedded Data Source, you can always mark the Workbook containing it.

Your Favorites page

Now that you know how to select your favorite content, let's look at your **Favorites** page. To open this, click **Favorites** on the left-hand side Navigation Pane. If your sidebar is collapsed, you will only see a star icon. Click this icon to open it. When you open your **Favorites** Page, you will see your **Contents Toolbar** just below the page title. Below that is where the content you have chosen to favorite will be featured.

The **Contents Toolbar** options on your **Favorites** page, shown at the top of the following figure, will appear very similar to what you have seen on other pages on Tableau Server:

Figure 3.23 – Favorites page in a grid view

Dashboard images created by Chimdi Nwosu

A more in-depth analysis of all the available content toolbar options on Tableau Server can be found in *Chapter 5, Filtering and Sorting Content*.

Here's a quick overview of the **Favorites** page's content toolbar options:

- **Select All**: Clicking this option allows you to quickly select all the content on the page. Once selected, a list of actions that are available will appear in a drop-down menu on the toolbar. The actions that are available to you will vary based on what you have selected in the content type menu, which we discussed in the previous section, and your permissions for that content.

- **Content Type**: Clicking this option will provide you with a drop-down list of options that allows you to filter your **Favorites** page by one or more types of content. The list of content options includes **Project**, **Workbooks**, **Views**, **Metrics**, **Data Sources**, and **Data Roles**. The interactivity of this drop-down filter mode is nearly identical to a **Multiple Values (List)** dimension filter on Tableau Desktop.

- **Sort by**: Clicking this option will provide you with a drop-down list of options that allows you to organize your **Favorites** page by a single option. The list of content options includes **Name**, **Type**, **Owner**, **Modified**, **Date Added**, and **Custom**. The interactivity of this drop-down filter closely resembles a **Single Value (Drop-down)** dimension filter on Tableau Desktop.

- **View Modes**: Clicking this option will provide you with a drop-down list of two view options a grid view or a list view. A grid view provides a series of thumbnail images or icons representing your content, while a list view presents your content and some of the data surrounding it in a tabular format.

- **Filtered Search**: Clicking this option will open a sidebar on the right-hand side of your screen with filter options. This sidebar contains a search box and filter options that include the ability to filter by **Owner**, **Modified on/after**, **Modified on/before**, **Created on/after**, and **Created on/before**. These options may vary, depending on what you have selected in the content type menu.

When you look at the content on your **Favorites** page, you will find that any recently favorited items will appear at the top left-hand side of the screen.

Like other pages on Tableau Server, your **Favorites** page can be viewed in either a grid view or a list view. However, unlike those other pages, if you have your view mode set to grid view, you have the unique ability to drag and drop items to reorder your favorite content as you see fit. This ordered preference appears as the custom option seen in the **Sort By** drop-down of your toolbar options.

As we wrap up the *Examining the Favorites page* section, consider what you have learned. You now understand how to favorite content, what content can and cannot be favorited, the available options on the **Contents Toolbar**, and how to use the unique drag and drop feature while in the grid view to organize the items on your **Favorites** page. In the next section, we will discuss how to find and navigate content that you have recently viewed.

Examining the Recents page

As its name suggests, the **Recents** page shows the views and metrics you have recently opened. This page is located on the Navigation Pane, on the left-hand side of your screen, and can be identified by the analog clock icon and the word **Recents**. Your **Recents** page defaults to showing the views sorted by what you have most recently looked at in the top left corner of the page.

The **Contents Toolbar** options, shown in the following figure, at the top of your **Recents** page will appear very similar to what you have seen on other pages on Tableau Server:

Figure 3.24 – Recents page in a grid view

Dashboard images created by Chimdi Nwosu and Mark Bradbourne

A more in-depth analysis of all available content toolbar options on Tableau Server can be found in *Chapter 5, Filtering and Sorting Content*.

Here's a quick overview of the **Recents** page's Contents Toolbar options:

- **Select All**: Clicking this option allows you to quickly select all the content on the page. Once selected, a list of actions will become available in a drop-down menu on the toolbar. The actions that are available to you will vary based on what you have selected in the content type menu, which we discussed in the previous section, and your permissions for that content.

- **Sort by**: Clicking this option will provide you with a drop-down list of options that allow you to organize your **Recents** page by a single option. The list of content options includes **Name**, **Workbook**, **Last Accessed At**, **Project**, and **Owner**. The interactivity of this drop-down filter closely resembles a **Single Value (Drop-down)** dimension filter on Tableau Desktop.

- **View Modes**: Clicking this option will provide you with a drop-down list of two view options: a grid view and a list view. A grid view provides a series of thumbnail images or icons representing your content, while a list view presents your content and some of the data surrounding it in tabular format.

- **Filtered Search**: Clicking this option will open a sidebar on the right-hand side of your screen that contains a list of filter options. The sidebar contains search options such as a search box and filter options that include the ability to filter by **Owner**, **Tag**, **Modified on/after**, **Modified on/before**, **Created on/after**, and **Created on/before**. Lastly, there is a checkbox for **My favorites** that shows content that you have visited recently and favorited.

The following screenshot shows the **Recents** page, with the views displayed in grid view format:

Figure 3.25 – Recents page thumbnails with timestamps

Dashboard images created by Chimdi Nwosu and Mark Bradbourne

You'll notice that the difference between the thumbnail images shown here and those on other pages is that a time is displayed in the bottom left corner of each view. This feature is unique to your **Recents** page and provides you with a timestamp of when you last visited the view.

> **Note**
>
> Tableau wisely caps the number of views that appear on your **Recents** page. This ensures that you are not forced to navigate through every view you have ever clicked on while on Tableau Server. As a result, no more than 14 of your most recently visited views will be prominently displayed on the page.

Now that you have completed this section, you possess a much deeper understanding of how to utilize your **Recents** page. You should feel comfortable with identifying timestamps and navigating the toolbar options. In the next section, we will discuss content that has been shared with you.

Examining the Shared with Me page

The **Shared with Me** page contains items that other users have created and shared with you on Tableau Server. This page conveniently stores this shared content in a single location for you to find when you need it. This is helpful because it is easy to forget to bookmark content that is sent to you. When another Tableau Server user shares an item, you will receive an email with a link to that item on the server. Content on the **Shared with Me** page will show the corresponding thumbnail or icon, the title, and information about when it was shared. We will discuss how you, too, can share content with others in *Chapter 8, Interacting with Views on Tableau Server*.

It is important to note that even though an item has been shared with you, the permissions rules will have to be adjusted for you to be able to view and interact with the content. The process of altering or adjusting permissions will vary by organization. We will discuss this in more detail in *Chapter 7, What is in the More Actions (…) Menu*.

Here's a quick overview of the **Shared with Me** page's Contents Toolbar options:

- **Select All**: Clicking this option allows you to quickly select any or all content that has been shared with you and gives you the option to add a tag.

- **View Modes**: Clicking this option will provide you with a drop-down list of two view options: a grid view and a list view. A grid view provides a series of thumbnail images or icons representing your content, while a list view presents your content and some of the data surrounding it in tabular format.

Only the most recently shared item will appear on your **Shared with Me** page when the same content is shared with you more than once. If versions of the same view are shared with you that have different filters and selections than previous versions, a **Shared Versions** icon will appear, as shown in the following screenshot:

Figure 3.26 – Shared with Me page – Shared Versions

Clicking this icon will provide you with a detailed history of who shared the view, if it is a customized or modified view, the date and time it was shared with you, any comments from the sharer, and a link to open that view.

Examining the Recommendations page

The **Recommendations** page contains a compilation of content that has been suggested based on your viewing habits on your server site. You may also see content being recommended that is popular, or trending, on the site. You can hover over a recommended view for additional information, such as why it was recommended, the workbook's name, the owner's name, and the modified date. An example of this page is shown in the following screenshot:

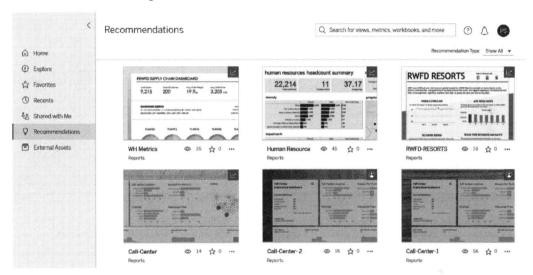

Figure 3.27 – Recommendations page

Dashboard images created by Chimdi Nwosu, Mark Bradbourne, and Luther Flagstad

You'll notice an icon in the top right corner of each thumbnail view image on the **Recommendations** page. A *trending* icon appears as an image of a line graph moving upward because it has been recently trending, while a *for you* icon appears as a cartoon headshot and is shown because people with similar viewing habits to yours looked at this.

> **Note**
>
> Server administrators can determine whether you see the **Recommendations** page at all and what types of additional details are available to you on this page. If you have questions or concerns about what you can see, your administrator should be able to assist you.

This page can be a useful way to discover new content and find information that may be useful to you. If a recommended view is not helpful, you can hide it using the actions menu, which is represented by an ellipsis (…). Rest assured that only users that have permission to view an item can see it listed on their **Recommendations** page.

Summary

In this chapter, we examined the Tableau Server Navigation Pane, and you learned how to utilize its most common options. We discussed how the **Home** page serves as a quick way to provide you with much of your desired content in one place. Next, we reviewed how to browse content using the **Explore** page. You then learned how to mark and organize your most frequently used items on the **Favorites** page. We then discussed how to use the **Recents** page to find the content you have most recently viewed. Lastly, we looked at where to discover and interact with content that has been shared with you by other users.

Gaining a basic understanding of how to interact with this sidebar and its contents is relatively straightforward. However, by completing this chapter, you now have a much deeper understanding of the Navigation Pane than just the basics. You know how and why you would want to use the options available. The knowledge you have gained here will help you maximize your use of Tableau Server.

In the next chapter, we'll look at the top toolbar, which will help you quickly search for and find items, get help, locate notifications, and modify your settings in Tableau Server.

4
Tableau Server Top Toolbar

In this chapter, you will learn how to utilize the features that are available from Tableau Server's top toolbar. Because the top toolbar is so useful, the options you will learn about here will always be available to you as you navigate the server interface.

You will learn how to quickly search for content, find Tableau Server help, recognize received notifications, explore your content, and manage your personal account settings. A solid understanding of how to use the top toolbar will greatly enhance your Tableau Server experience, by helping you identify and resolve important notifications and quickly find the items you need.

By the end of this chapter, you will know how to utilize all the options featured on your top toolbar. We will be covering the following topics:

- Understanding the top toolbar
- Examining Quick Search
- Examining the Help Menu
- Examining Notifications
- Examining My Content and Account Settings

Understanding the top toolbar

The **top toolbar** can be found in the top-right corner of your Tableau Server window. It provides a quick way to search for important items, receive Tableau Server help or support, see notifications, access all your content, and change your account settings. The following screenshot shows an example of your top toolbar within the Tableau Server window:

Figure 4.1 – Tableau Server top toolbar

In this chapter, we will review the options that are available in the top toolbar. Let's begin by quickly explaining each of these options:

- **Quick Search**: This appears as a magnifying glass icon with the word **Search** next to it contained in a search box. It is located in the top-right corner of your page. This option is a fast way to look for items on the server using a text search.

- **Help Menu**: This appears as a question mark icon in the top-right corner of your page. Clicking this icon will provide you with shortcuts to online Tableau support and information.

- **Notifications**: This appears as a bell icon in the top-right corner of your page. A green circle will appear on the bell icon if one or more of your reports experiences an extract issue. Clicking this icon will provide you with more detailed information on the issue or issues that you are being alerted about.

- **My Content and Account Settings**: This appears as a circle icon with your initials inside it or your selected profile image in the top-right corner of your page. Clicking this icon will present you with a drop-down menu of options that will allow you to quickly view all your content, update your account settings, change your start page, or sign out of Tableau Server.

After completing this chapter, you will know how and when to use the options available via your top toolbar. Many of the things you will learn about here will allow you to efficiently navigate, search, identify issues, and find help on Tableau Server. Let's begin by looking at an item you will use frequently on your top toolbar, Quick Search.

Examining Quick Search

Quick Search is a search box that provides a fast way to enter a query and search for associated items. After submitting a search term, Tableau Server will analyze its contents for matching words in things such as names, descriptions, tags, comments, captions, owners, metadata, and other additional information. This search box can be found on the top right-hand side of your page and can be identified by the magnifying glass icon, with the words **Search for views, metrics, workbooks, and more** next to it.

Your Quick Search option functions much like a web search engine. When you click the search box, your cursor will begin to flash, indicating that Quick Search has been selected. As you enter the search terms you want to query, items that share the same text will automatically begin to populate in a drop-down menu below your search box, as shown in the following screenshot:

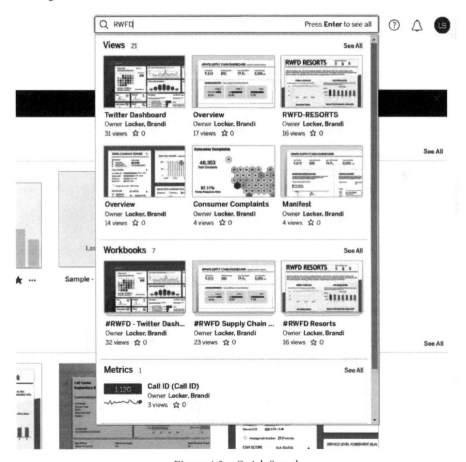

Figure 4.2 – Quick Search

Dashboard images created by Chimdi Nwosu, Luther Flagstad, and Mark Bradbourne

> **Note**
>
> When typing a query into the Quick Search box, there is no need to worry about case sensitivity or the order of words. For example, searching for %
> `Profit` will yield the same results as searching for `PROFIT %`.
>
> This is also true for the **Filtered Search** feature, which we will discuss in *Chapter 5, Filtering and Sorting Content*.

Search Operators

Tableau Server allows you to use commands, referred to as **Search Operators**, to assist you in refining and filtering your search results. The Search Operator commands that are available for you to use on Tableau Server are **and**, **or**, **not**, and *****. Let's take a look at these:

- **and**: This Search Operator restricts your returned search results to only those that contain both the search term preceding and following it. For example, if you type `profit and loss` in the search box, it will only return results that contain both the word `profit` and the word `loss`.

- **or**: This Search Operator returns search results that match either the search term preceding or following it. For example, if you type `profit or loss` in the search box, it will return results that contain either the word `profit` or the word `loss`.

- **not**: This Search Operator only returns search results that exclude the search term you put into the search box. For example, if you type `not profit` in the search box, it will only return results that do not contain the word `profit`.

- *****: This Search Operator serves as a wildcard for a word, character, or partial search term. This can be a useful tool when you are trying to search for a phrase but are having trouble remembering the exact term or phrase. For example, you can type `Customer Ac*` in the search box if you are having trouble remembering how to spell a term or finding search results on `Customer Acquisitions`.

> **Note**
>
> Surrounding a search such as `profit and loss` with double quotation marks informs Tableau Server that you want the returned results to contain that exact phrase. Make sure that you wrap any queries with double quotation marks if the text you enter into your Search Box includes most Search Operators (**and**, **or**, or **not**), spaces, or punctuation.

After typing in your query, there are several ways to select the content you want to view based on your search entry. The easiest way is to simply select the item if you see it appear in your drop-down menu. That action will transport you directly to the item you selected. Another way is to click the blue **See All** hyperlink, shown in *Figure 4.2*, located on the right-hand side of your search box drop-down menu and organized by type. Clicking this option will take you to a **Search Results** page showing all the items that share that type.

Finally, to see all the results of your query, press *Enter* on your keyboard to submit the search term in your search box. This will transport you to a **Search Results** page, similar to the one shown in the following screenshot:

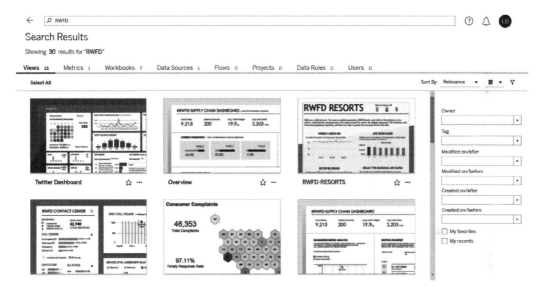

Figure 4.3 – Search results

Dashboard images created by Chimdi Nwosu, Luther Flagstad, and Mark Bradbourne

This page provides you with all the results based on your query, broken down by content type. You will find a row of tabs directly above the page showing your results. Clicking a tab will allow you to view all the items associated with that content type. The tabs you can use to select and organize your search results by are **Views**, **Metrics**, **Workbooks**, **Data Sources**, **Flows**, **Projects**, **Data Roles**, and **Users**.

You can reorder your results by clicking the drop-down menu entitled **Sort By** on the right-hand side of your page, as shown in the following screenshot. You have the option to order your search results by **Relevance**, **Name**, **Viewed by Users**, **Workbook**, **Worksheet**, **Project**, **Owner**, and **Modified Date**. In addition, if you want to see more details, such as the number of views, owner, or when a view was last modified, simply switch your **View Mode** from a grid to a list by clicking on the icon located to the right of the **Sort By** option:

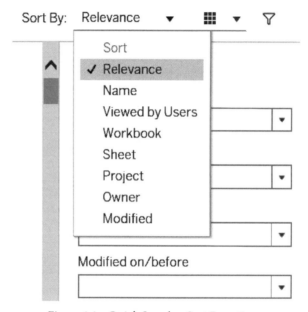

Figure 4.4 – Quick Search – Sort By options

> **Note**
>
> When using the Quick Search option, please remember that it only searches through **published** data sources. Make sure that you use a **Filtered Search** if you know that you are searching for an embedded data source. The Filtered Search will be discussed at length in the next chapter, *Chapter 5, Filtering and Sorting Content*.

You now have an awareness and understanding of how and when to use the Search Operator commands. The information we have discussed here will help you create more nuanced queries, when needed, resulting in better search results being returned.

> **Tip**
>
> Creating and using **Tags** is a great way to improve your ability to find content when using a Quick Search. A Tag is a keyword that you attach to items (views, workbooks, and data sources) on Tableau Server to aid you in finding, filtering, and categorizing content. A good Tag can help ensure that you and others will be able to quickly and easily locate specific content in an ocean of published workbooks. We will cover how to effectively write, create, and use Tags in *Chapter 7, What is in the More Actions (…) Menu.*

Search Attributes

You can further refine your searches by using **Search Attributes**. This option allows you to enter specific attributes directly into the search box to further limit your returned search results on Tableau Server. Some common attributes you can search by include name, title, owner, project, and tag.

To utilize a search attribute, you simply need to enter the following syntax into your search box:

```
<attribute name>:<search term>
```

Here is an example of a simple query using a single search attribute and search term:

```
name:profit
```

Finally, here is a slightly more complex example using multiple search attributes and search terms:

```
owner:sarsfield name:profit
```

Make sure that when you are using search attributes, no spaces exist on either side of the colon between the attribute name and your search term. *Figure 4.5* provides an example of both a correctly and an incorrectly entered search attribute:

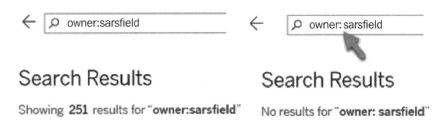

Figure 4.5 – Search attributes entered correctly and incorrectly

A full list of Search Attribute options can be seen in the following table:

This attribute...	Followed by...	Returns
name:	Search term	Items with names that match the search term.
title:	Search term	Views with titles that match the search term.
caption:	Search term	Applies to views with captions.
owner:	Username	Items that are owned (published) by the specified users. **Note**: Prior to 8.2, owners were listed as publishers in Tableau Server. The **publisher** serch attribute is still supported and returns the same results as the **owner** attribute.
publisher:	Username	(See owner above).
project:	Search term	Items that are part of a project whose name matches the search term.
comment:	Search term	Views whose comments match the search term.
tag:	Search term	Items whose tags match the search term.
field:	Search term	Views with matching fields on the rows, columns, level of detail, pages, or encoding shelves.
sheettype:	View, dashboard, or story	Views that are of the matching sheet type.
class:	Type of data source (for example, mysql)	Views and data sources that are associated with the matching type of data source.
dbname:	Name of database	Published data sources that are associated with the matching data source.
nviews:	Number	Workbooks that contain the specified number of views.

Figure 4.6 – Search Attributes
(information available at `https://help.tableau.com/current/pro/desktop/en-us/search.htm`)

With that, you have become familiar with how to use the Tableau Server Quick Search box option to quickly find items. You understand how and when to craft better queries by using Search Operators and Attributes. You are also aware of the different options available so that you can navigate your search results. In the next section, we will discuss how you can find help and other online Tableau resources.

Examining the Help Menu

The **Help Menu** is a shortcut you can use to find Tableau Server product support when you need it. It is represented by a question mark icon and can be found in the top-right corner of your page on the top toolbar, between the Quick Search (search box) and the Notifications icon, as shown in *Figure 4.7*:

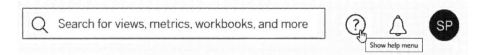

Figure 4.7 – Help Menu icon

Clicking this icon will open the drop-down menu shown in *Figure 4.8*:

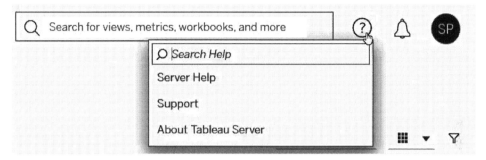

Figure 4.8 – Help Menu drop-down options

The first option that's available to you at the top of your Help Menu is the **Search Help** feature. The Help Menu search box allows you to type your search criteria directly into the Tableau Server window. After hitting *Enter*, a new web browser tab or window will open with your search result options on Tableau's Support website.

This shortcut enables you to seamlessly find solutions without ever having to leave the Tableau Server environment to open a new window to search for help. The **Search Help** box does this all for you in one convenient step.

> **Note**
>
> The Help Menu search is not to be confused with the Quick Search feature within the top toolbar, which we discussed in the previous section. Quick Search allows you to search for content on your Tableau Server, while the Search Help feature of Help Menu functions as a shortcut to the help and support pages on the Tableau website.

The next option in the **Help Menu** drop-down is a selection called **Server Help**. Clicking on this option will open a new web browser tab or window directly to a page on the Tableau website, designed to help you get started with Tableau Server. From this page, you can browse through various Tableau Server help topics. You can also find links to explore what is new or has changed on the server. Please note that some of these pages may be directed toward Tableau Server administrators and may not be as applicable to a developer or analyst.

The third option in the **Help Menu** drop-down is a selection called **Support**. This option takes you directly to the main support page on the Tableau website. From this page, you can browse through the various specific support pages for each Tableau product, read Support FAQs, find contact information for Tableau Support, and more. If you are unable to find what you need in the provided links, you can also search the Support pages for your specific issue.

The last option in the **Help Menu** drop-down is the **About the Server** option. Your organization or administrator may have customized the wording to include the company name or other details. Clicking this option will open a pop-up window that identifies which version of Tableau Server you are using and contains Tableau Software copyright information.

You are now familiar with the Help Menu, which can be found within the top toolbar of Tableau Server. Using this menu provides quick navigation to Tableau Support for a seamless product experience. Next, you will learn about notifications.

Examining Notifications

Tableau Server **Notifications** is a feature designed to inform you of changes occurring with server content that may be important to you, such as shares, comments, and data extract information. The Notifications center is represented by a bell icon and is located on the top toolbar, between the Help Menu and your profile icon, as shown in *Figure 4.9*:

Figure 4.9 – Notification icon (with a notification)

When you have a new notification, you will notice a red dot appear on the bell icon. You can click the bell icon at any time to look at new and previous notifications. An example of the notifications drop-down is shown in *Figure 4.10*:

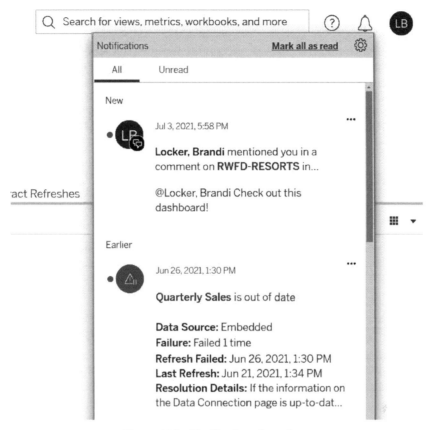

Figure 4.10 – Notifications drop-down

You can use the tabs at the top of the **Notifications** drop-down to toggle the view to show **All** of your notifications or only the **Unread** ones. A blue dot to the left of the notification indicates that it is unread. Once the notification has been read, the blue dot will disappear. To clear all of the unread notification indicators, click the **Mark all as read** option at the top of the **Notifications** drop-down.

Each notification describes what's new or has changed on the server that is relevant to the content you own or have been tagged in. You can hover over a notification for even more information in a pop-up, also known as a tooltip, or you can click on the notification to be redirected to the content indicated.

On the top-right corner of each notification is an ellipsis button (...). Clicking this button will open a menu that allows you to apply certain actions to that particular notification, such as marking it as read or unread, removing the notification, or viewing the connection details if the notification pertains to a data extract. Your notifications will remain in the **Notifications** center until you choose to remove them using the ellipsis button. This menu is shown in the following screenshot:

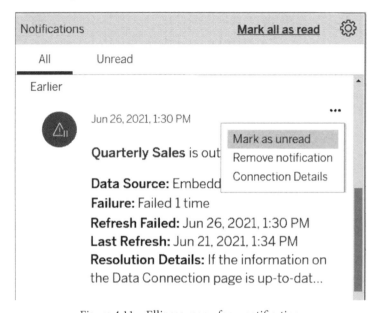

Figure 4.11 – Ellipses menu for a notification

One of the most common notifications that you may see is if you own a workbook that contains data that is out of date, as illustrated in the previous two screenshot. This happens when a workbook's data extract fails to refresh.

The details provided in this notification can provide important troubleshooting information to help you resolve any issues, including the following:

- Data source type
- Failure count
- Date of refresh failure
- Last refresh date
- Resolution details (potential solutions to resolve the error)

At the top of the **Notifications** center is a gear icon. Clicking this icon will open your **Settings** page, where you can adjust your own **Notifications** preferences. You can choose to be notified on Tableau Server or by email. Adjusting your settings will be covered in the next section.

With that, you have learned about Notifications center, which is available on Tableau Server. This feature can provide you with useful details if you need to troubleshoot regarding with your content, inform you of shared content or new comments, and more. Next, let's continue learning about the last item in the top toolbar, which is all about accessing your content and settings menu.

Examining My Content and Account Settings

The last feature available in the top toolbar is the **My Content and Account Settings** menu. By default, this option appears as a circle with your initials inside of it in the top-right corner of your page, as shown in the following screenshot:

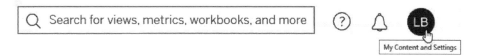

Figure 4.12 – My Content and Account Settings icon

This menu provides a shortcut that you can use to access your content on Tableau Server, a location to adjust your server settings, and more. It contains conveniences that can aid you in quickly navigating the server and help you customize your server experience.

We will examine each option that's available, starting with My Content.

My Content

The first selection that's available in the **My Content and Account Settings** drop-down menu is **My Content**. This option is shown in the following screenshot:

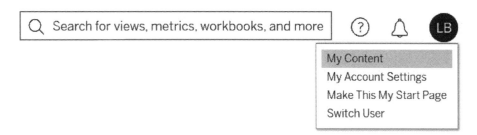

Figure 4.13 – My Content menu option

As the name indicates, this page provides you with a quick look at the items that you will likely need to find most often as you manage and maintain your content on Tableau Server. At the top of the **My Content** page, you will see your user icon, name, user information, site role, last sign-in date, and your linked account email address. Below that information is tabs that allow you to access your **Content**, **Alerts**, **Subscriptions**, and **Settings**, as shown in the following screenshot:

Figure 4.14 – My Content page

Dashboard images created by Chimdi Nwosu and Mark Bradbourne

The **Contents** tab is the default page that opens when you select **My Content** from the **My Content and Account Settings** drop-down menu. It only contains items that you own. This includes content that you have published and content that was published by others with ownership transferred to you. Your owned content includes views or workbooks, metrics, and data sources. By default, your content page will be sorted alphabetically. It will also default to a grid view unless you have previously selected to view content in a list view.

The **Alerts** tab contains a summarized view of alerts that you create for yourself and others within workbooks. From this page, you can manage your alerts from the actions menu by removing yourself from the alert, editing the alerts, changing the owner, and deleting the alert. If you have created an alert for someone else, you can also add yourself to that alert using the actions menu. These alerts have links to their corresponding dashboards so that you can easily navigate directly to that item. You will learn about alerts and how to create them in *Chapter 8, Interacting with Views on Tableau Server*.

> **Tip**
>
> You can access the actions menu by clicking the ellipsis button (…) under the actions column in the view, or by selecting the checkbox to the left of an item and using the actions drop-down that appears when an item is selected.

The **Subscriptions** tab is similar to the **Alerts** tab in that it summarizes all of your subscriptions to views in one convenient place for you to manage them. On this page, you will see subscriptions to views you have chosen yourself and views that you have been subscribed to by others. From this page, you can see the subscription's schedule, the last and next update, who created the subscription, and more. You can also use the actions menu to change the frequency, subject, select what happens when the view is empty, format, or unsubscribe. Like alerts, subscriptions also have links to their corresponding dashboards so that you can easily navigate directly to that item. You will learn about subscriptions and how to create them in *Chapter 8, Interacting with Views on Tableau Server*.

The **Settings** tab is another way to navigate to the same account settings page that we will discuss in the next section. It is simply a shortcut so that you can go directly to that page without returning to the drop-down in the top toolbar.

> **Tip**
>
> You can use the **Back to Content** button at the top left of the page or the **Home** button on the Navigation Pane on the left-hand side to return to the Tableau Server **Home** page.

The **My Content** page provides a convenient way to quickly manage and review your content by utilizing the additional actions, view, and filter options available in the toolbar shown previously in *Figure 4.14*. We will discuss this toolbar in depth in *Chapter 5, Filtering and Sorting Content*.

With that, you have learned about the first selection that's available in the **My Content and Account Settings** drop-down menu, **My Content**. Selecting this option will default to a page showing the content you own. Additionally, this page will have tabs available that, when clicked, provide quick access to items you have set up with alerts, are subscribed to, and access to your personal settings. Let's continue by learning about the next item in the drop-down menu: **My Account Settings**.

My Account Settings

The next option that's available in the **My Content and Account Settings** drop-down is **My Account Settings**, as shown in the following screenshot:

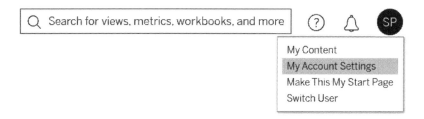

Figure 4.15 – My Account Settings menu option

On this page, you can check the settings for your account and customize your server settings to suit your needs and preferences. The options that are available to you on this page may vary based on your organization's server and administrators' specifications. We will review the common setting selections that are available. If you have questions about additional options that are not discussed in this chapter, please contact your server administrator for assistance.

Similar to the **My Content** page, you will see your user icon, name, user information, site role, last sign-in date, and your linked account email address at the top of your account settings page.

> **Tip**
> From the **Settings** page, you can use the **Content**, **Alerts**, and **Subscriptions** tabs to navigate directly to those pages without having to return to the **My Content and Account Settings** drop-down menu.

You can change your Tableau Server profile image by clicking on the icon next to your name in the top-left corner of your account settings page, as shown in the following screenshot:

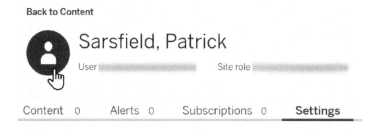

Figure 4.16 – My Account Settings – changing your user photo

Making this selection will open the **Edit User Photo** page, as shown in the following screenshot. Simply click the **Upload from computer** button to add your own personalized custom profile image:

Figure 4.17 – My Account Settings – Edit User Photo

At the top of the **Settings** page, you will see your Tableau Server **Username**, **Display Name**, and **Email**. Depending on your site role and the settings that have been established by your organization, you may also have the ability to edit these items and manage your account password here. If your organization has integrated your server credentials and your Windows credentials, this option will likely not be available to you.

Let's review some of the common options you are likely to see below your personal information (**Username**, **Display Name**, and **Email**) when you open **My Account Settings**:

- **Saved Credentials for Data Sources** is where you can view and manage data sources where you have saved connection details, such as tokens or usernames and passwords. You can edit connection details individually, or you can also **Clear All Saved Credentials**. If you select this button, you will be prompted to **Cancel** or confirm that you wish to **Clear Credentials**. Your options to save credentials will be managed by your server administrator.

- **Connected Clients** is where you can view and manage other Tableau applications or services that are connected to your server. By default, this connection is automatically established after your initial sign-in.

- **Personal Access Tokens** is where you can view and manage existing tokens or create new tokens. A personal access token is used to connect with the Tableau Server REST API, which allows you to program server tasks. Like a personal password, your tokens must be created individually and cannot be created by an administrator.

> **Note**
>
> An in-depth discussion of advanced settings, such as Saved Credentials for Data Sources, Connected Clients, Personal Access Tokens, and the REST API will not be discussed in this book due to their complexity and variations among different server environments. However, you can learn more by referring to the Help pages available on the Tableau website.

The **Settings** page also enables you to personalize your server preferences, as shown in the following screenshot:

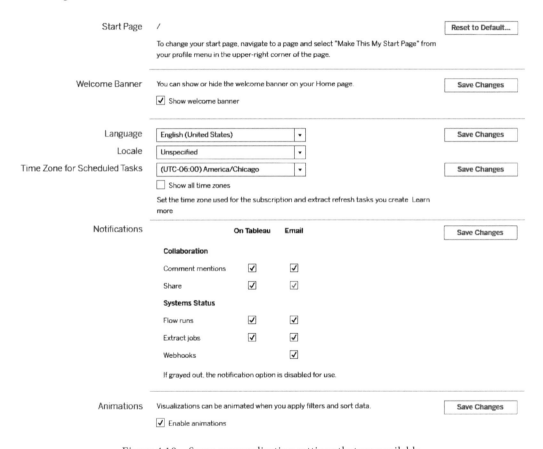

Figure 4.18 – Some personalization settings that are available

Let's quickly review these options:

- The **Start Page** section of the **Settings** page allows you to review your customized start page's path or restore it to the default setting. We will discuss this more in the next section of this chapter.

- The **Welcome Banner** section of the **Settings** page allows you to choose whether to show the welcome banner on the Tableau Server home page, which you learned about in *Chapter 3, Tableau Server Navigation Pane*.

- The **Language** and **Locale** sections of the **Settings** page allow you to identify your preferred language. This will be used throughout the Tableau Server interface. You can also select your location, which will be used in visuals when displaying details such as number formatting.

The language and locale settings are determined by different variables. These variables have an order of priority, as shown in the following diagram:

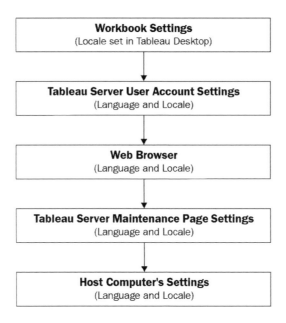

Figure 4.19 – Priority order of location and locale settings

As you can see, your selected server locale settings can only be overridden by the settings of an individual workbook. Your user account and web browser selections for language and locale will override selections made by your server administrator. You can also leave these options unspecified if you wish.

The **Settings** page has additional options that allow you to adjust the functionality of your content. Let's take a look at them:

- The **Time Zone for Scheduled Tasks** section allows you to adjust the time zone for your subscriptions and extract refresh schedules that you create. This option may be managed by your server administrator.

- The **Notifications** section allows you to choose which activities trigger a notification on Tableau Server and/or an email. These include activities such as comment mentions, content shares, and extract job notifications.

- The **Animations** section is where you can enable or disable animations for all the content that you view on the server. Animations are a feature that leverages the pre-attentive attribute of motion. This can be a useful feature to enable as our attention will naturally be directed toward any movement on a chart or graph. Enabling movement of your data visualizations allows you to see marks on a view move from one location to another.

After making your desired changes, you can use the **Save Changes** button on the right-hand side of the window next to each setting selection to implement the changes.

With that, you have learned about the second option available in the **My Content and Account Settings** drop-down menu: **My Account Settings**. This page provides you with many useful setting options for customizing your Tableau Server experience. Let's continue learning about the next item in the drop-down menu: **Make This My Start Page**.

Make This My Start Page

The **Make This My Start Page** option is the third item that's available in the **My Content and Account Settings** drop-down, as shown in the following screenshot:

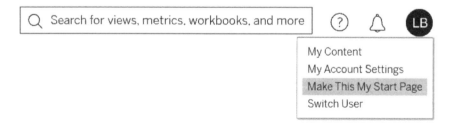

Figure 4.20 – Make This My Start Page menu option

As you may have guessed, this selection allows you to choose any page on the server to be your default start page, which is the page that will open when you sign into Tableau Server. It is a simple and convenient feature that helps you customize your Tableau Server experience. If you find yourself navigating to the same location on the server consistently, it may be convenient for you to make that page your start page. Remember, you can change the start page selection as often as you like.

You can check your start page path and/or reset the start page to the default settings using the **My Account Settings** page, which you learned about in the previous section:

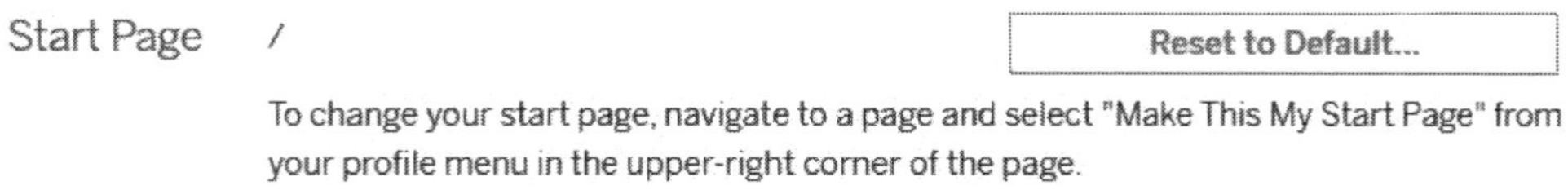

Start Page   /

Reset to Default...

To change your start page, navigate to a page and select "Make This My Start Page" from your profile menu in the upper-right corner of the page.

Figure 4.21 – Start Page setting options

Your selections will override any start page selection that's been established by your server administrator. If you do not choose a customized start page, and if your server administrator has not chosen a start page for your organization's users, the default will be your **Home** page, which you learned about in *Chapter 3, Tableau Server Navigation Pane.*

Switch User

The **Switch User** option is the fourth item that's available in the **My Content and Account Settings** drop-down, as shown in the following screenshot:

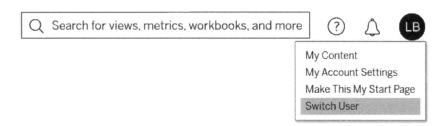

Figure 4.22 – Switch User menu option

As the name indicates, this is where you can sign out of your Tableau Server account and log in as a different user. Your organization may have single sign-on enabled, which allows you to use your Windows credentials to log onto the server. In this case, you can use the **Sign in using your Windows Credentials** link on the Tableau Server sign-in page. You will need to contact your administrator with further questions about signing into your account.

Summary

In this chapter, you learned how to best utilize the available options on the Tableau Server top toolbar. We discussed how the Quick Search box serves as a great way to enter a query and easily obtain fast results. You also learned efficient ways to refine searches through the use of Search Operators and Attributes. We then reviewed how the Help Menu works to streamline your experience with Tableau products and Support. The Notifications section taught you how to identify when an extract refresh failure requires attention. Finally, we looked at how **My Content and Account Settings** can help you quickly find your content, manage alerts and subscriptions, and customize your experience on Tableau Server to your preferences.

After finishing this chapter, you have a more thorough understanding of the top toolbar than just what you can quickly observe. You know when and how you would want to use these available options. This knowledge will help you efficiently navigate and personalize your use of Tableau Server.

In the next chapter, we'll look at how to filter for and sort content, which will help you understand how to search, sort, and filter through available items by utilizing the Contents Toolbar.

5
Filtering and Sorting Content

In this chapter, you will learn how to search, sort, and filter available items using the **Content Toolbar**. A solid understanding of how to filter and sort your content is useful when you are working on a Tableau Server site with a large amount of published content, and you want to find a specific item or piece of information.

By the end of this chapter, you will know how to utilize the options featured on your Content Toolbar:

- Understanding the Content Toolbar
- Examining the **New** menu
- Examining the **Select All** option
- Examining the **Content Type** menu
- Examining the **Sort By** menu
- Examining **View Modes**
- Examining Filtered Search

Understanding the Content Toolbar

The Content Toolbar is available on almost every page in Tableau Server. When it is available, the Content Toolbar options can be found directly above the first row of views displayed on your page. This toolbar gives you the ability to create a new project or workbook directly on the server, select and modify all or some content on a page, filter your page by its content type, sort by different options to organize the items on your page, switch between views best suited for visual content or reading content, and carry out comprehensive searches to find content using a combination of search terms and filters. *Figure 5.1* highlights an example of all the options you have available when using the Content Toolbar:

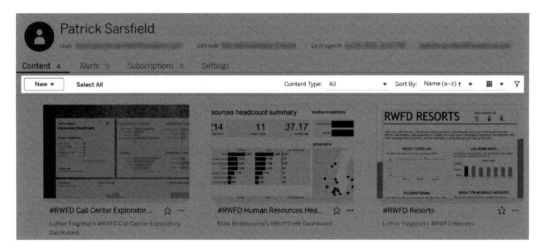

Figure 5.1 – Tableau Server Content Toolbar

Dashboard images created by Luther Flagstad and Mark Bradbourne

> **Note**
>
> It's important to remember that the options on your Content Toolbar will vary depending on the type of content you are viewing. *Figure 5.1* presents potential Tableau Server Content Toolbar options, but you may see fewer options depending on what you are looking at.

Let's look at each of these options one by one:

- **New**: This appears as a square button with the word **New** inside it and is located on the left side of your Content Toolbar. Clicking this option will provide you with a drop-down list of options that allows you to create a new project or workbook or to upload a workbook directly to the server without needing to open Tableau Desktop.

- **Select All**: When available, this option appears with the words **Select All** and is located on the left side of your Content Toolbar. Clicking this option is a fast way to select all the content displayed on the page. Once content is selected, you are provided a list of available actions in a drop-down menu on the toolbar.

- **Content Type**: When available, this option appears with the words **Content Type** and is located on the right side of your Content Toolbar. Clicking this option will provide you with a drop-down list of options that allows you to filter the page you're on by one or more types of content. If you are familiar with Tableau Desktop, the interactivity of this drop-down filter mode is nearly identical to a **Multiple Values (List)** dimension filter.

- **Sort By**: When available, this option appears with the words **Sort By** and is located on the right side of your Content Toolbar. Clicking this option will provide you with a drop-down list of options that allows you to organize items on your page by a single selection. The list of available options will also vary based on your server location and by what is selected in the **Content Type** menu. If you are familiar with Tableau Desktop, the interactivity of this drop-down filter most closely resembles a **Single Value (Drop-down)** dimension filter.

- **View Modes**: Clicking this menu will provide you with a drop-down list of two view options, **Grid View** or **List View**. The **Grid View** icon appears as a 3x3 grid of 9 squares, while the **List View** icon appears as 3 rows. **Grid View** provides a series of thumbnail images or icons representing your content. **List View** presents your content and some of the data surrounding it in a tabular format.

- **Filtered Search**: When available, this option appears as a funnel icon and is located on the far-right side of your Content Toolbar. Clicking this option will open a sidebar on the right side of your screen with search and filter options. The sidebar filter options will vary depending on your **Content Type** menu selection.

After completing this chapter, you will understand how to use the options on your Content Toolbar. The choices made available to you here will aid you in *creating, selecting, organizing, sorting,* and *filtering* the content on a page. Let's begin by looking at the **New** menu.

Examining the New menu

The **New** menu is a drop-down option that, depending on your Tableau Server permissions, can give you the ability to quickly create a new project, a new workbook, or upload an existing workbook within Tableau Server. You can find the **New** menu button on your **Home**, **Explore**, or any content page. This menu appears on the left side of your Content Toolbar and can be identified by the square button with the word **New** inside of it, as shown in *Figure 5.2*:

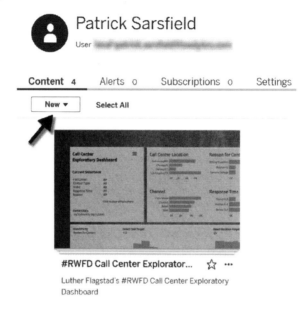

Figure 5.2 – New menu location within the Content Toolbar

Dashboard image created by Luther Flagstad

The next screenshot, *Figure 5.3*, provides an example of the menu you will see after clicking the **New** button:

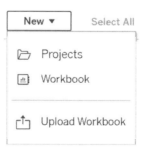

Figure 5.3 – New menu

Let's examine each of the options in this menu.

Creating a project

The first option you will see under the **New** drop-down menu is **Projects**. This option allows users with a site role of **Server Administrator** or **Site Administrator** to create a new project. Site roles are discussed in depth in *Chapter 1, What is Tableau Server?*. A project houses content such as workbooks, metrics, and data sources. You can think of a project as a folder that contains specific items, typically categorized or organized by what it contains. Selecting the **Projects** option automatically opens the **New Project** window, where you can enter details such as name and description.

Creating a workbook

The next option you will see in the **New** drop-down menu is **Workbook**. This option provides you with the ability to connect to data sources and perform data analysis via the web, without ever having to leave Tableau Server. Selecting the **Workbook** option will automatically open another web browser tab or window linking to Tableau Server's **Web Authoring** feature. You will be presented with the **Connect to Data** window, which will appear similar to *Figure 5.4*:

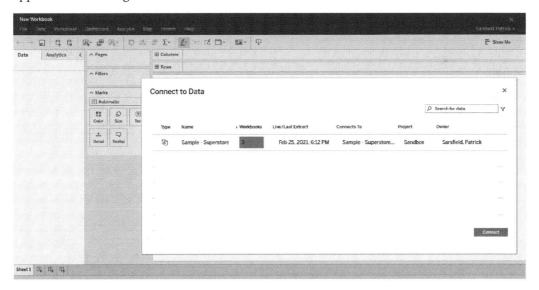

Figure 5.4 – Connect to Data window

This feature is available to you if you have the Explorer site role; however, you must have at least the Explorer (can publish) site role to save your work. Those with a site role of Viewer will not have access to save these features.

> **Note**
>
> If you do not have access to some of the options we listed, it's possible you do not have permissions, or the default permissions were changed by your site administrator. If you believe some of your permissions have been removed, contact your site administrator to see whether they will regrant them.

This feature provides a quick and easy way to explore your data and create data visualizations without ever needing to open the Tableau Desktop application. Web authoring will be discussed in depth in *Chapter 8, Interacting with Views on Tableau Server*.

Upload Workbook

The last option you will see in the **New** drop-down menu is **Upload Workbook**. This choice provides the ability to upload Tableau workbooks directly to Tableau Server. Selecting this option from the drop-down menu will open the **Upload Workbook** window shown in *Figure 5.5*:

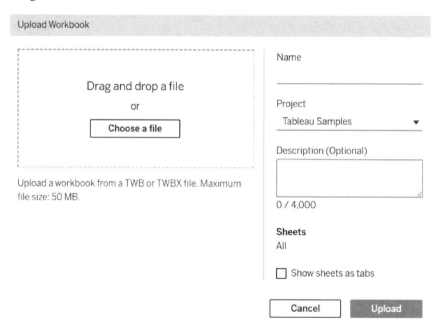

Figure 5.5 – Upload Workbook window

The left side of the window advises you of your two options to upload a workbook. You can either **drag and drop a file** directly to this window or **choose a file** from a saved location on your computer. You can upload either a Tableau workbook (.twb) or a packaged workbook (.twbx).

> **Note**
>
> When using the **Upload Workbook** option, the file size of an uploaded Tableau workbook or packaged workbook cannot exceed 50 MB.

The workbook will prepopulate in the **Name** field with the name of the file you select. However, if you want to enter a new name or edit the existing one, click the **Name** field in the top-right side of your **Upload Workbook** window.

Below the **Name** field, you will see a **Projects** drop-down menu. Use this menu to select the project where you want your workbook to be published.

Next, you can add a **description** to your workbook. You have the option to add a description of your workbook up to 4,000 characters. While a brief description of your workbook can be helpful to end users, it is not a requirement.

> **Tip**
>
> **Upload Workbook** publishes all **sheets** within the workbook. If you only want to publish select items, such as only dashboards, then you will need to publish the workbook from Tableau Desktop.

Last, in the bottom-right corner of the window, you will see a **Show sheets as tabs** checkbox. Clicking this checkbox will add tab-based navigation to your workbook on Tableau Server. Tabs provide users with the ability to navigate your published workbook similar to a web browser window with multiple tabs. If you check this option, you will see tabs at the top of the screen for workbooks that contain multiple worksheets, dashboards, or stories. *Figure 5.6* provides an example of tabs in a published workbook:

Figure 5.6 – Sheets shown as tabs in a published workbook

Click the **Cancel** button in the **Upload Workbook** window to exit the window without uploading or click **Upload** to proceed,

> **Note**
>
> Whether or not you choose **Show sheets as tabs** will affect your content's permissions. When tabs are shown, workbook-level permissions automatically apply to the sheets. When tabs are not shown, view-level permissions must be set individually. Changes to the workbook permissions will not apply to the views. We will discuss permissions in more depth in *Chapter 7, What is in the More Actions (...) Menu*.

As we end this section, you have become familiar with how to use the **New** menu. You should now understand how and when you would want to create a project or workbook directly on Tableau Server. You also know how to upload a workbook via Tableau Server and how it differs from uploading a workbook from Tableau Desktop.

In the next section, we will discuss how you can utilize the **Select All** option.

Examining the Select All option

The **Select All** option is a convenient way to select and make certain changes in bulk to many or all of the items on a page. You can find the **Select All** button on the left side of your Content Toolbar identified by the words **Select All**. *Figure 5.7* shows the location of the **Select All** button on your **My Content** page:

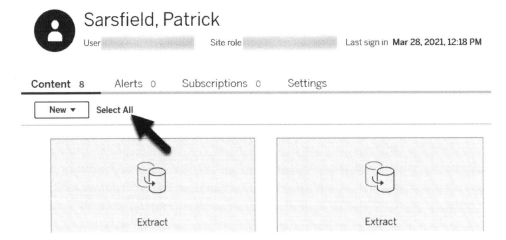

Figure 5.7 – Select All option location on the My Content page

Figure 5.8 provides a screenshot of the two things that will occur after you click the **Select All** button. First, all the content appearing on your page will be selected. This is denoted by a filled checkbox in the top-left corner of each thumbnail item on your page when your view mode is set to **Grid View**. In **List View**, the unfilled checkboxes appearing in the first column on the left side of your page become checked. Second, you will notice that the **Clear All** and **Actions** options appeared to the right of the **Select All** button, along with a count of the items you have selected:

Figure 5.8 – Select All option selected

Dashboard images created by Luther Flagstad, Mark Bradbourne, and Chimdi Nwosu

Let's examine the functionalities available after you select all items.

Clear All

Selecting the **Clear All** button will simply deselect the items. After clicking this option, you will see your page return to the same state prior to clicking the **Select All** button.

> **Note**
> Don't panic, clicking the **Clear All** button **WILL NOT** delete all the items that you have selected from Tableau Server.

To the right of the **Clear All** button, you will see a notification that identifies the total number of items you have selected on your page. This number will automatically update anytime you select or unselect a checkbox.

Selecting individual items

If your goal is to only select or deselect a few items on the page, instead of all or most of the content presented on your screen, then you can simply hover over a thumbnail image when in **Grid View** to select or deselect the checkbox in the upper-left corner of that item. *Figure 5.9* presents an unselected item to the left, an unchecked checkbox in the middle, and a selected item to the right:

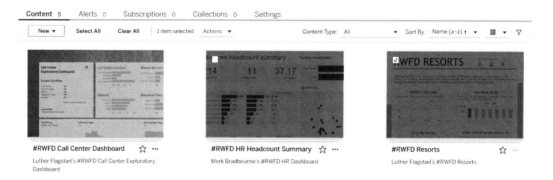

Figure 5.9 – Select individual items

Dashboard images created by Luther Flagstad and Mark Bradbourne

After you select an individual checkbox, the same **Clear All** and **Actions** options that appeared when you clicked **Select All** will appear.

Actions

Actions represent a series of options that are available to you and allow you to implement a specific change across all the items you have selected. *Figure 5.10* provides an example of an **Actions** menu opened after clicking **Select All**:

Figure 5.10 – Actions menu

The actions you see will vary depending on the type of content you have selected and your permissions. In general, the more items you select, the fewer actions you should expect to have available. The following list provides brief descriptions of some of the most common actions you may see in the menu when you click **Select All**:

- **Tag**: This option opens a window that allows you to tag selected content with searchable keywords.

- **Move**: This option opens a window that allows you to move your selected content to another project.

- **Change Owner**: This option opens a window that allows you to transfer ownership of an item to another person.

- **Refresh Extracts**: This option opens a window that provides you with options to **refresh now or schedule a refresh**. **Refresh Now** will perform a full refresh on the data sources for all the items you have selected. **Schedule a Refresh** will allow you to select a refresh schedule for the content you have selected.

- **Delete**: This option opens a window that gives you the option to permanently delete the items you have selected if you have permission to do so.

We discuss each of these individual options at length in *Chapter 7, What is in the More Actions (…) Menu.*

> **Note**
>
> Rest assured, you cannot delete items from Tableau Server of which you are not the owner, have administrator permissions, or **Delete** permissions have been granted through a custom template under **Permissions**. If you don't have permissions to delete an item, the option will be grayed out, or you will receive an error message stating that the item could not be deleted.

In this second section of this chapter, you have learned about the **Select All** option. This option provides you with many helpful ways to make quick changes to the selected items on your page. Let's continue learning about the next item on the Content Toolbar, the **Content Type** menu.

Examining the Content Type menu

The **Content Type** menu is a drop-down menu that allows you to limit the content shown in your server window by its type, such as a workbook or data source. This menu is found near the right side of your screen in the Content Toolbar, as shown in *Figure 5.11*:

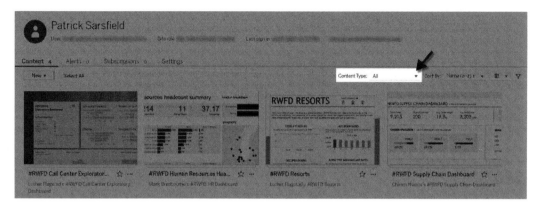

Figure 5.11 – Content Type menu
Dashboard images created by Luther Flagstad, Mark Bradbourne, and Chimdi Nwosu

This particular **Content Type** menu is unique to certain locations on Tableau Server, such as the **Favorites** page and the **My Content** page. You will also see this menu appear as you browse through the projects on the server. It has a similar function as the **Content Type** menu on the **Explore** page discussed in *Chapter 3, Tableau Server Navigation Pane*. Clicking on the drop-down menu will provide options similar to those shown in *Figure 5.12* and the number of those item types available in your current location on Tableau Server. The exact options in the drop-down may vary based on your server page location:

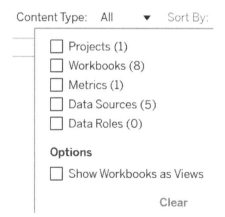

Figure 5.12 – Content Type menu drop-down options

> **Note**
>
> The counts provided in this **Content Type** menu found on the Content Toolbar are limited to the count of each item type found in your current location on the server. The counts provided by each type on the **Explore** page's **Content Type** menu tell you how many items of that type are available to you on the entire Tableau Server site.

The first option in the menu is **Projects**. Notice that this menu does not contain a **Top-Level Projects** option like the **Content** menu found on the **Explore** page. This is because the **Explore** page allowed you to see all items available to you on the server, while this menu focuses your options to your current location, whether that is an individual project or your own content page. Selecting projects from this menu will filter the content shown on your screen to the projects within your current server location.

In the same way, selecting **Workbooks, Metrics, Data Sources**, or **Data Roles** from this **Content Type** menu will filter items on your screen to that particular content type for your current server location. For example, if you are on the **My Content** page, selecting **Workbooks** will filter the page to show workbooks that you own. For another example, let's say your organization has a top-level project named `Sales` that contains additional projects for each of its four regions. Filtering to the **Projects** content type from within the top-level `Sales` project would filter your page to only those four regional projects. Using the same example, if you were to select **Data Sources** from the filter, you would see all of the data sources available within that `Sales` top-level project.

One of the key differences between the **Content Type** menu found in the Content Toolbar and the menu found on the **Explore** page is the ability to select multiple options from the drop-down menu. You may select as many options as you need. The **Clear** button at the bottom of the drop-down menu allows you to clear all selections, which resets the view to show all content types.

Another difference is that this menu has the additional **Show Workbooks as Views option**, as shown in *Figure 5.13*:

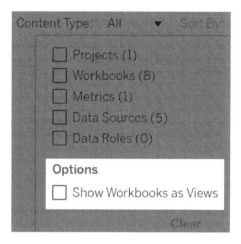

Figure 5.13 – Content Type menu Options

Recall that a single workbook can contain many views. Selecting this option allows you to see all of the views available within the workbooks on your current server location without having to open those individual workbooks. Notice that if you click this option, the drop-down menu will change dynamically to be relevant to your selection, as shown in *Figure 5.14*:

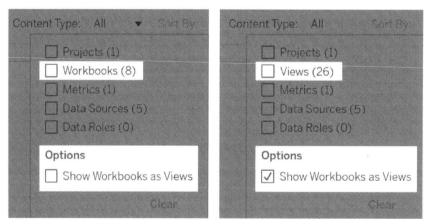

Figure 5.14 – Comparison of the Content Type menu with Options selected and deselected

To return to the default workbook view, simply click the **Show Workbooks as Views** option again to deselect the option box. This feature is not available in the menu on the **Favorites** page, but it does offer **Views** as an option from the drop-down, instead.

The **Content Type** menu is a convenient feature that allows you to browse and efficiently locate items on Tableau Server. You have learned how to utilize this menu to help you customize your page view, monitor, and manage content. In the next section, you will learn how to use the **Sort By** menu to tailor your server view to your needs.

Examining the Sort By menu

The **Sort By** feature is a drop-down menu that allows you to customize how items on your server page are organized. This feature is located on the content toolbar between the **Content Type** menu and the **View Mode** menu, as shown in *Figure 5.15*:

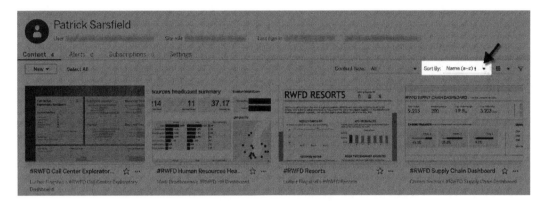

Figure 5.15 – Sort By menu in the Content Toolbar

Dashboard images created by Luther Flagstad, Mark Bradbourne, and Chimdi Nwosu

The options available in the **Sort By** menu are generally broken down into two sections, **Order** and **Sort**, as indicated in *Figure 5.16*. We will review examples of the available options:

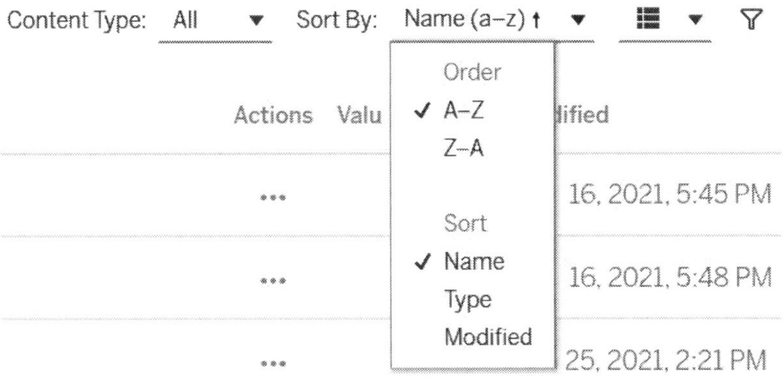

Figure 5.16 – Sort By menu options with Order and Sort sections

> **Note**
>
> All of the **Sort By** options are available to you in both Grid and List View, but the details will be more noticeable in List View. These two view options will be discussed in the next section.

The **Order** options at the top of this menu will dynamically update based on what you have selected in the **Sort** section at the bottom. If **Name** is selected, you can choose to order the names alphabetically, either ascending or descending. If **Modified** is chosen, then you can choose to order items by **Newest** or **Oldest**, according to the item's modified date. Sorting by type does not provide an option to order items.

> **Note**
>
> The meaning of **Modified Date** for an item can be confusing as it may vary based on its content type. The modified date of a workbook will depend on the data source(s) to which it is connected, but it could refer to either the last date the workbook was published or edited, or to the last extract refresh date. The modified date of a published data source could refer to the last time it was published or edited, or to the last server refresh date.

Additionally, all of these options will vary depending on where you are on the server and what you have selected in the **Content Type** menu, as discussed in the previous section. On the **My Content** page, and with **All** selected in the **Content Type** menu, your options will resemble the previous screenshot. If you have **Workbooks** selected in the **Content Type** menu on the **My Content** page, then your options may resemble *Figure 5.17*:

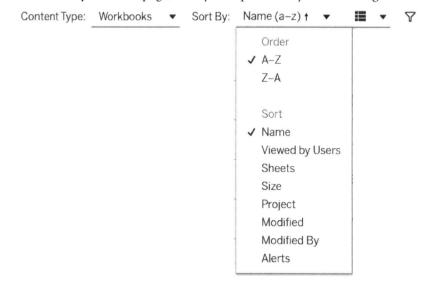

Figure 5.17 – Sort By menu options for Workbooks

Again, selecting any of the items in the **Sort** section on the lower part of the drop-down menu will dynamically update the **Order** options available in the upper part of the menu. For example, in the previous screenshot, content is sorted by **Name** and ordered alphabetically. If you select **Viewed by Users**, your **Order** options will change to a selection of timeframes: **1 Month**, **3 Months**, **12 Months**, and **All-Time** views, as illustrated in *Figure 5.18*:

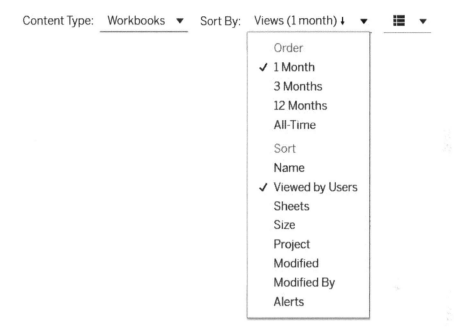

Figure 5.18 – Sort By menu option for Workbooks when Viewed by Users is selected

You can also select to sort by **Project**, which will organize all of your workbooks, grouped by their corresponding project location. It is easier to see the sort details in List View because you will have headers corresponding to the sort criteria, such as **Project** or **Modified** date. Since Grid View primarily presents you with a thumbnail image of the content and a title, the applied sort criteria are less obvious.

If you have **Data Sources** selected in the **Content Type** menu on the **My Content** page, then your options in the **Sort By** menu will resemble *Figure 5.19*:

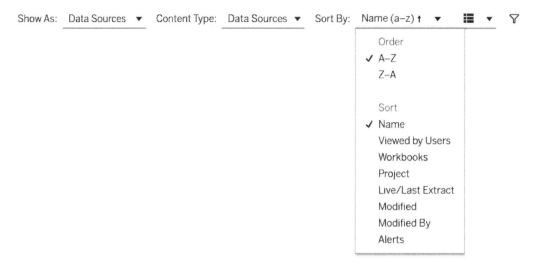

Figure 5.19 – Sort By menu options for Data Sources

Notice that in this screenshot, when the **Content Type** menu is filtered to **Data Sources**, an additional menu option appears to the left called **Show As**. This menu was discussed in *Chapter 3, Tableau Server Navigation Pane*. There, you learned that you can choose to view by **Data Source** or by **Connections**. When you choose to view by **Connections**, the options available in the **Sort By** menu will change to reflect that selection.

> **Note**
> If you have two or more items selected in the **Content Type** menu, then your **Sort By** options will resemble the same options shown in *Figure 5.16*, when the **Content Type** menu was set to **All**.

The **Sort By** menu is available on most locations within Tableau Server, particularly as you browse the server using the **Explore** page and look through projects. The options available will continue to vary depending on your server location and what you have selected in other filters or menus. However, there are some exceptions. For example, when viewing your **alerts and subscriptions** from the **My Content** page, there are fewer Content Toolbar options. Even though you cannot sort these items with the drop-down menu as we have discussed so far, you can also use many of the column headers on these pages to sort. Simply hover over a column name that you wish to sort the content by to see whether a link appears, as shown in *Figure 5.20*:

Figure 5.20 – Link to sort by column header

If it does, you can click on the header name to sort. As it sorts, a small arrow indicating the sort order will appear next to the header name, as shown in *Figure 5.21*:

Figure 5.21 – Sorting content with headers

In this screenshot, the subscriptions' **subject** will be sorted in descending order. Simply click the header again to reverse the sort order to ascending. When viewing these pages, you will only see one sort arrow next to the column headers. This indicates to you which column the sort is currently applied to.

> **Tip**
>
> You can use the sort by header technique as an alternative method to sort and order content from other pages while in List View, regardless of whether or not the **Sort By** drop-down menu is available. For example, if you are viewing content within a project and wish to sort by the item owner, you can either select **Owner** from the **Sort By** drop-down, or you can click on the column header for the **Owner** column. In this case, the sort order would default to ascending alphabetical (A-Z). If you wish to order the items in descending alphabetical order (Z-A), simply click the column header again to reverse the order.

You are encouraged to continue exploring the many options available from the **Sort By** menu as you browse content on Tableau Server on your own. This menu provides an efficient way to review and manage content on the server, and you should now feel confident to use its available selections to your advantage. Next, you will learn about the **view modes** available on Tableau Server.

Examining view modes

There are two view modes available on Tableau Server: **Grid View** and **List View**. The view menu can be found on the right side of your screen within the Content Toolbar, as shown in *Figure 5.22*:

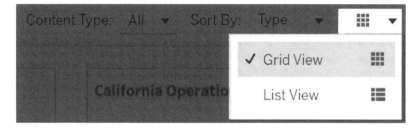

Figure 5.22 – View Mode toggle on the Content Toolbar

This menu allows you to change your server viewing preference as often as you need. The default view for Tableau Server is **Grid View**, although if you change this selection to **List View,** the server will remember your selection as you continue browsing through content. This feature is one of the few Content Toolbar menus that is available on almost every server page or location.

Grid View

As the name suggests, **Grid View** displays items on the server with a preview, also referred to as a thumbnail, of the content or an icon representing the content type, arranged in rows and columns that form a grid shape. In this view, you will also see the name of the item, a description if available, an option to favorite the item, and a More Actions button represented by an ellipsis (…). You can see additional information about an item by hovering over the thumbnail until a tooltip appears, as shown in *Figure 5.23*:

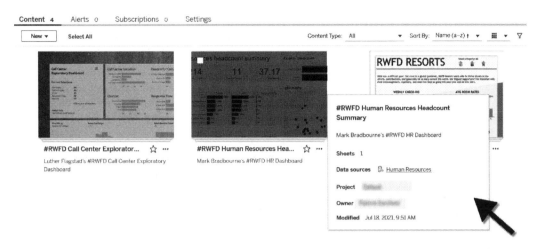

Figure 5.23 – Content tooltip when in Grid View

Dashboard images created by Luther Flagstad and Mark Bradbourne

The details shown in the tooltip will vary based on what type of content that item is, but may include the item owner, modified date, tags, number of sheets for workbooks, and data source information.

List View

List View displays content in a tabular format, with each item given its own record of details. The details are displayed in columns and vary depending on that item's content type. Some details shown may include the item owner, file size, project location, view count, and modified date. Next to each item name in **List View**, you will also see an icon representing the content type. Some of these icons are illustrated in *Figure 5.24*:

Figure 5.24 – Content types and their corresponding icons

Recall that these icons and view modes were briefly discussed in *Chapter 3, Tableau Server Navigation Pane*.

You can adjust the width of a column in **List View** by hovering between two header names until an icon with expand arrows appears, as shown in *Figure 5.25*:

Figure 5.25 – Adjust width of a column in List View

Once this icon appears, left-click and hold down the mouse button, then move your mouse left or right until the column is the appropriate width.

Choosing between Grid View and List View

Grid View is a good choice when you need to browse content in a visual format. It may be more helpful if you want to explore what is available on Tableau Server. The grid format allows for equal attention to all items on the screen. One drawback to this view is that the visuals take up more space on the screen, causing you to scroll more. However, this view can be a convenient way to find a dashboard that you cannot remember the name of because it provides a visual cue with a thumbnail of the content.

List View contains more detailed text information and fewer visual cues. It provides a more structured viewing format that follows a natural reading pattern in left-to-right reading cultures, such as the F-shaped pattern, illustrated in *Figure 5.26*:

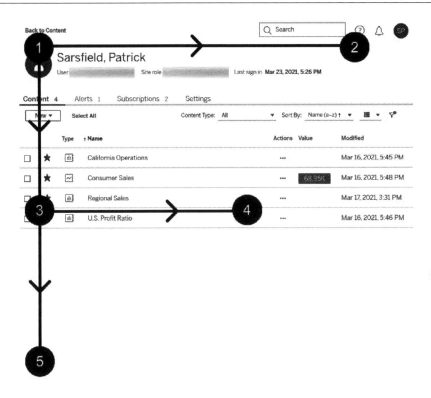

Figure 5.26 – Illustration of the F-shaped reading pattern

This pattern illustrates the order that users typically examine content on a page. The design of the page creates a good visual hierarchy as the level of attention given to content decreases as users scroll down the screen. Finally, **List View** allows more items to be shown on the screen at a given time, which reduces scrolling and improves your ability to scan content.

You may also notice that even more details appear in a list view if you select a single content type using the **Content Type** menu discussed earlier in this chapter. For example, selecting **Data Sources** from the **Content Type** menu will provide an additional column called **Workbooks** in **List View** that indicates how many workbooks are connected to that data source. If you were to select **Workbooks** from the **Content Type** menu, a column called **Sheets** would appear that indicates how many views are published from within that workbook.

You can easily see if an item has an alert by looking at the far-right column in **List View**. When there are no alerts, this column will be empty. When there is an alert for an item, that row will have an icon of an exclamation mark within a red triangle. Clicking on that icon will present a tooltip with additional details, much like the one shown in *Figure 5.27*:

Figure 5.27 – Alert icon in List View

List View can be a useful way to manage content by quickly checking details such as view counts, size, modified date, or alerts.

> **Tip**
>
> To monitor your data sources and ensure that your monthly reports have all updated correctly, simply navigate to your **My Content** page and use the **Content Type** menu to filter to **Data Sources**. Next, you can use the **Sort By** menu to sort your results by the **Modified** date and choose your order preference of **Newest** or **Oldest**. You can also choose to sort by ascending or descending modified date by clicking on the **Modified** column header in **List View**.
>
> This method works in both **Grid View** and **List View** but may be more effective in **List View**.

As we end this section, you are now comfortable using the **View Mode** menu in Tableau Server. You have learned the differences between **Grid View** and **List View** and the benefits of each selection. You should feel confident in selecting the view mode that best suits your needs and preferences at any given time.

In the next section, we will examine the final feature on the Content Toolbar, Filtered Search.

Examining Filtered Search

Filtered Search is a helpful feature that enables you to refine content on Tableau Server to suit your needs using both search and filter functions. This feature is indicated by a funnel icon located on the right side of the Content Toolbar, as indicated in *Figure 5.28*:

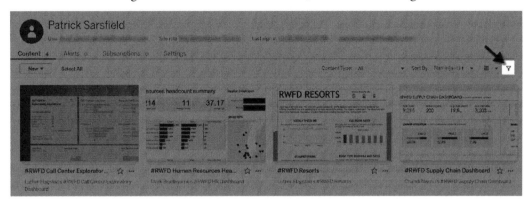

Figure 5.28 – Filtered Search in the Content Toolbar

Dashboard images created by Luther Flagstad, Mark Bradbourne, and Chimdi Nwosu

When you click the funnel icon, a search pane appears to the right of your server window. Once you have identified all of your required filters, you can collapse this pane to allow a larger view of your filtered content by clicking on the funnel icon a second time. When you have applied a search or filter from this pane, you will notice that a green dot appears on the funnel icon, as illustrated in *Figure 5.29*:

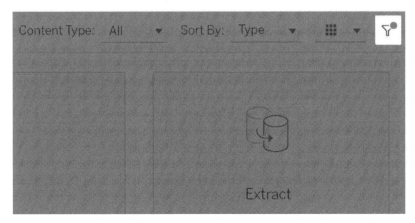

Figure 5.29 – Icon indicating filters have been applied

This serves as a helpful reminder that you are viewing limited server items, particularly if you have collapsed the pane and are browsing the content on a page.

The search options available in the Filtered Search pane will vary depending on what you have selected in the applicable **Content Type** menu for your server location. Recall from *Chapter 3, Tableau Server Navigation Pane*, that if you are on the **Explore** page, the **Content Type** menu is at the top of the page, above the Content Toolbar. All other applicable pages or locations will utilize the **Content Type** menu found in the Content Toolbar that you learned about previously in this chapter. If you are on a page that contains multiple content types, or **All** is selected in the **Content Type** menu, the options in the Filtered Search pane will contain only the general filter options, shown in *Figure 5.30*:

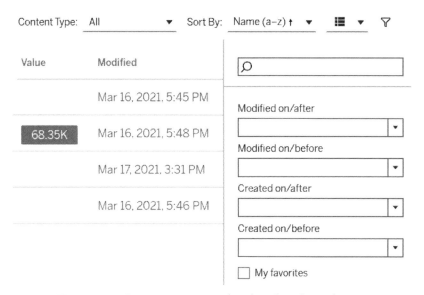

Figure 5.30 – Common options within the Filtered Search pane

First, we will explore the search box feature and its discrete, but powerful, capabilities. Then, we will review the remaining common options. We will end this section by exploring some of the more advanced filters available as the Filtered Search pane dynamically updates its options depending on your selected content type.

Search box within the Filtered Search pane

The first option available in the Filtered Search pane is a search box, indicated by the empty textbox with a magnifying glass icon. This search is similar to the **Quick Search** found at the top of your server window that you learned about in *Chapter 4, Tableau Server Top Toolbar*, which searches the entire Tableau Server site for matching content. However, the Filtered Search pane in the Content Toolbar differs in that it looks for matching content within the server location that you are currently viewing.

> **Tip**
>
> If you would like to search the entire server using the additional filters available in the Filtered Search pane, you can do so by navigating to the **Explore** page and opening Filtered Search from there. Remember to be mindful of what is selected in the **My Content** menu at the top of the **Explore** page, as having this selected will impact your results.

Both the Quick Search and Filtered Search features support the use of search operators and attributes. Recall that a search operator is a command that assists you in refining your search results. Operators available on Tableau Server are and, or, not, and *. A search attribute is a command that allows you to narrow your search results using the characteristics of your desired content. Some of the search attributes supported on the server are name:, owner:, project:, or tag:. To use a search attribute, you simply type the attribute, followed by a colon, followed by your search term, with no spaces, such as name:sales. A complete overview of search operators and attributes is provided in *Chapter 4, Tableau Server Top Toolbar*.

> **Tip**
>
> Some of the filter options available in the Filtered Search pane allow you to search attributes without having to type commands into the search box, such as the **Owner** filter. These options may be simpler to use; however, both methods are available to you.

After entering a search term into the Filtered Search pane, Tableau Server will analyze its contents for matching words in things such as names, descriptions, tags, comments, captions, owners, metadata, and other additional information. Filtered Search is not case-sensitive. Typing Sales will yield the same search result as typing SALES or sales.

The search box in the Filtered Search pane is a powerful feature that helps you refine your content selection within Tableau Server. Next, we'll review the remaining common options in the filter pane.

Other common options in Filtered Search

Recall from the beginning of the section that if you are on a page containing multiple content types, the options in the Filtered Search pane will contain only the most common filter options. We just learned about the first option in the filter pane, the search box, and will now quickly review the rest of the options, as shown in *Figure 5.31*:

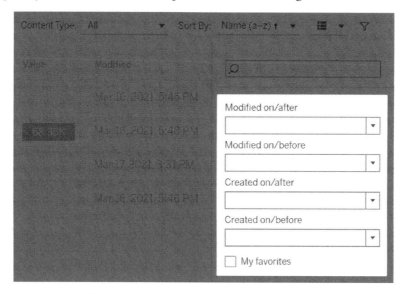

Figure 5.31 – Remaining common filter options

The remaining common options on the Filtered Search pane are as follows:

- **Modified on/after**: Clicking on this option opens a calendar window to allow you to select a specific modified date. You can use the left and right arrows in the header next to the month and year to go forward or backward in time. Your results will show items that were modified on that date or after it.

- **Modified on/before**: Clicking on this option opens a calendar window to allow you to select a specific modified date. Your results will show items that were modified on that date or prior to it.

- **Created on/after**: Clicking on this option opens a calendar window to allow you to select a specific created date. Your results will show items that were created on that date or after it.

- **Created on/before**: Clicking on this option opens a calendar window to allow you to select a specific created date. Your results will show items that were created on that date or prior to it.

- **My favorites**: Checking this box will limit your search results to only items that you have marked as a favorite.

These options are available in the Filtered Search pane with almost any selection of the **Content Type** menu. Depending on your server location and selections, you may see additional common options, such as **Owner** or **Tag** (not shown in the previous screenshot). As you may have guessed, the **Owner** filter allows you to select items by a particular owner. This filter only allows single-value options and does not support filtering by multiple owners. **Tag** allows you to filter items by searching for applicable tags associated with an item. Tags are discussed more in *Chapter 7, What is in the More Actions (…) Menu*.

Tip

You can use the various Content Toolbar features in conjunction with each other to optimize your content search or review. For example, you can use the **Content Type** menu and Filtered Search to limit results to workbooks created or modified in the current year. Then you can use the **Sort by** feature to quickly see what items were created this year by scrolling through content in **List View**. You can then choose to see which items are the most popular with users by sorting your results by their view counts.

Next, let's examine how the Filtered Search pane options vary the most with workbook and data source content types. These options will cover additional filter possibilities available with other content types.

Filtered Search for specific content types

Like many other Tableau Server features, the Filtered Search options dynamically update based on your server location and what you have selected in the **Content Type** menu. If you select **Workbooks** or **Data Sources** from the **Content Type** menu (either from the **Explore** page or within the Content Toolbar), you will notice that more filter options appear in the Filtered Search pane, as shown in *Figure 5.32*:

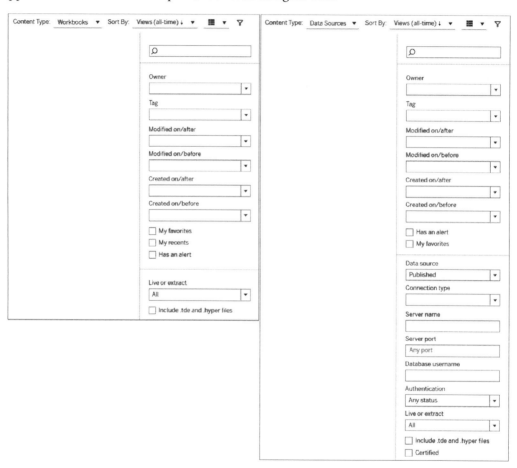

Figure 5.32 – Filtered Search options for workbooks or data sources

Let's review the options available in the Filtered Search pane for workbooks and data sources.

Filtered Search options for workbooks

In addition to the generic options you have learned about, selecting **Workbooks** allows you to filter results by **Owner** or **Tag**, with options to only show items listed in your favorites, recent items, or items that have an alert. You can also filter results by their data source type from the filter named **Live or extract**. This filter allows you to select from a list of options, including **All**, **Live**, **Extracts**, and **Published**, and various encryption options, such as **Unencrypted Extracts** and **Encrypted Extracts**.

> **Note**
> Encrypting data sources is an advanced feature that is managed at the site level by your organization's server administrators and will not be discussed in this book. Please reach out to an administrator if you need assistance encrypting data.

Finally, you can choose whether or not to **include .tde and .hyper files**. Files with a `.tde` or `.hyper` extension are data extract files, which are local copies of datasets that Tableau uses to optimize performance and share data with others. Recall that data source types were discussed in *Chapter 2, How to Connect and Publish to Tableau Server*.

Filtered Search options for data sources

When **Data Sources** is selected in the **Content Type** menu, you will see the generic Filtered Search options and an additional section of filters at the bottom of the pane that are unique to data sources.

Here is a quick overview of the Filtered Search options for data sources:

- **Data Source**: Produces a drop-down menu that allows you to select data sources that are published separately, embedded in a workbook, or both

- **Connection Type**: Produces a searchable drop-down menu with a list of your available databases (Cloudera Hadoop, Oracle, Snowflake, and so on)

- **Server Name**: Provides a textbox where you can enter the name of a specific server

- **Server Port**: Provides a drop-down menu that allows you to filter between **Any port** or **Default port**

- **Database username**: Filters data sources using the database username credential that you identify in the textbox

- **Authentication**: Produces a drop-down menu to filter data sources by whether or not database login credentials are embedded in the connection, not embedded, or both (all)

- **Live or Extract**: Produces a drop-down menu that allows you to select the type of data source, such as live, extract, and multiple encryption options

- **Include .tde and .hyper files**: A checkbox to select whether or not to include Tableau data extract files in your results

- **Certified**: A checkbox that allows you to filter your data sources to only data sources that have been verified by your site administrator or project leader

> **Tip**
>
> While the Quick Search discussed in *Chapter 4, Tableau Server Top Toolbar*, only searches **published** data sources from your entire server site, Filtered Search provides you with the ability to search for an **embedded** data source from your current server location.

You have learned about the more detailed filter options available in the Filtered Search pane. To wrap up this chapter, let's learn how to remove the search and filter criteria and reset the page view.

Removing applied filters from a filtered search

Notice that as soon as you enter text into the search box or select a filter, a **Clear all filters** text button appears at the top of the pane, as shown in *Figure 5.33*:

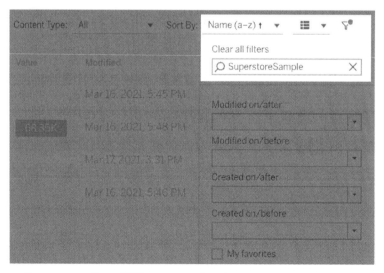

Figure 5.33 – Clear all filters option found in the Filtered Search pane

As the name indicates, this is a way for you to reset your current page view by clearing all of the filters within the Filtered Search pane. If you have multiple filters and search criteria selected in the pane, you can choose to remove specific ones individually, as illustrated in *Figure 5.34*:

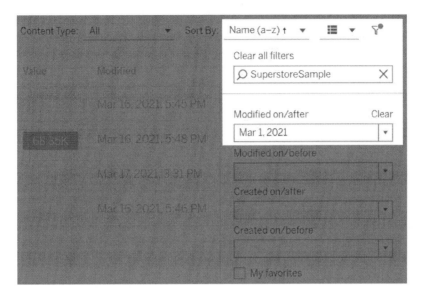

Figure 5.34 – Clear specific filters from the Filtered Search pane

To clear text from the search, simply click the **X** that appears on the right side of the search box. To remove any selected filters, simply click the **Clear** button that appears next to that particular filter option.

Filtered Search is not only a helpful search tool, but also provides a way to easily manage or monitor content on Tableau Server. You should feel comfortable using the features available in the Filtered Search pane in conjunction with the other options in the Content Toolbar to search for and refine content search results.

Summary

In this chapter, we examined the Tableau Server Content Toolbar, and you learned how to take advantage of all its available options. First, we discussed how to create and upload workbooks using the **New** menu. Next, we reviewed how to capture some or all the items on a page and perform actions on the selected content using the **Select All** option. You then learned how to filter the content on your page by type using the **Content Type** menu. We then covered how to easily arrange the content displayed on a page by utilizing the **Sort by** menu. This was followed by learning how to switch between **Grid View** and **List View** and when to use each for effective server navigation and content management. Finally, we went over the Filtered Search option and discussed how it is similar to and differs from Quick Search.

Learning how to use the Content Toolbar will help the way you interact with any page by knowing how to quickly make bulk changes, rearrange content, apply detailed filters, and perform in-depth searches. Now that you have this knowledge, you can apply these options as convenient organizational and time-saving tools.

In the following chapter, we'll look at navigating through a workbook in Tableau Server, where you will learn how and when to use the different options you have available to view the information contained within an individual workbook.

Section 3: Managing Content on Tableau Server

In this section, you will learn how to share, manage, and customize your content, as well as how to automate certain tasks. You will also learn how to leverage Tableau Server features to drive the utilization of content on the server.

This section comprises the following chapters:

- *Chapter 6, Navigating Content Pages in Tableau Server*
- *Chapter 7, What is in the More Actions (...) Menu*
- *Chapter 8, Interacting with Views on Tableau Server*

6
Navigating Content Pages in Tableau Server

The content pages in Tableau Server help to organize additional details about a particular item. In this chapter, you will learn to navigate through workbooks, data sources, and metrics in Tableau Server. As you browse the server and click on one of these items, a content page will open. Each page contains a series of tabs that correspond to that content type. When selected, these tabs allow you to see what views are available, monitor the data connections, see connected metrics, check when data is scheduled to refresh, view existing subscriptions, identify workbooks connected to a data source, and view metrics.

Learning how to utilize these pages will give you a deeper understanding of the content on Tableau Server. This chapter will enable you to manage server content and troubleshoot potential issues by understanding where to find and interact with pertinent information for each content type. By the end of this chapter, you will know how to navigate any standard content page within Tableau Server that you are presented with.

In this chapter, we will cover the following topics:

- Navigating a workbook in Tableau Server

- Navigating a data source in Tableau Server

- Navigating a metric in Tableau Server

Navigating a workbook

Navigating a workbook in Tableau Server is very similar to navigating **My Content** as discussed in *Chapter 4, Tableau Server Top Toolbar*. Viewing a workbook in Tableau Server is a great way to get a quick overview of its components. *Figure 6.1* presents an example of the top portion of a workbook page:

Figure 6.1 – Top portion of a workbook page

Dashboard image and table view created by Luther Flagstad

A chart icon and the title of your workbook appear in the top-left corner of your page. Directly to the right of the workbook title are three icons. The following list provides brief descriptions of these icon options:

- **Add to favorite**: Appears as a star icon and is located directly to the right of the workbook title. Clicking this icon will add this workbook to your personal **Favorites** page.

- **Details**: Appears as an information icon and is located directly to the right of the **Add to favorite** icon. Clicking this icon opens a **Workbook details** page that contains the information shown in *Figure 6.2*:

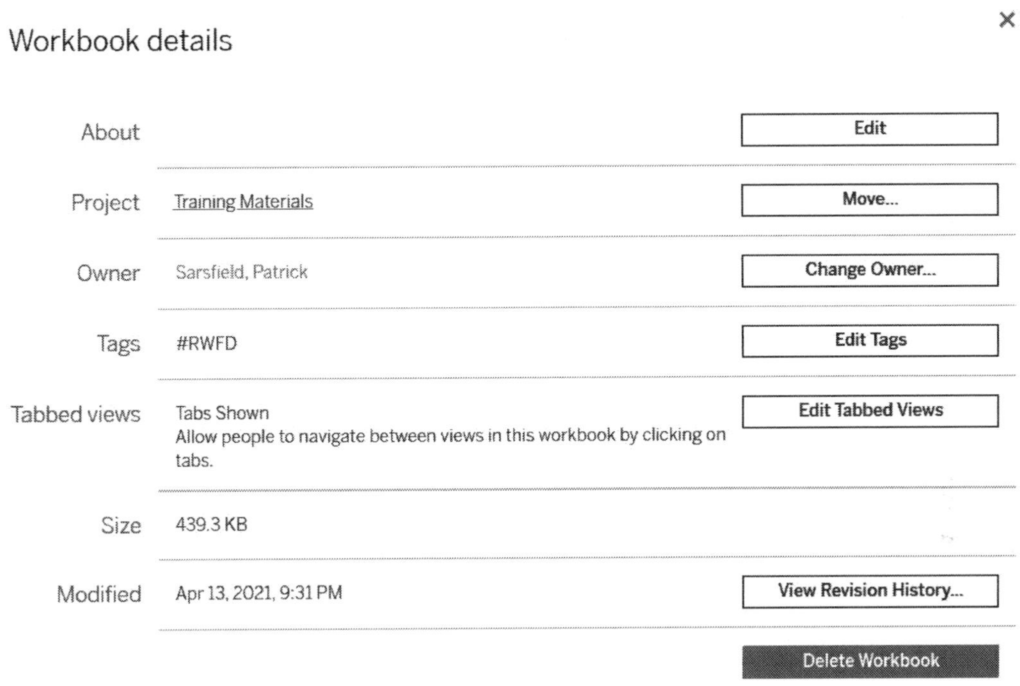

Workbook details

About		Edit
Project	Training Materials	Move...
Owner	Sarsfield, Patrick	Change Owner...
Tags	#RWFD	Edit Tags
Tabbed views	Tabs Shown Allow people to navigate between views in this workbook by clicking on tabs.	Edit Tabbed Views
Size	439.3 KB	
Modified	Apr 13, 2021, 9:31 PM	View Revision History...
		Delete Workbook

Figure 6.2 – Workbook details page

The Workbook details page presents you with both useful workbook information and additional options. Here are brief descriptions of the available details:

- **About**: This section presents a brief description of a workbook, if one has been entered. Clicking the **Edit** button opens a menu that provides you with the ability to add a description to a workbook. You have the option to add a description of up to 4,000 characters. A brief description of your workbook can help inform users about the contents within.

- **Project**: This section provides the name of the project where a workbook is located in Tableau Server. The project name also serves as a link to the project itself. Clicking the **Move...** button opens a menu that provides you with the ability to move a workbook to a new project.

- **Owner**: This section provides the name of the owner of a workbook. Clicking the **Change Owner...** button opens a menu that provides you with the ability to change the owner of a workbook if you have permission to do so. Generally, you must own the workbook currently in order to transfer it to someone else.

- **Tags**: This section provides the tags associated with a workbook. A tag is a keyword that can be attached to an item on Tableau Server to aid you in finding, filtering, and categorizing content. We cover how to effectively write, create, and use tags in *Chapter 7, What is in the More Actions (…) Menu*. Clicking the **Edit Tags** button opens a menu that provides you with the ability to add or remove tags associated with a workbook.

- **Tabbed views**: This section informs you if tabs in a workbook have been shown or hidden. When tabs are available, they allow people to navigate between views in a workbook by clicking on them. Clicking the **Edit Tabbed Views** button opens a menu that provides you with the ability to show or hide the tabs in a workbook if you have the permission to do so.

- **Size**: This section provides the size of a workbook in bytes.

- **Modified**: This section provides the last date and time a workbook was modified. Clicking the **View Revision History…** button opens a menu that provides you with the ability to revert a workbook to a previous version.

- **Delete Workbook**: This option will appear as a red button if you are the owner of a workbook or have the necessary permissions. Clicking this button will open a menu that provides you with the ability to permanently delete a workbook from Tableau Server.

- **More actions**: Appears as an ellipsis icon (…) and is located directly to the right of the **Details** icon. Clicking this icon will open a drop-down menu that presents you with the options shown in *Figure 6.3*:

Figure 6.3 – More actions ellipsis icon and menu

Depending on your permissions, some options on your menu may appear grayed out and will not be available to you. The **More actions** menu options are discussed at length in *Chapter 7, What is in the More Actions (…) Menu.*

Directly below the workbook title is the workbook owner's name, the last modified date, and the most recent extract date.

- **Edit Workbook**: Appears as a button containing the words **Edit Workbook**. If this button is visible to you, it means that you have permission to make changes to that workbook in Tableau Server. Clicking this button will open the workbook in Web Edit and allow you to make edits and connect to different published data sources. This **Edit Workbook** button has the same functionality as the **Edit Workbook** option from the **More actions** drop-down menu featured in the previous screenshot.

> **Tip**
> When adding content from a workbook to your **Favorites** by selecting the star icon, you have the option to select an entire workbook, an individual view within that workbook, or both.

Below the **Edit Workbook** button, you will see various tabs that allow you to access a workbook: **Views, Data Sources, Connected Metrics, Custom Views, Extract Refreshes**, and **Subscriptions**, as shown in *Figure 6.4*. We'll discuss each of these in depth as we continue through this chapter:

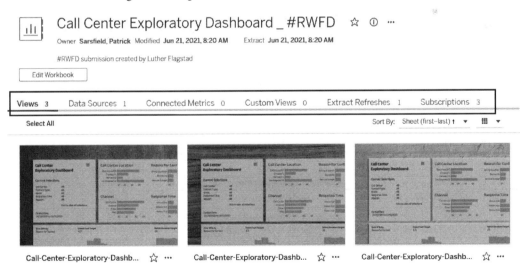

Figure 6.4 – Workbook page tabs

Dashboard images created by Luther Flagstad

After completing this chapter, you will understand how to use the options available on your content pages in Tableau Server. In addition, the information covered here will help you better utilize the content toolbars and tabbed pages on Tableau Server. Let's begin by looking at **Views**.

Examining the Views page

The **Views** page contains all the published views in a workbook. It's the first tab on the left side of your page, and it is also the default tab that opens when you select a workbook. On the tab, to the right of the word **Views**, you are presented with the total number of dashboards and worksheets within your selected workbook.

> **Note**
>
> When selecting what to upload in a workbook to Tableau Server, a worksheet, dashboard, or story would all be considered a View, if selected.

Figure 6.5 presents an example of a standard **Views** page:

Figure 6.5 – Views page

Dashboard image and table view created by Luther Flagstad

Directly below the tab options is a content toolbar. The following list provides brief descriptions of the content toolbar options that are available when looking at the **Views** page:

- **Select All**: This option appears with the words **Select All** and is located on the left side of your content toolbar. Clicking this option is a fast way to select all of the content displayed on the page. Once selected, you are provided with a list of actions available in a drop-down menu on the toolbar.

- **Sort By**: This option appears with the words **Sort By** and is located on the right side of your content toolbar. Clicking this option will provide you with a drop-down list of options that allows you to organize items on your page by a single selection. If you are familiar with Tableau Desktop, the interactivity of this drop-down filter most closely resembles a Single Value (drop-down) dimension filter.

- **View Modes**: This option appears as one of two icons and is located on the right side of your content toolbar. Clicking this menu will provide you with a drop-down list with two view options, **Grid View** and **List View**. **Grid View** provides you with the ability to visually identify specific views based on their thumbnail images, while **List View** presents your content and some of the data surrounding it in tabular format.

If you want to learn more about your content toolbar, please refer to *Chapter 5*, *Filtering and Sorting Content*, where we take a deep dive into each of these options. You'll notice that the **Content Type** menu and **Filtered Search** are not available as content toolbar options. The absence of the **Content Type** menu makes sense. By selecting a specific workbook, the menu becomes unnecessary, as the content you want to examine has already been determined to be a workbook.

The individual views are all the items shown on the page below the content toolbar. While in **Grid View**, you can hover over a specific view to see a tooltip containing additional details, such as tags, project location, and workbook name. Clicking on a view will open the dashboard, worksheet, or story you selected.

Examining the Data Sources page

The **Data Sources** page contains all the data sources connected to a workbook. It's the second tab starting on the left side of your page. On the right side of the **Data Sources** tab, you are presented with the total number of data sources within your selected workbook. *Figure 6.6* presents an example of a standard **Data Sources** page:

Figure 6.6 – Data Sources page

Directly below your tab options is a content toolbar. The following list provides brief descriptions of the Content Toolbar options that are available when looking at the **Data Sources** page:

- **Select All**: This option appears with the words **Select All** and is located on the left side of your content toolbar. Clicking this option is a fast way to select all of the content displayed on the page. Once selected, you are provided with a list of actions available in a drop-down menu on the toolbar.

- **Show As**: This option appears with the words **Show As** and is located on the left side of your content toolbar. This option is unique to the Data Sources page. There are two available options in the drop-down: **Data Sources** (the default selection) and **Data Connections**.

- **Sort By**: This option appears with the words **Sort By** and is located on the right side of your content toolbar. Clicking this option will provide you with a drop-down list of options that allows you to organize items on your page by a single selection. If you are familiar with Tableau Desktop, the interactivity of this drop-down filter most closely resembles a Single Value (drop-down) dimension filter.

- **View Modes**: This option appears as one of two icons and is located on the right side of your content toolbar. Clicking this menu will provide you with a drop-down list with two view options, **Grid View** and **List View**. **Grid View** provides you with the ability to visually identify specific views based on their thumbnail images, whereas **List View** presents your content and some of the data surrounding it in tabular format.

The individual data sources are the items shown on the page below the content toolbar. While in **Grid View**, a data source will be represented by an icon, instead of a thumbnail or view preview. If a workbook contains a data source that is a Tableau Server data source, meaning that it was published separately, you can find a link to navigate to that data source location on the server. This link is available in the item tooltip, or in the **Connects to** column in **List View**.

> Tip
> If a workbook has multiple data sources with different refresh schedules, you can use the data sources page to review when all of the data last refreshed.

Examining the Connected Metrics page

The **Connected Metrics** page contains the metrics that were created from views within that workbook. It's the third tab starting on the left side of your page. On the right side of the **Connected Metrics** tab, you are presented with the total number of connected metrics within your selected workbook. *Figure 6.7* presents an example of a standard **Connected Metrics** page:

Figure 6.7 – Connected Metrics page

Directly below your tab options is a content toolbar. The following list provides brief descriptions of the content toolbar options that are available when looking at the **Connected Metrics** page:

- **Select All**: This option appears with the words **Select All** and is located on the left side of your content toolbar. Clicking this option is a fast way to select all of the content displayed on the page. Once selected, you are provided with a list of actions available in a drop-down menu on the toolbar.

- **Sort By**: This option appears with the words **Sort By** and is located on the right side of your content toolbar. Clicking this option will provide you with a drop-down list of options that allows you to organize items on your page by a single selection. The list of available options will also vary based on your server location and what is selected in the **Content Type** menu. If you are familiar with Tableau Desktop, the interactivity of this drop-down filter most closely resembles a Single Value (drop-down) dimension filter.

- **View Modes**: This option appears as one of two icons and is located on the right side of your content toolbar. Clicking this menu will provide you with a drop-down list with two view options, **Grid View** and **List View**. **Grid View** provides a series of thumbnail images or icons representing your content, whereas **List View** presents your content and some of the data surrounding it in tabular format.

The individual metrics are all the items shown on the page below the content toolbar. You can hover over a metric to see a tooltip containing additional detail, such as tags or owner information, while in **Grid View**, or you can switch to **List View** for even more information. Clicking on a metric will open the item you selected. We will discuss metric pages later in this chapter along with how to create a metric in *Chapter 8, Interacting with Views on Tableau Server*.

Examining the Custom Views page

A custom view is a saved version of a view that retains all of the filters and selections that have been applied. The **Custom Views** page shows all of the custom views that you have created or views that were created by others and made visible to other users. It's the fourth tab starting on the left side of your page. On the tab to the right of the **Custom Views** label, you are presented with the total number of custom views within your selected workbook. *Figure 6.8* presents an example of a standard **Custom Views** page:

	Name	Actions	Original view	Owner	Views (all-time)	Last accessed at	Modified
☐	The Chord dashboard	•••	RWFD-RESORTS	Locker, Brandi	5	last week	May 10, 2021, 8:33 PM
☐	The Sankey dashboard	•••	RWFD-RESORTS	Locker, Brandi	3	19 minutes ago	Jun 21, 2021, 8:22 AM

Views 2   Data Sources 1   Connected Metrics 0   **Custom Views** 2   Extract Refreshes 0   Subscriptions 0

Select All

↑ Name

Figure 6.8 – Custom Views page

Directly below your tab options is a content toolbar. The following list provides brief descriptions of the content toolbar options that are available when looking at the **Custom Views** page:

- **Select All**: This option appears with the words **Select All** and is located on the left side of your content toolbar. Clicking this option is a fast way to select all of the items displayed on the page. Once selected, you are provided with a list of actions available in a drop-down menu on the toolbar. The **Actions** options provided on the **Custom Views** page are as follows:

  - **Change Owner…**: This option allows you to change the owner of the selected custom view(s).

  - **Delete…**: This option allows you to remove the selected custom view(s) from Tableau Server.

Custom Views are displayed in a **List View** format only. This tabular view contains the view name, individual action menus, the original view name, the owner name, a view count, the last accessed date, and the last modified date. You can click on some of the headers, such as **Name**, to change the sort order. You can also change the view count timeframe from all-time to 1 month, 3 months, or 12 months, by clicking on the **Views (all-time)** header. *Figure 6.9* provides an example of these options:

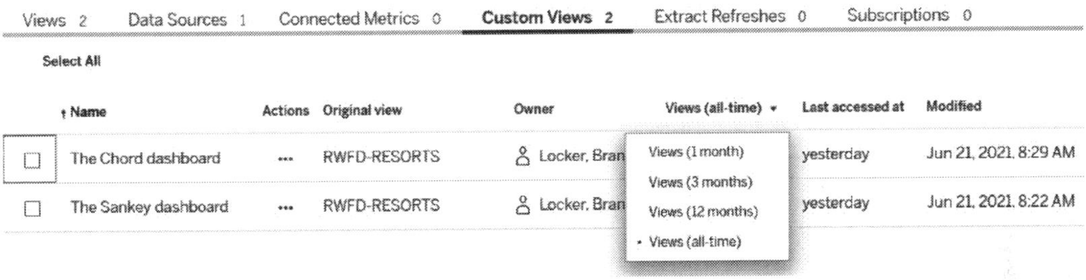

	Views 2	Data Sources 1	Connected Metrics 0	**Custom Views 2**	Extract Refreshes 0	Subscriptions 0	

Select All

	↑ Name	Actions	Original view	Owner	Views (all-time) ▾	Last accessed at	Modified
☐	The Chord dashboard	⋯	RWFD-RESORTS	Locker, Bran	Views (1 month)	yesterday	Jun 21, 2021, 8:29 AM
☐	The Sankey dashboard	⋯	RWFD-RESORTS	Locker, Bran	Views (3 months)	yesterday	Jun 21, 2021, 8:22 AM
					Views (12 months)		
					• Views (all-time)		

Figure 6.9 – Custom Views drop-down option for the Views column

Clicking on the name of the custom view will open that view. You can also navigate to the workbook containing the view by clicking on the **Original View** link for that item. Lastly, you can click on a custom view owner's name to be taken to that person's user page. You will learn how to create a custom view in *Chapter 8, Interacting with Views on Tableau Server*.

Examining the Extract Refreshes page

The **Extract Refreshes** page shows the data extract refresh schedule for a workbook. It's the fifth tab starting on the left side of your page. To the right of the **Extract Refreshes** tab, you are presented with the total number of extract refreshes occurring within your selected workbook. *Figure 6.10* presents an example of a standard **Extract Refreshes** page:

	Views 2	Data Sources 1	Connected Metrics 1	**Extract Refreshes 1**	Subscriptions 1	

New Extract Refresh   Select All

	Refresh type	Actions	↑ Schedule	Priority	Last update	Next update
☐	Full refresh	⋯	Daily at 1:00 PM CST – Every 24 hours starting at 1:00 PM	5	Apr 15, 2021, 1:22 PM	Apr 16, 2021, 1:00 PM

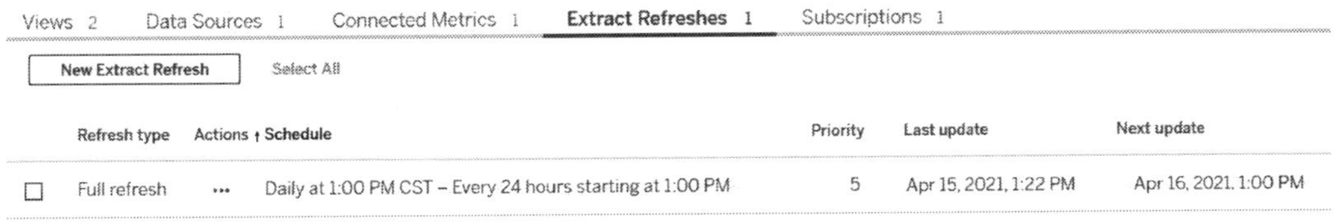

Figure 6.10 – Extract Refreshes page

You may notice that the **Last Update** time does not precisely match what is identified in the scheduled time. This is because, when an item is scheduled to refresh, it goes into a queue at that time. The **Priority** column indicates when this item will refresh relative to others in the queue.

Directly below your tab options is a content toolbar. The following list provides brief descriptions of the content toolbar options that are available when looking at the **Extract Refreshes** page:

- **New Extract Refresh**: This option appears with the words **New Extract Refresh** and is located on the left side of your content toolbar. Clicking this option opens a page that allows you to choose a refresh schedule for a workbook.

- **Select All**: This option appears with the words **Select All** and is located on the left side of your content toolbar. Clicking this option is a fast way to select all of the items displayed on the page. Once selected, you are provided with a list of actions unique to refresh schedules available in a drop-down menu on the toolbar. The actions provided on the **Extract Refreshes** page are as follows:

  - **Run Now…**: This option allows you to execute a full refresh on a data source when you click **Full Refresh**.

  - **Resume…**: This option allows you to resume a suspended extract refresh.

  - **Change frequency…**: This option allows you to select a different schedule for a workbook's extract refresh.

  - **Delete…**: This option allows you to delete a workbook's extract refresh schedule.

Your extract information is presented in a **List View** format only. As a result, your data is presented in a tabular format with columns containing information for the refresh type, available actions, the refresh schedule, assigned priority number, the last update, and the next scheduled update.

> **Note**
>
> To understand an item's extract refresh priority, the lower the number, the higher the priority. Priority can range from 1 to 100.

We will discuss how to create an extract refresh in the *Navigating a data source in Tableau Server* section of this chapter.

> **Note**
>
> The Extract Refreshes page will not be available if your workbook only has a server data source connection. You can find the extract refresh schedule for a Tableau Server data source by going to its Data Sources page and clicking on the **Extract Refreshes** tab.

Examining the Subscriptions page

The **Subscriptions** page shows the subscriptions to a workbook. It's the sixth tab option starting on the left side of your page. To the right of the **Subscriptions** tab, you are presented with the total number of scheduled subscriptions. *Figure 6.11* presents an example of a standard **Subscriptions** page:

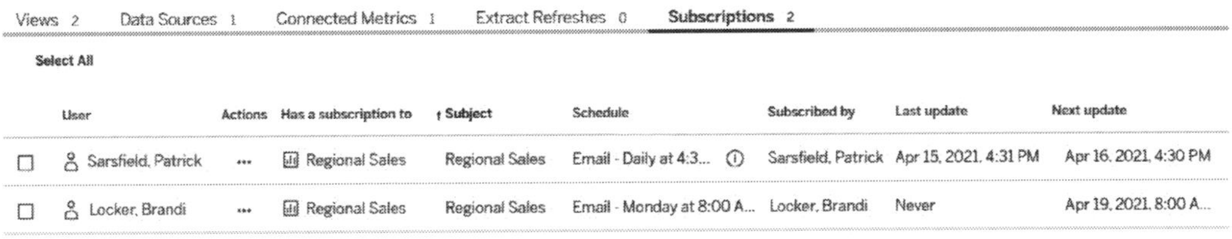

	User		Actions	Has a subscription to	↑ Subject	Schedule		Subscribed by	Last update	Next update
Views 2	Data Sources 1	Connected Metrics 1	Extract Refreshes 0	**Subscriptions** 2						
Select All										
☐	👤 Sarsfield, Patrick		⋯	📄 Regional Sales	Regional Sales	Email - Daily at 4:3...	ⓘ	Sarsfield, Patrick	Apr 15, 2021, 4:31 PM	Apr 16, 2021, 4:30 PM
☐	👤 Locker, Brandi		⋯	📄 Regional Sales	Regional Sales	Email - Monday at 8:00 A...		Locker, Brandi	Never	Apr 19, 2021, 8:00 A...

Figure 6.11 – Subscriptions page

Directly below your tab options is a content toolbar. The following list provides brief descriptions of the content toolbar options that are available when looking at the **Subscriptions** page:

- **Select All**: This option appears with the words **Select All** and is located on the left side of your content toolbar. Clicking this option is a fast way to select all of the content displayed on the page. Once selected, you are provided with a list of actions available in a drop-down menu on the toolbar. The actions options provided on the **Subscriptions** page are as follows:

  - **Change Frequency…**: This option allows you to change the schedule when selected subscriptions will be received.

  - **Change Format…**: This option allows you to change the format in which you receive your subscription. You have the options to receive your subscriptions as an **Image**, **PDF**, or **Image and PDF.**

  - **Unsubscribe…**: This option allows you to unsubscribe from selected subscriptions.

Just like the **Extract Refreshes** page, your subscription information is presented in a **List View** format only. You are presented with columns containing information for the subscribed user, actions to change aspects of a subscription, the view being subscribed to, the subscriptions subject line, the subscription schedule, who created the subscription, the last update, and the next update. We discuss how to create a subscription in *Chapter 8, Interacting with Views on Tableau Server.*

As we conclude this section, you are now acquainted with workbook content pages. You now understand how the content that you select to upload to Tableau Server is displayed in a workbook's content page. You should feel confident in using the **Views**, **Data Sources**, **Connected Metrics**, **Extract Refreshes**, and **Subscriptions** pages. In the next section, we will discuss how to navigate a data source page in Tableau Server.

Navigating a data source in Tableau Server

Viewing a published data source on Tableau Server is similar to viewing a workbook. It is a page that contains helpful information about that particular data source. This page has multiple tabs that contain the data connection information, extract refresh information, and show connected workbooks that you have permission to view. **Ask Data** is another feature you may see here that is available for an additional cost. Because it is not a standard feature within Tableau Server, it will not be covered in this book. You can learn more about Ask Data on the Tableau website at `https://www.tableau.com/products/new-features/ask-data`.

> **Note**
> Recall from *Chapter 1, What is Tableau Server?* that a published data source is one that has been published to the server independently of a workbook. It can be used as a server data source connection for multiple workbooks.

When you open a data source page, shown in *Figure 6.12*, you will see that the top portion of the page appears identical to a workbook content page:

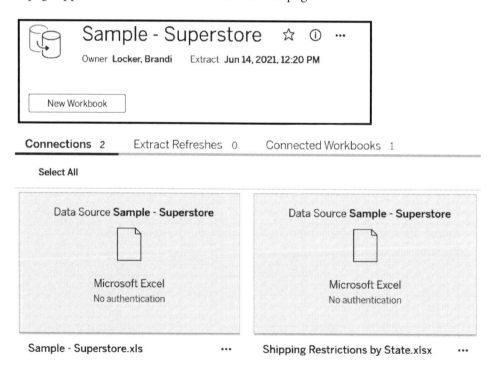

Figure 6.12 – Top portion of a data source page

You will find the name of the data source, a star icon that allows you to add the data source as a favorite item, an information button, an ellipsis button that opens an actions menu, the data source owner, and the most recent extract refresh date. The three icons next to the data source name were discussed thoroughly in the previous section, *Navigating a workbook*.

> **Note**
>
> Clicking the information button for a data source opens a window containing almost the same detail as the information included for a workbook. You will see sections including **About**, **Project**, **Owner**, **Tags**, and the **Modified** date. Data sources also include an **Ask Data** section and a **Certification** section.
>
> The **Ask Data** section allows you to choose **Enabled**, **Disabled**, or **Site Default**. (**Ask Data** is only available through the **Data Management** add-on.) The **Certification** section informs you whether or not a data source has been verified by your administrator or the project leader.

Data sources also display an icon that indicates whether it is an **Extract** or a **Live** connection. The icon for an extract is illustrated in *Figure 6.13*:

Figure 6.13 – Icon indicating that a data source is an extract

The icon for a live connection is illustrated in *Figure 6.14*:

Figure 6.14 – Icon indicating that a data source is a live connection

These icons are similar to the data source icons that you see in Tableau Desktop.

Following this information is a button to create a new workbook. Clicking this option opens a new web browser tab or window using the **Tableau Server Web Edit** feature that contains a new workbook with the data connection already established for the particular data source you were viewing. This can be a convenient way to explore the data available from that source without having to open Tableau Desktop and establish a new server connection. If you create a view or dashboard that you would like to save to Tableau Server, you can do so by selecting **File** and choosing **Save As** from the drop-down menu. Please note that you must have the appropriate permissions to save the workbook to the server. Clicking **Save As** will open a pop-up box that allows you to give the workbook a name, select its project location, show sheets as tabs, and embed a password for the data source. Alternatively, when you close the **Web Edit** window by clicking the **X** in the upper-right corner of the window, you will see the pop-up box shown in *Figure 6.15*:

Figure 6.15 – Save a Copy window

Clicking **Save a Copy** from this box will open the same window that allows you to choose a name and location to save the workbook. Clicking **Don't Save** will close the web edit window without saving any changes.

Below the **New Workbook** button on a data source page are three tabs: **Connections**, **Extract Refreshes**, and **Connected Workbooks**, shown in *Figure 6.16*:

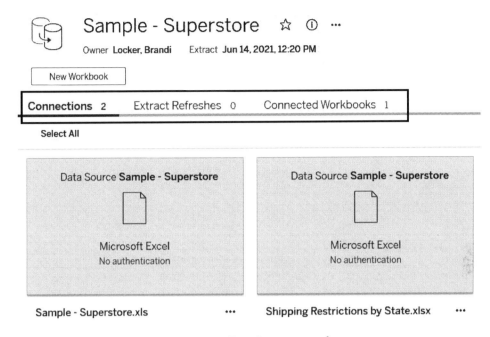

Figure 6.16 – Data Source page tabs

We will examine each of these tabs in turn, beginning with **Connections**.

Examining Connections

The **Connections** tab within a data source page shows all of the individual data connections that exist within that single published data source. As we have discussed, a data source can have multiple connections. For example, two data tables can be connected using relationships or joins using the data model within Tableau Desktop. When you create the extract and publish this data source to Tableau Server, you will have a single data source that contains both of those two data table connections. Details for each of those connections are displayed on the **Connections** page.

Figure 6.17 illustrates a single data source that contains multiple data connections:

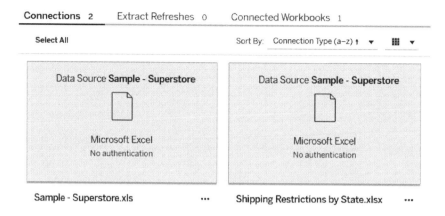

Figure 6.17 – Connections within a data source

The data connections can be viewed in either **Grid View** or **List View**. **Grid View** visually represents each data connection with an icon, the connection type name, credential or authentication information, the database name, and a more actions menu. **List View** provides the same detail in a tabular format.

> **Tip**
>
> You can use the **Actions** menu to edit a connection directly on Tableau Server without having to open Tableau Desktop, make changes, and republish your data source. This is particularly helpful for simple changes, such as updating a password. To do this, open the data connection **Actions** menu by clicking the ellipsis button directly on the item or by using the **Select All** or checkbox option that was learned in *Chapter 5, Filtering and Sorting Content*. Next, click **Edit Connection**. A window will pop up that enables you to update connection details, such as the server name, server port, username, and password.
>
> Note that you can only edit connection details for multiple connections at the same time if they are the same connection type.

Examining Extract Refreshes

The **Extract Refreshes** tab within a data source page shows the refresh schedule for the data source extract in a **List View**. An extract is a subset of your data that has been optimized for Tableau using the Tableau data engine. Data extracts can be scheduled to refresh at regular intervals on Tableau Server so that you do not have to manually refresh your data or consume excess server resources with a live data connection.

The **Extract Refreshes** page has unique options within the content toolbar to help you manage extract refresh schedules. The first option is a button labeled **New Extract Refresh**, located to the left of the **Select All** option, shown in *Figure 6.18*:

Figure 6.18 – New Extract Refresh option in the content toolbar

Clicking this button will open a window that allows you to search for a schedule or to scroll through a list of refresh schedules available with your site. An example of this window is shown in *Figure 6.19*. Note that your exact refresh schedule options will likely differ from what is shown and are based on your administrator settings.

Schedule an Extract Refresh

Choose a refresh schedule for data source "Sample - Superstore".

Search

Daily at 7:45 AM UTC

Daily at 7:45 PM UTC

Daily at 8:00 AM UTC

Daily at 8:00 PM UTC

Daily at 8:15 AM UTC

Daily at 8:30 AM UTC

Daily at 8:30 PM UTC

Daily at 8:45 AM UTC

Daily at 9:00 AM UTC

Refresh type

⦿ Full Refresh

◯ Incremental Refresh

| Cancel | Schedule Refresh |

Figure 6.19 – Schedule an Extract Refresh window

You may have the option to choose between **Incremental Refresh** or **Full Refresh**. A full refresh replaces the entire data extract with new data. An incremental refresh only adds new rows of data to the existing file. The **Incremental Refresh** option is only available if you configured the data to do so in Tableau Desktop prior to publishing the item to the server. For information on configuring incremental data refreshes, please refer to the Tableau Help pages or your Tableau Server administrator. Once you have located the refresh schedule that you need, select it and click **Schedule Refresh**.

> **Note**
>
> Depending on the settings of your organization established by your server administrators, the ability to schedule an extract refresh may be disabled for you. Please contact an administrator if you need assistance refreshing data.

A Tableau Server site has a default time zone of **Coordinated Universal Time (UTC)** for data extracts. This time zone can be customized by an administrator. This time zone will determine how published content displays the time.

The second option in the content toolbar on this page is the **Select All** button. This feature was discussed in depth in *Chapter 5, Filtering and Sorting Content*.

The **Extract Refreshes** page is displayed only in **List View** and has unique columns that are relevant to data sources. These columns include the following:

- **Refresh Type**: Identifies whether an extract refresh is a full refresh or an incremental refresh.

- **Actions**: Each row contains an ellipsis icon. Clicking this icon opens a drop-down menu of options that allow you to manage an extract refresh schedule, including:

  - **Run Now…**: This option allows you to execute a full refresh on a data source when you click **Full Refresh**.

  - **Resume…**: This option allows you to resume a suspended extract refresh.

  - **Change frequency…**: This option allows you to select a different schedule for a workbook's extract refresh.

  - **Delete…**: This option allows you to delete a workbook's extract refresh schedule.

- **Schedule**: Identifies the extract refresh frequency for that data source.

- **Priority**: Identifies the priority order of an extract refresh in a queue of multiple refresh schedules.

- **Last Update**: Identifies the date of the most recent data extract refresh.

- **Next Update**: Identifies the date of the next data extract refresh.

An example of the **Extract Refreshes** page is shown in *Figure 6.20*:

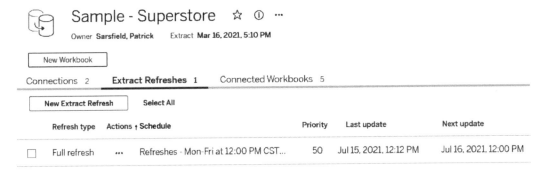

Figure 6.20 – Extract Refreshes page with a scheduled refresh

Recall from earlier in the chapter that the refresh schedules on Tableau Server have a priority assigned that can range from 1 to 100. The lower the number, the higher the priority.

Examining Connected Workbooks

The **Connected Workbooks** tab within a data source page shows all of the workbooks that use, or are connected to, that data source. An example of this is shown in *Figure 6.21*:

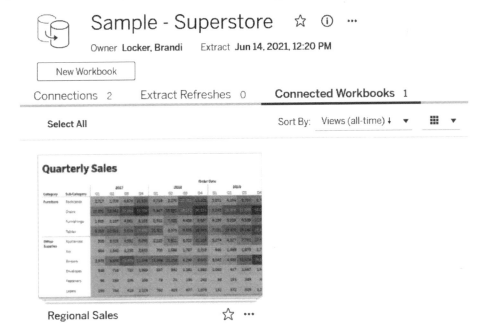

Figure 6.21 – Connected Workbooks tab

You can view these workbooks in **Grid View** to see a small preview of that item or in **List View** to see more detail, such as the view count, size, or whether or not the item has an alert. Both **Grid View** and **List View** provide a link to view that workbook.

Tip

In most cases, **List View** shows the most detail for an item. However, items in **Grid View** have a tooltip that appears when you hover over the thumbnail or icon. This tooltip shows all of the data sources used in that workbook. This information is not available in **List View**.

This page is helpful because it allows you to see which workbooks will be affected by any change in the underlying data or impacted by an extract refresh failure on the server. You can also use this page to help you understand which workbooks should match each other compared to workbooks that might use a similar, but different, data source. It can also help you confirm whether there are workbooks that rely on a particular data source before deleting or making changes to that data source on the server. It is wise to contact the owner of workbooks that use a data source before making any changes to the data to avoid negatively affecting another user's content.

Note

If you do not have access to view a workbook, you will not be able to see it on the **Connected Workbooks** page, even if you own the server data source that it connects to. It may be wise to have your server administrator confirm that there are no other workbooks that you are aware of that use the data before changing or deleting an item.

As we conclude this section, you are now acquainted with your data source pages. You now understand how to find useful information about a data source. You should feel confident using the Connections, Extract Refreshes, and Connected Workbook pages. In the next section, let's examine what is included in a metric page.

Navigating a metric in Tableau Server

Tableau **Metrics** is a type of content that allows users to easily view and monitor **Key Performance Indicators** (**KPIs**) from dashboards at a glance. Metric pages are unique from the other content pages. They can be opened from within a workbook page, as discussed previously in this chapter, or they can be opened directly from other locations on Tableau Server, such as from a project. Selecting a metric will open a window that contains all of the metric details in one view, along with a visual display of the metric data that is automatically formatted by Tableau, as demonstrated in *Figure 6.22*:

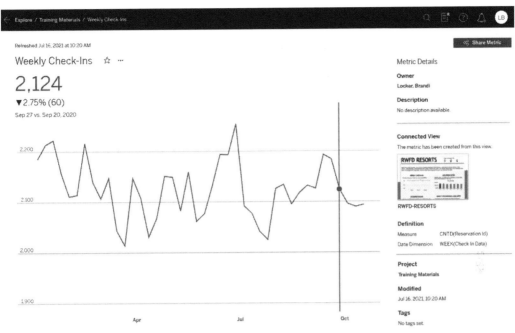

Figure 6.22 – Metrics page on Tableau Server
Dashboard image created by Luther Flagstad

The top of a metric page will be similar to that of a workbook or data source page. You will see the metric name, an option to add the metric to your favorites, and an actions button that looks like an ellipsis (…). Above that information, you will see the date and time of the last metric refresh date. Below the metric name, you will see a large **Big Aggregated Number (BAN)** of the latest data point of the metric. Below that number, you will see the percent change from the previous value and the value difference in parentheses, with the comparison date values shown at the bottom of the section. The KPI number, or the BAN, will dynamically update as you move your cursor over the trend line values.

> **Note**
> Your metric will only include a trend line if the data point selected when creating the metric contained a date field. If the selected point did not include a date field, then you will only see the aggregated number, or BAN.

On the right side of the metric page, you will see a button to share the metric, shown in *Figure 6.23*:

Figure 6.23 – Share Metric button

To share a metric, follow these steps:

1. Click the **Share Metric** button shown in the preceding screenshot. Clicking this button will open the window shown in *Figure 6.24*, which allows you to share directly with certain users or to copy a link:

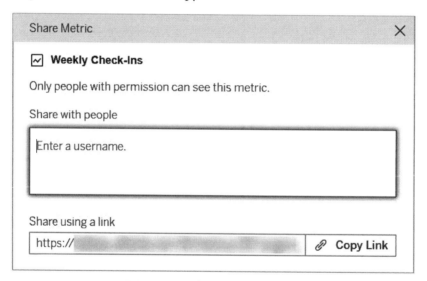

Figure 6.24 – Share Metric window

2. To share a metric with other users directly, enter the usernames of those people with whom you wish to share the metric in the **Share with people** box. As you start typing a name in the box, suggested users will appear in a drop-down menu to help you quickly find who you are looking for. You can enter or select the names of multiple people in this box. Notice that once you enter a name, another box appears that allows you to type an optional message, shown in the following screenshot, *Figure 6.25*. To continue using the **Share with people** method, proceed to step 3.

In the window shown in *Figure 6.24*, you can also use the **Share using a link** method by clicking **Copy Link** in the lower-right corner of the window. Once the link is copied, you can paste it anywhere you wish, such as in a direct message or email. When you are finished with the **Share Metric** window, you can close it by clicking the **X** in the top-right corner.

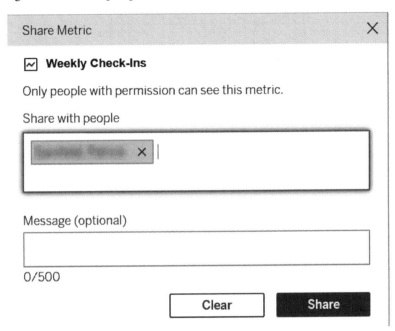

Figure 6.25 – Sharing a metric with other users

3. Enter any message that you wish to include when you share the metric. Messages in this window have a limit of 500 characters. If you click on **Clear** from this window, the users and any message you have entered will be removed, and the window will return to the image shown previously in *Figure 6.24*.

4. Click **Share** when you are ready to send the metric to others.

Below the **Share Metric** button are additional details, illustrated in *Figure 6.26*:

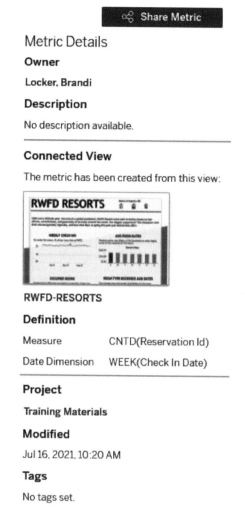

Figure 6.26 – Additional information available on the Metric page
Dashboard image created by Luther Flagstad

The additional metric information includes the metric owner and its description, if any was given. You will also see a **Connected View** section that includes a preview of the dashboard that the metric was created from and a link to open that dashboard. If you hover over this preview, a tooltip will appear that provides detail about that dashboard, such as any tags, the workbook name, project location, the item owner, and the last modified date. You can also use the links within the tooltip to navigate directly to that workbook, project, or owner's content page.

Below the **Connected View** section, you will see the measure and dimension that the metric consists of.

> **Note**
>
> A **measure** is a quantitative value, meaning it can be measured and aggregated, such as the speed of a car. A **dimension** is a qualitative value that provides detail to your data, such as customer names, sales categories, or geographical data.

The lower-right corner of the metric page lists the project location, the last modified date, and any tags associated with it.

Metrics are a convenient way to track KPIs within a dashboard without having to create a separate view. The metrics page allows you to further explore a particular KPI and provides a convenient way to navigate to the corresponding dashboard for a deeper understanding of the data driving that metric number.

Summary

As we conclude this chapter, you now understand how to find particular details about workbooks, data sources, and metrics by examining their individual content pages. You know how to navigate through the unique information tabs available on each page to help you see the views within a workbook, review a workbook's data sources and extract refresh schedules, examine metrics created from a view, and examine or edit subscriptions connected to a workbook. Likewise, you know how to review a Tableau Server data source to see the connections within, review and edit its extract refresh schedule, and see which workbooks are connected to it. Finally, you understand how to interpret a metric page and how it differs from that of a workbook or server data source.

Throughout the previous chapters, you have been briefly introduced to the **More Actions** menu, which is available in almost every Tableau Server location and is usually shown as an ellipsis button (…). In the next chapter, we will take a closer look at this menu and explore the various utilities that it offers.

7
What is in the More Actions (...) Menu

In this chapter, you will learn how to utilize the most valuable options located inside the **More actions** ellipsis (**...**). This menu provides you with the ability to make important changes to the content on Tableau Server. This is where you can set and review access privileges, view and edit data connection details, view and manage data extract refresh information, monitor the usage of your content, and more.

After completing this chapter, you will have a better understanding of how to utilize the most important options featured within your **More actions** ellipses.

In this chapter, we will cover the following topics:

- Examining the More actions ellipsis
- Examining Edit Workbook/Edit View
- Examining Share
- Examining Download
- Examining Tag
- Examining Rename
- Examining Move
- Examining Permissions

- Examining Change Owner
- Examining Revision History
- Examining Delete
- Examining Who Has Seen This View?
- Examining Edit Connection
- Examining Refresh Extracts
- Examining Tabbed Views

Examining the More actions ellipsis

The **More actions** menu can be found in various locations for all types of content throughout Tableau Server. It is usually represented by an ellipsis (...) near the item(s) that you are viewing. An example of a **More actions** menu that is available for a workbook is shown in *Figure 7.1*:

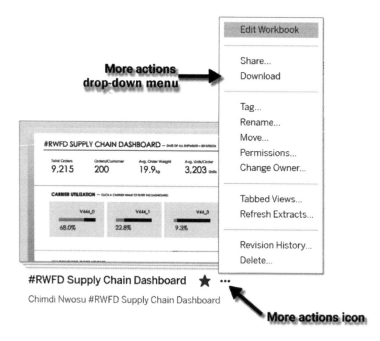

Figure 7.1 – The More actions ellipsis icon and drop-down menu for a workbook
Dashboard image created by Chimdi Nwosu

When you hover over the ellipsis, a tooltip showing **More actions** will appear. Clicking on the ellipsis will open the drop-down menu.

> **Note**
>
> In some places, the menu is referred to as **More actions**. In other places, you will only see it labeled as **Actions**. Both menus have the same functionality, and we will use the two terms interchangeably throughout this book. The major difference between the **More actions** ellipsis (**...**) and the **Actions** option available on **Select All** is that the ellipsis button performs a selected action on a single piece of content, whereas the **Actions** option can apply an action to multiple selections. One drawback to the **Actions** option is that only those actions that can be performed on all of your selections are available. This means that the more selections you make, the fewer menu options you are likely to see.

As you browse through the content that is available to you on your server site, you will find that the **Actions** menu appears throughout the following :

- The **Explore**, **Favorites**, **Recents**, and **Shared with Me** pages

- Content pages, including projects, workbooks, metrics, and data sources

- Your **My Content** page

When your view is set to **Grid View**, the ellipsis button appears at the top of a project or content page after the item title and near the lower-right corner of each item on the page, as shown in *Figure 7.2*:

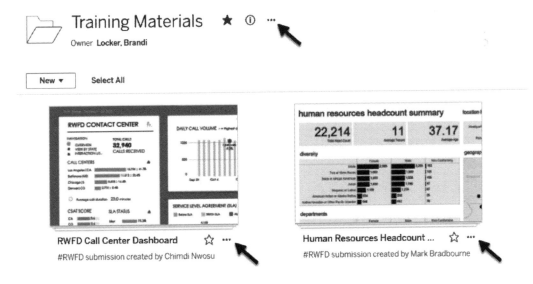

Figure 7.2 – The More actions ellipsis buttons in grid view

Dashboard images created by Chimdi Nwosu and Mark Bradbourne

> **Note**
>
> If you are viewing the content of a project and have individual items selected, the ellipsis button on the right-hand side of the project name will be disabled.

When your view is set to list view, the ellipsis button appears at the top of a project or content page after the item title and next to the name of each item in the list, as shown in *Figure 7.3*:

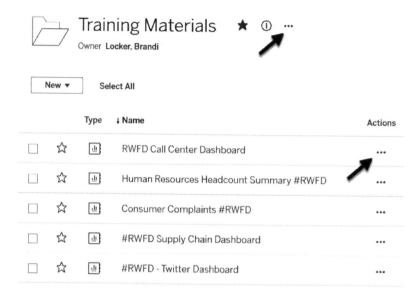

Figure 7.3 – The More actions ellipsis buttons in list view

The **Actions** menu can also be found in the content toolbar after selecting individual items or after clicking on **Select All**. We discussed this method in the *Examining the Select All option* section in *Chapter 5, Filtering and Sorting Content*. An example of navigating to the **Actions** menu using this method is shown in *Figure 7.4*:

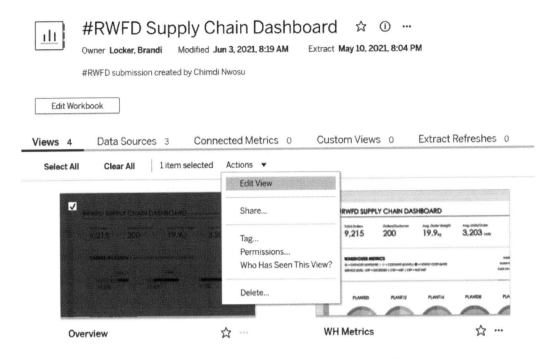

Figure 7.4 – The Actions menu in the content toolbar

Dashboard images created by Chimdi Nwosu

You can also find **Actions** menus when viewing your **Alerts** and **Subscriptions** from your **My Content** page to manage those items, as illustrated in *Figure 7.5*:

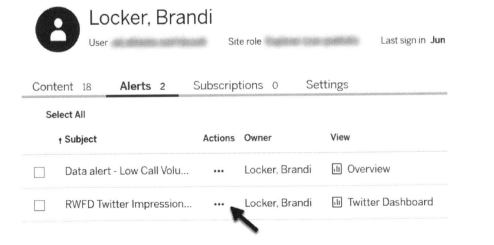

Figure 7.5 – The Actions menus on the Alerts page

The options available in each **Actions** menu will vary depending on the content type of the item(s) you are viewing, on your site role, and on your capabilities, as determined by the permissions rules of the item, or the project(s), it is stored in. If you select multiple content types, such as a workbook and a metric, you will only see the options shared by both types in the **Actions** menu. If you select multiple items and attempt to perform an action, but do not have the correct permission rules to perform that action for each of the items, you will receive an error.

Now that you know where to find the **More actions** menu throughout your Tableau Server site, we will examine the most common options available within the drop-down menu. Note that you might encounter additional options that are not covered in this chapter. Most options are straightforward, and many are discussed throughout this book. However, if you require further assistance, you can contact your Server Administrator or search for information within the Tableau Help resources. Let's begin by examining the **Edit** option. We'll do this in the next section.

Examining Edit Workbook/Edit View

The **Edit Workbook** or **Edit View** feature is available for workbooks and views, respectively, from the **More actions** ellipsis (…) menu. If you can see one of these options available, that means you have the proper permissions. Selecting the **Edit Workbook** or **Edit View** option will open a **Web Edit** page that will allow you to make edits to a view or workbook within Tableau Server without leaving your web browser. After clicking on the **More actions** ellipsis (…), the **Edit Workbook** feature or the **Edit View** feature will be located at the top of their respective drop-down menus. Examples of where these features are located inside a **More actions** drop-down menu is shown in *Figure 7.6*:

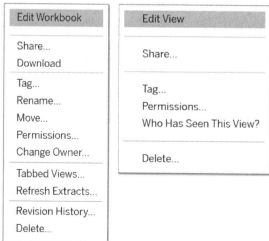

Figure 7.6 – The locations of Edit Workbook and Edit View inside a More actions drop-down menu

After selecting either **Edit Workbook** or **Edit View**, a **Web Edit** page will open. Here, you will see an online layout that appears almost identical to Tableau Desktop. In this environment, you have the ability to make edits to workbooks or views directly on Tableau Server. We discuss **Web Edit** permissions, layouts, and their differences to Tableau Desktop, at length, in the *Examining the Web Edit button* section of *Chapter 8, Interacting with Views on Tableau Server*. An example of a **Web Edit** page after selecting **Edit Workbook** is shown in *Figure 7.7*:

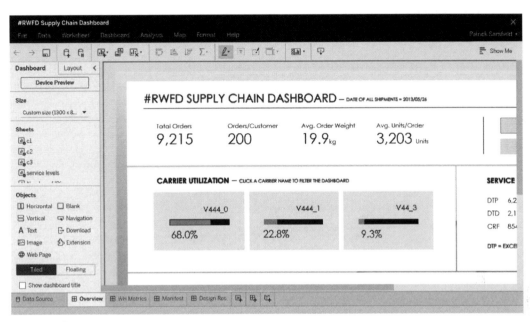

Figure 7.7 – A Web Edit page after selecting Edit Workbook

Dashboard image credit: Chimdi Nwosu

In this section, you learned how to quickly access a way to make edits to your workbooks and views without needing to leave the Tableau Server environment. Now, let's take a look at another item from your **More actions** drop-down menu, that is, the **Share...** feature.

Examining Share

A simple, but useful, Tableau Server feature that is available for projects, workbooks, views, metrics, and data sources within the **More actions** ellipsis (…) is the **Share…** feature. Selecting this option will open a window that will provide you with the ability to either copy a link to share content or share content directly with others. After you click on the **More actions** ellipsis (…) button, the **Share…** feature will appear near the top of the drop-down menu. An example of where this feature is located inside a **More actions** drop-down menu for a workbook is shown in *Figure 7.8*:

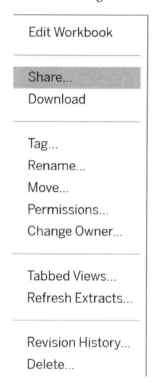

Edit Workbook

Share…
Download

Tag…
Rename…
Move…
Permissions…
Change Owner…

Tabbed Views…
Refresh Extracts…

Revision History…
Delete…

Figure 7.8 – The location of Share… inside a More actions workbook drop-down menu

After you click on **Share…** from the **More actions** menu, a new window will open that provides you with the ability to share your selected content. The **Share** window reminds you that **Only people with permission can see this [content type]**. *Figure 7.9* shows an example of the **Share Workbook** window:

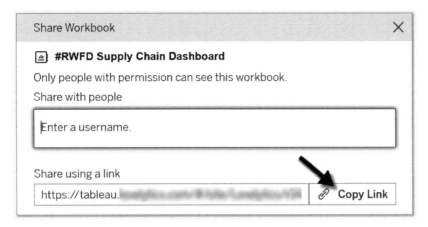

Figure 7.9 – The Share Workbook window

This feature presents you with two options to share: **Share with people** and **Share using a link**. Both options have their own time and place.

Share with people

The **Share with people** option allows you to share content directly with other Tableau Server users by entering usernames into the **Share with people** box. Entering a username will open an optional **Message** box that allows you to add up to 490 characters, which will be attached to your shared content. An example of a **Share Workbook** window is shown in *Figure 7.10*:

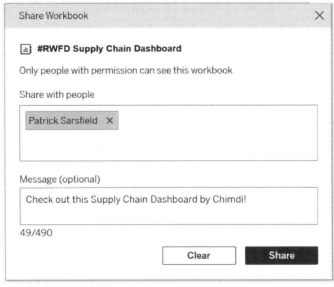

Figure 7.10 – The Share Workbook window with the name and an optional message

Sharing content with other users will generate an email that links to your selected content and your message (if a message has been entered). Click on the **Share** button to complete the process or select **Clear** to cancel without saving.

Additionally, any content that you share with a user is added to their **Shared with Me** page.

Share using a link

The **Share using a link** option allows you to share content directly with other Tableau Server users by copying and sharing a link. Using this option is great if you simply want to share a piece of content with other users via a link and want to avoid automatically generating an email or adding a piece of content to other users' **Shared with Me** pages. It can also be used in presentations, across your organization's communication channels, or as a link within an email that you create.

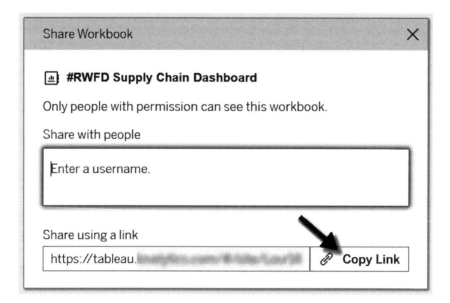

Figure 7.11 – The Share Workbook window

In this section, you learned about two ways in which you can easily share projects, workbooks, views, metrics, and data sources with other Tableau Server users. Now, let's take a look at another item from your **More actions** drop-down menu, that is, the **Download** feature.

Examining Download

A commonly used Tableau Server feature that is available for workbooks and data sources within the **More actions** ellipsis (**...**) is the **Download** feature. Clicking on this option automatically downloads a Tableau workbook that you can open with Tableau Desktop. After clicking on the **More actions** ellipsis (**...**), the **Download** feature can be found near the top of the drop-down menu, just below **Share....** An example of where this feature is located inside a **More actions** drop-down menu is shown in *Figure 7.12*:

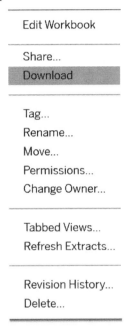

Figure 7.12 – The location of Download inside a More actions workbook drop-down menu

> **Tip**
>
> If you would like the option to download a workbook in a different version of Tableau Desktop, you can do this by going into a view, clicking on the **Download** button, and selecting **Tableau Workbook**. This will provide you with a window titled **Download Tableau Workbook**, and you will have the option to select the current or past versions of Tableau. It's important to remember that if you open a workbook in an older version of Tableau Desktop, any functions that were made available after the version you selected will no longer work.

In this section, you learned how to quickly download a workbook or data source. Next, let's take a look at another item from your **More actions** drop-down menu, that is, the **Tag...** feature.

Examining Tag

Tableau Server offers many tools to aid you in finding information. However, the **Tag…** feature might be one of the most underutilized. A tag is a keyword that can be attached to workbooks, views, metrics, and data sources to help you filter and categorize your content. If you author a piece of published content, then you can add tags to it or remove tags from it. Additionally, if you are assigned a Creator or Explorer site role, then you can add or remove tags on content that you have been granted permission to. After clicking on the **More actions** ellipsis (**…**) button, the **Tag…** option can be found near the top of the drop-down menu. An example of where this feature is located inside a **More actions** drop-down menu is shown in *Figure 7.13*:

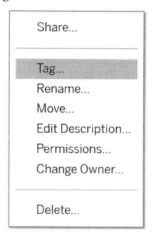

Figure 7.13 – The location of Tag… inside a More actions drop-down menu

Adding a Tag

To add a tag, begin by clicking on **Tag…** inside the **More actions** drop-down menu. This will open the **Change Tags** window. In the **Change Tags** window, there is a textbox where you can add one or more tags. An example of this is provided in *Figure 7.14*:

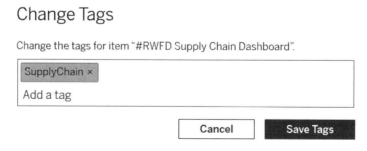

Figure 7.14 – The Change Tags window

Here are some best practices to bear in mind when using or creating tags:

- Review existing tags.

- Keep a tag short but descriptive.

- Use keywords.

- Try to keep your tags to a few words or less.

- Check your spelling.

> **Tip**
>
> When creating a tag, there is no requirement for it to be a continuous word that contains either underscores or no spaces. To create tags on Tableau Server that include spaces, simply wrap your tag in quotations. Additionally, tags are not case sensitive, so don't worry about this when creating or using one in search. Lastly, consider including common misspellings of keywords as tags. This can help ensure that users will still be directed to their desired content despite any typographical errors (typos).

After you have entered the tag or tags you want to be associated with your content in the **Change Tags** window, click on the **Save Tags** button to complete their creation or select **Cancel** to exit without saving.

If you are looking at your content in a grid view format and hover over a thumbnail image, you will see a tooltip appear. If you look at a tooltip, you will see that any tags added to a piece of content now appear. *Figure 7.15* presents an example of a thumbnail with a tooltip containing tags:

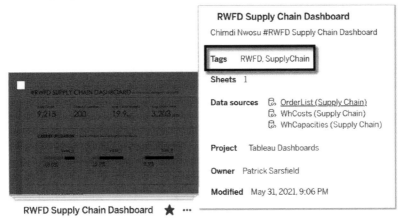

Figure 7.15 – Tags displayed in a tooltip

Dashboard image credit: Chimdi Nwosu

The tooltip contains two tags: one for the **Real World Fake Data** Tableau community initiative, indicated by the acronym of "RWFD," and another for "SupplyChain."

Finding a tag

When looking for a tag, you can utilize a quick search or filtered search. The **Quick Search** option is a search box that provides a quick way to search through content on Tableau Server. It is located in the upper-right corner of your page and can be identified by the magnifying glass icon with the word "Search" next to it. *Figure 7.16* presents an example of a basic quick search:

Figure 7.16 – Searching for a tag using the quick filter

Dashboard images created by Chimdi Nwosu and Mark Bradbourne

The results of this search successfully returned all content that contained the RWFD acronym. The search found content with the RWFD tag. However, it also returned content with RWFD in its name, description, comments, and more. In most cases, this might not be an issue. However, if you only want the results of your quick search to return the tag you are searching for, then you can use a **Search Attribute**. This option allows you to enter specific attributes directly into the search box to further limit your returned search results. *Figure 7.17* presents an example of a quick search using the tag: search attribute:

Figure 7.17 – Using search attributes for a tag

Dashboard image credit: Chimdi Nwosu

In the preceding example, the tag:RWFD search attribute is entered inside the quick search box. For this to work, you'll just need to remember to leave no spaces between the search attribute (tag:) and the tag you want to search for (RWFD). In this instance, the results of the quick search using a search attribute only returned the items that contained the RWFD tag. For more information regarding the quick search feature and search attributes, please refer to *Chapter 4, Tableau Server Top Toolbar.*

Alternatively, you can use a filtered search to find tags. A filtered search allows you to refine your searches on Tableau Server with the use of both the search and filter options. When this feature is available, it appears as a funnel icon and is located on the right-hand side of your content toolbar. Clicking on the funnel icon will open a sidebar on the right-hand side of your screen and display your filtered search options. To access the tag filter on a filtered search, you need to be looking at a single type of content that can be tagged, such as a view. *Figure 7.18* presents an example of a filtered search with the **Tag** filter shown:

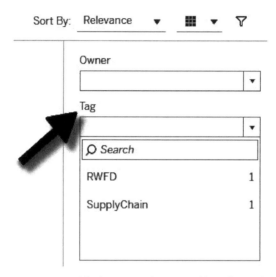

Figure 7.18 – The location of Tag in a filtered search

We reviewed the filtered search feature at length in *Chapter 5*, *Filtering and Sorting Content*.

Removing a tag

Removing a tag is very similar to the process of adding one. You begin by clicking on the **Tag...** feature on the **More actions** drop-down menu. This will open the **Change Tags** window. In this window, you will be able to view the existing tags associated with that piece of content. Put simply, find the tag that you want to remove, and click on the **x** located at the end of the tag you want to delete. To finalize the removal of a tag, click on the **Save Tags** button. You can view an example of this in *Figure 7.19*:

Figure 7.19 – Deleting a tag

In this section, you learned how to add and remove tags. Now, let's take a look at another item from your **More actions** drop-down menu, that is, the **Rename** feature.

Examining Rename

There may be times when you need to rename an item that has already been published to Tableau Server. One way to do this is by completely republishing the item from Tableau Desktop to Tableau Server. However, this method requires you to not only republish an item but remove the original item and fix or replicate any broken connections, such as favorites, metrics, subscriptions, and more. Fortunately, you can avoid this by renaming the item directly on Tableau Server using the **Rename…** option in the **Actions** menu, as presented in *Figure 7.20*:

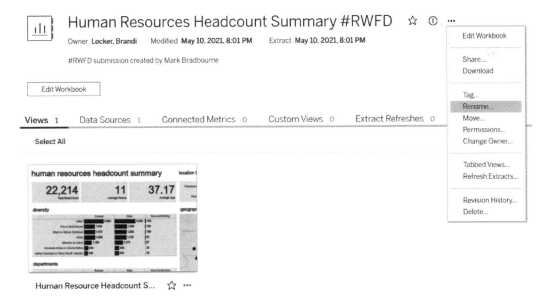

Figure 7.20 – The Rename… option

Dashboard image created by Mark Bradbourne

Clicking on this option will open the **Rename Workbook** pop-up window, as shown in *Figure 7.21*:

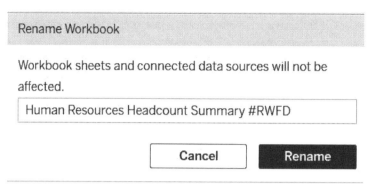

Figure 7.21 – The Rename Workbook pop-up window

From this window, you can edit the existing text or enter a new name and click on **Rename** to save or **Cancel** to exit without saving your changes.

> **Note**
>
> If you rename a workbook on Tableau Server, but later need to republish the workbook, the **Publish Workbook to Tableau Server** window that you learned about in *Chapter 2, How to Connect and Publish to Tableau Server*, will automatically reflect the current name listed on Tableau Server. This is a convenient feature that saves you from having to remember if the content was renamed on the server when republishing a workbook.

You will need the **Save** capability to rename content that you do not own. You should already have the necessary permissions for content that you own. Likewise, you can remove the ability of others to rename an item by removing their **Save** capability. Editing permissions will be discussed later in this chapter.

Projects, workbooks, and metrics can all be renamed on Tableau Server. If you do not have the appropriate permissions, the **Rename…** option will appear grayed out in the **Actions** drop-down menu.

> **Note**
>
> Changing the name of a project will not affect the content within it or the URLs to those items. Likewise, changing the name of an item, such as a workbook, will not affect the URL to that item. This is a helpful feature that prevents content links that have been saved by others from breaking.

Data sources and views cannot be renamed on the server. They must be republished to implement a name change. It is important to be aware of workbooks connected to any data source that you change and confirm that the appropriate data connections are updated to the new data source within those workbooks.

> **Tip**
>
> Even though there is not a rename option for views within the **Actions** menu, you can rename a view from the server by using the **Web Edit** feature, which we will discuss in *Chapter 8, Interacting with Views on Tableau Server*.
>
> To edit a name using **Web Edit**, click on the **Edit** option from the **Actions** drop-down menu that we discussed earlier in this chapter. In the edit window, double-click on the worksheet tab so that the worksheet name is highlighted and enter the new name. Save your changes before exiting the view in **Web Edit**.

As we conclude this section, you should now have a good understanding of how to rename content directly on Tableau Server without republishing items, when this option is not available, and how to determine whether you or other users have the capability to rename an item based on the permissions settings. In the following section, we will examine the next option in the **More actions** menu, that is, **Move**.

Examining Move

Sometimes, there is a need to reorganize items on the server by changing their project location. After content has been published, Tableau Server conveniently allows you to move it within a site. Depending on your site role and permissions settings, content that can be moved within the server includes projects, workbooks, metrics, and data sources. Individual views cannot be moved because they are considered to be part of a workbook.

To move an item, click on the **More actions** menu and locate the **Move…** option, as indicated in *Figure 7.22:*

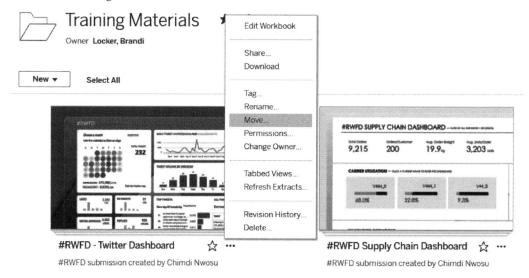

Figure 7.22 – The Move… option

Dashboard images created by Chimdi Nwosu

Clicking on this option will open the **Move Content** pop-up window. This contains each project available to you on the Tableau Server site. Once you have identified the desired project location, click on **Move Content** to confirm the change, or click on **Cancel** to close the window without saving any changes. *Figure 7.23* shows an example of the **Move Content** pop-up window:

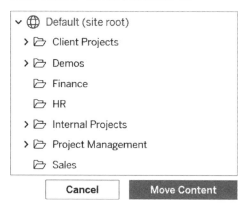

Figure 7.23 – The Move Content window

> **Tip**
> Moving content will not affect the URL, so you do not have to worry about notifying your users to update navigation links.

The **Move** option is only available to you if your site role is, at the very least, that of a Creator or Explorer (who can publish). Additionally, you must have the *View* and *Publish* capabilities for the project that you are moving an item to, and either be the content owner or have the *Move* capability granted in the permissions templates. These capabilities will be briefly discussed in the next section.

> **Note**
> Project leaders and owners have the capability to move nested projects and content between their projects. Only administrators can make a project a top-level project.

Moving an item removes it from the original location and saves it in the selected location. It is important to be aware of the potential impact on the permissions settings for items that are moved. A project can be **locked** or **unlocked**; this is also referred to as **customizable**. Locked projects have permission templates set at the project level that dictate the applied permissions for all content within them. Note that this may or may not affect any nested projects within. A customizable project has established permission templates but allows content owners to manage specific permission templates for each item in the project.

Moving an item into a locked project will replace all of its existing permissions templates with the permissions templates of the project. This means that if you do not have the capability to *Move* or *Set Permissions* in the locked project, then you will not be able to edit the permissions settings going forward or even relocate that item again without seeking help from an administrator or project leader.

Moving an item into a customizable project will retain the existing explicit permissions settings for that item. Those that only have implicit access, such as a project leader of a higher-level project, would lose access and need to be added to the permissions templates. Additionally, project owners or leaders will gain access to content moved into their projects.

You should now have a good understanding of how to move an item on Tableau Server along with a basic understanding of the potential effect of this change on the content permission settings. In the next section, you will learn how to edit those permissions.

Examining Permissions

Permissions determine what content Tableau Server users can access, interact with, edit, and manage. They can be managed at multiple layers throughout the server, such as projects, workbooks, views, metrics, and data sources. Permissions can also be applied to groups of users or specific individuals.

Understanding permissions can be overwhelming. In this section, we will only focus on the basics of editing the permission settings for content-level permissions using the **Actions** menu. A broad understanding of permissions is presented in *Chapter 1, What is Tableau Server?* For further information regarding this topic, please refer to the Tableau Help pages at `https://help.tableau.com/current/server/en-us/permissions.html`.

> **Note**
>
> Throughout various Tableau communities and resources, you might see a phrase such as "download permission." This phrase is easy to understand and is fine to use in a broad context, but when studying permissions, it is important to understand its precise definition.
>
> Permissions are comprised of capabilities. A capability is a specific ability to perform an action, such as view, edit, save, download, or delete. A permission rule determines which capabilities are allowed and which are denied for a group or user. Permission templates group common sets of capabilities together for your convenience while establishing a new rule, but these can be adjusted, as needed, using a custom template.

When an item is published to Tableau Server, it will automatically inherit the permissions settings for the project that it is published to. If the project is customizable, these settings can be adjusted using the **More actions (…)** menu. Recall that locked and customizable projects were briefly discussed in the previous section.

To edit the permissions settings for an item, open the **Actions** menu and locate the **Permissions…** option from the drop-down menu, as illustrated in *Figure 7.24*:

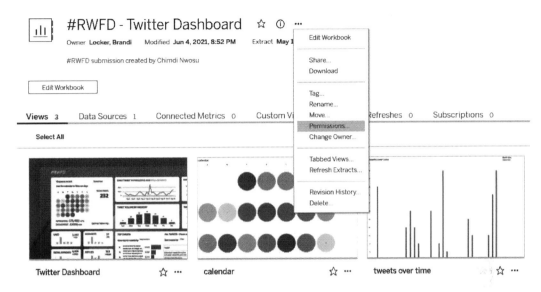

Figure 7.24 – The Permissions... option

Dashboard images created by Chimdi Nwosu

Clicking on this option will open the **Permissions** dialog, as shown in *Figure 7.25*:

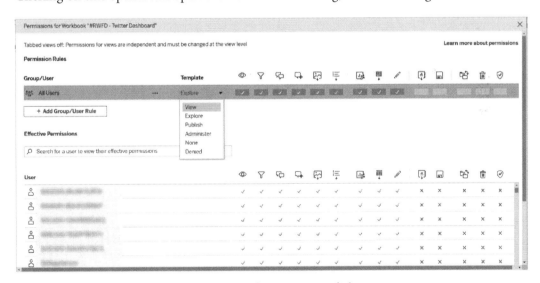

Figure 7.25 – The Permissions dialog

This window presents the existing **Permissions Rules**. The first column indicates the **Group/User** that the permission rule applies to, the second column provides a list of **Templates** to choose from, and the remaining columns are made up of a series of icons that represent individual interaction capabilities. These include capabilities to **View**, **Filter**, **View Comments**, **Add Comments**, **Download Image/PDF**, **Download Summary Data**, **Share Customized**, **Download Full Data**, **Web Edit**, **Download/Save A Copy**, **Overwrite**, **Move**, **Delete**, and **Set Permissions**. Hovering over each icon will identify what it is within a tooltip.

Each group or individual given a rule will be represented by their own record or row. You can use the **Template** column to select existing rule options, or you can individually select each capability to create a custom template. To add a rule, click on the **Add Group/User Rule** button in the **Permissions** dialog, as shown in *Figure 7.26*:

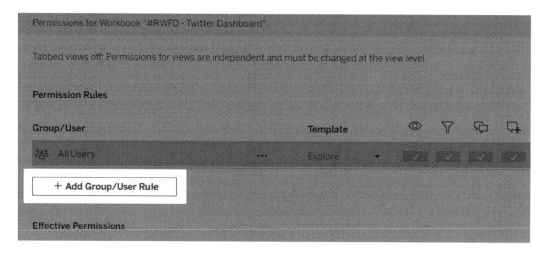

Figure 7.26 – The Add Group/User Rule button in the Permissions dialog

Clicking on this button will create a new row and provide a box for you to search for a group or individual user. Once you have identified the correct user or group, you can choose a template or create a custom permissions rule. Click on **Save** to create the new rule or **Cancel** to exit without saving any changes.

The lower half of the **Permissions** dialog contains the **Effective Permissions** section, as shown in *Figure 7.27*:

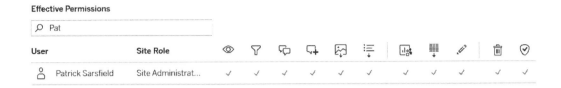

Figure 7.27 – The Effective Permissions section

You can use the search box in this section to search for groups or individuals and view what capabilities they possess for the selected item. This can be a particularly helpful feature to check a specific user's permission rule if the item contains many rules or if only groups are used and you are not certain which group, if any, that user is a part of.

Notice that at the top of the screenshot shown in *Figure 7.25*, there is a notice regarding **Tabbed Views**. When a workbook is located in a customizable project, meaning that content within the project can have its own permissions settings, and **Tabbed Views** are turned off, changes to the permissions rules must be made for each view.

> **Note**
>
> As discussed in the *Examining Move* section, if an item is located in a locked project, you will not be able to adjust individual workbook permissions. If you do not have the permissions option available, this could be a reason. Other potential reasons to investigate include understanding your site role, your **View** and **Publish** capabilities for the project, and your **Set Permissions** capabilities for the item in question.

You will also find a link to **Learn more about permissions** in the upper-right corner of the **Permissions** dialog. Clicking on this will open the Tableau Help pages for permissions. Once you have finished reviewing the permissions settings and saving any changes, you can close the window using the **X** in the upper-right corner.

This section provided a brief overview of how to edit permission rules on Tableau Server. You should now have a better understanding of how to edit, remove, and create new rules to effectively manage content on the server. In the next section, you will learn about the option to change the owner of an item.

Examining Change Owner

Another interesting Tableau Server feature that is available for projects, workbooks, metrics, and data sources on the **More actions** ellipsis (…) is the **Change Owner** feature. Selecting the **Change Owner...** option will allow you to transfer ownership of an item to another user. After you click on the **More actions** ellipsis (…) button, the **Change Owner...** feature can be found around the middle of the drop-down menu. An example of where this feature is located inside a **More actions** drop-down menu for a workbook is shown in *Figure 7.28*:

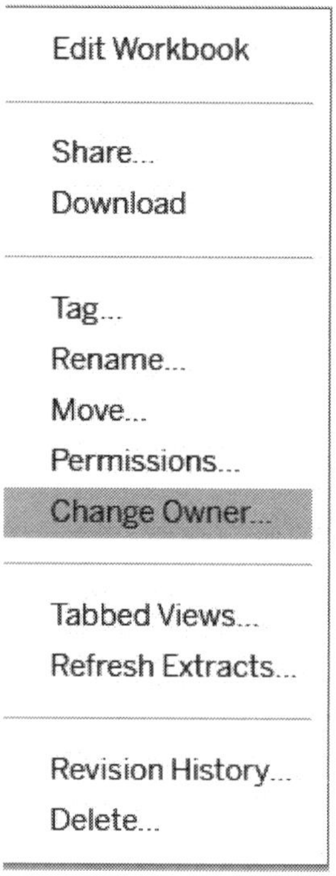

Figure 7.28 – The location of Change Owner… inside a More actions workbook drop-down menu

After you click on the **Change Owner...** option, a **Change Owner** window will open. This window advises you to transfer the ownership of a selected piece of content. The **Change Owner** window advises you to **Choose an owner for [your selected piece of content]**. You can select the user you would like to transfer ownership to via a drop-down menu with a list of usernames. Alternatively, you can type in a username using a search box. *Figure 7.29* shows an example of the **Change Owner** window:

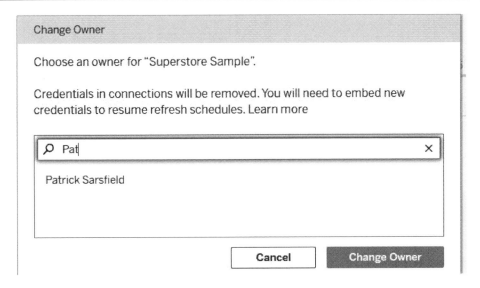

Figure 7.29 – The Change Owner window

After you have chosen the user you would like to assign ownership to on the **Change Tags** window, click on the **Change Owner** button to complete the transfer process or **Cancel** to exit without saving.

In this section, you learned how to transfer ownership of the content on Tableau Server. Now, let's take a look at another item from your **More actions** drop-down menu, that is, the **Revision History** feature.

Examining Revision History

Tableau Server tracks changes to workbooks and data sources in its **Revision History**. Any time a change is made using the **Web Edit** feature or from overwriting an existing workbook or data source by publishing from Tableau Desktop, a new version is saved in **Revision History**. Understanding how to view and manage content using this history allows you to recover earlier versions of files that might have been inadvertently changed, edited to accommodate fluctuating business requirements, are experiencing unknown errors, or other issues.

This option can be found in both workbooks and data sources. You can view **Revision History** using the **Actions** menu by clicking on the **More actions** ellipsis (**…**) button and selecting **Revision History…**, which is located near the bottom of the drop-down menu. An example of where this feature is located inside a workbook's **More actions** menu is shown in *Figure 7.30*:

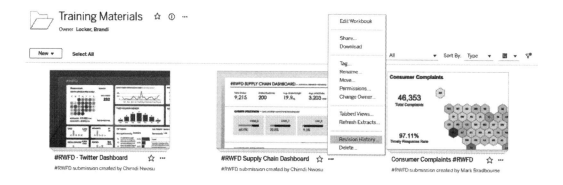

Figure 7.30 – The Revision History… option

Dashboard images created by Chimdi Nwosu and Mark Bradbourne

> **Note**
>
> If you do not see **Revision History…** in this menu when viewing a workbook or data source, or if the option is grayed out, that means you do not have the necessary site role or content permissions. You are required to have an Explorer (who can publish) or Creator site role and specific permissions depending on the type of content you are trying to access. The **Revision History…** option can also be disabled at the site level by a server administrator. If you need access to a previous version of a workbook or data source and are experiencing issues, you should verify your site role and contact the content owner or your Tableau Server administrator.

Clicking on the **Revision History…** option on the **Actions** drop-down menu opens a pop-up window that contains a list of the current and previous revisions for the selected item. The history indicates the **Revision Number**, **Publisher**, and **Publish Date** for each version. By default, Tableau Server stores up to 25 revisions for each item; however, this option could differ for you as it is managed by your Tableau Server administrator. To restore a previous version, select the previous version you want and click on **Restore**. The older version that you selected will become the current version, and what was your current version will now appear as a previous version in **Revision History**.

Each record in **Revision History** has its own **Actions** menu represented by an ellipsis (**…**) on the right-hand side of the window, as shown in *Figure 7.31*:

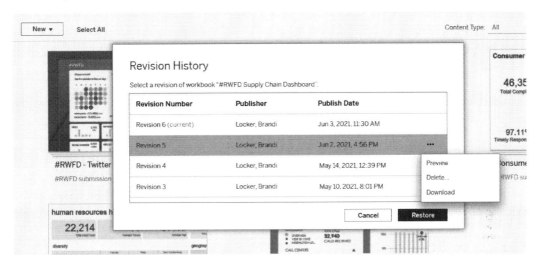

Figure 7.31 – The Revision History of a workbook

Dashboard images created by Chimdi Nwosu and Mark Bradbourne

When **Revision History** for a workbook has been selected, the first option available in this additional **Actions** menu is **Preview**. Clicking on **Preview** will open a new browser tab for Tableau Server that enables you to view and interact with that version as it would appear on the server. When you have finished examining the preview, you can select **Close Preview** to return to the previous window.

The next available option for a workbook revision is the **Delete** option. Deleting a revision only removes that particular version and does not delete the entire workbook.

Finally, clicking on the **Download** option will automatically initiate a download to your computer of that version as a packaged workbook with a .twbx filename extension.

> **Tip**
> If you need to make changes to a previous version before republishing, then you can download that version, make the necessary changes in Tableau Desktop, and overwrite the current version on Tableau Server. You can also use this technique if the **Restore** option is unavailable.

In this section, you learned how to revert a workbook or data source back to a previous version. Now, let's take a look at another item from your **More actions** drop-down menu, that is, the **Delete** feature.

Examining Delete

An important part of managing content on Tableau Server well includes removing unnecessary content, including items that are no longer in use. This is beneficial because it saves space on the server, and it helps you to keep your content organized. Removing excess server content also helps developers and users to avoid confusion on which items are currently being used and which items are no longer active or needed.

You must have an Explorer (can publish) or Creator site role and have the **Delete** capability for the item to remove it. You can also delete an item if you are the content owner or if you are the project owner or leader where the item is located.

To delete an item, first, you must navigate to it, then click on the **More actions** ellipsis (**…**) button. The **Delete** feature can be found at the bottom of the drop-down menu. An example of where this feature is located inside a **More actions** drop-down menu for a workbook is shown in *Figure 7.32*:

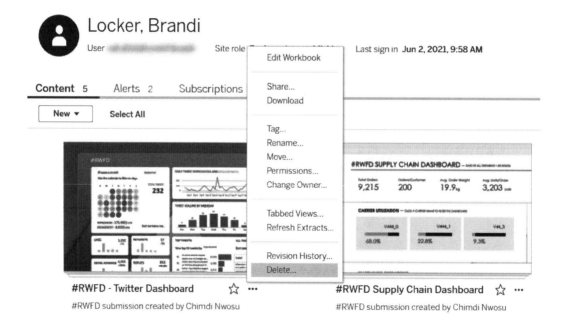

Figure 7.32 – The Delete… option

Dashboard images created by Chimdi Nwosu

From the drop-down menu that appears, select **Delete…** from the bottom of the menu list. After clicking on **Delete…**, you will get a pop-up window that asks you to confirm by selecting **Delete** again or to **Cancel** and go back. *Figure 7.33* shows an example of this pop-up window:

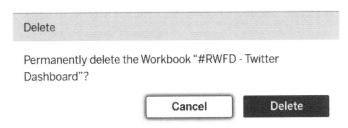

Figure 7.33 – The Delete pop-up window

While it is important to remove unnecessary content from the server, it is equally important to use caution when you consider deleting an item. Deleting content is a permanent action for all content types. The only exception to this is deleting views. You can hide recommendations or remove an item from collections without affecting the original content.

The resulting impact of the **Delete** feature on different content types are as follows:

- **Projects** are permanently deleted along with any content contained inside them.
- **Workbooks**, **Metrics**, **Flows**, and **Data Roles** are permanently deleted, and this action cannot be undone.
- **Views** are removed from your Tableau Server site but are still available if you download or edit a workbook.

As we conclude this section, you should now have a better understanding of the importance of keeping your Tableau Server site clear of excess content, know how to delete content from the server, and understand the potential consequences of this action. Next, we will explore some of the other options available in the **More actions** menu that are specific to certain content types, starting with **Who Has Seen This View?**

Examining Who Has Seen This View?

Who Has Seen This View? is a great option that is only available in the **More actions** drop-down menu of a view in which you are the owner. It helps to answer a question that plagues so many of us who publish content to Tableau Server regularly: "Is anybody looking at my dashboard?" Selecting this feature will open a window that lists all the users who have seen that view. After clicking on the **More actions** ellipsis (**...**), the **Who Has Seen This View?** feature can be found near the bottom of the drop-down menu. An example of where this feature is located inside a **More actions** menu is shown in *Figure 7.34*:

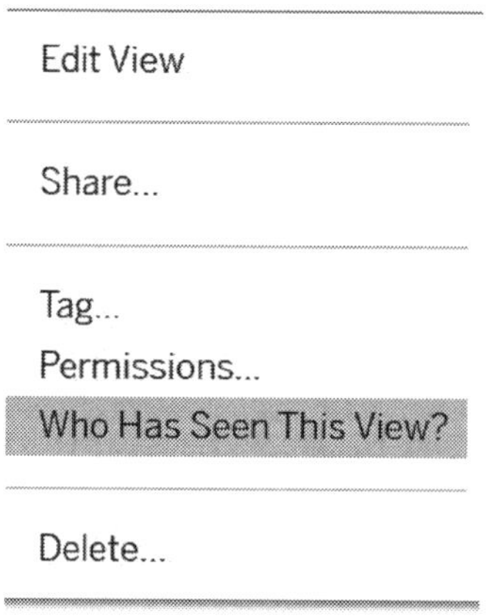

Edit View

Share...

Tag...
Permissions...
Who Has Seen This View?

Delete...

Figure 7.34 – The location of Who Has Seen This View? inside a More actions view drop-down menu

After you click on **Who Has Seen This View?** on the **More actions** menu, a new window will open that provides you with a list of all the users who have seen your view. This list provides you with the name of the user, the name of the view, the date and time each user last viewed it, and how many times each user has seen this view. *Figure 7.35* presents an example of this window:

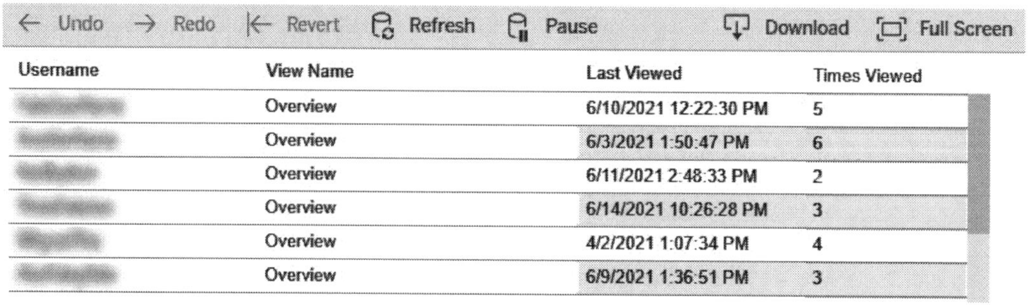

← Undo	→ Redo	⟵ Revert	↻ Refresh	⏸ Pause	⤓ Download	⛶ Full Screen

Username	View Name	Last Viewed	Times Viewed
	Overview	6/10/2021 12:22:30 PM	5
	Overview	6/3/2021 1:50:47 PM	6
	Overview	6/11/2021 2:48:33 PM	2
	Overview	6/14/2021 10:26:28 PM	3
	Overview	4/2/2021 1:07:34 PM	4
	Overview	6/9/2021 1:36:51 PM	3

Figure 7.35 – The Who Has Seen This View? window

You can sort the rows on your **Who Has Seen This View?** window. To view a **Sort By** option, simply hover over the column header. The **Username** and **View Name** columns can be sorted alphabetically, while the **Last Viewed** and **Times Viewed** columns can be sorted in ascending or descending order. These sorting options can come in handy when you have many rows and want to quickly do something, such as find a user, identify who recently looked at a piece of content, or discover who has looked at this view the greatest number of times. *Figure 7.36* zooms in on the previous screenshot to demonstrate the sort icon that appears when you hover over a column header. Clicking on this icon applies the sort feature to the highlighted column:

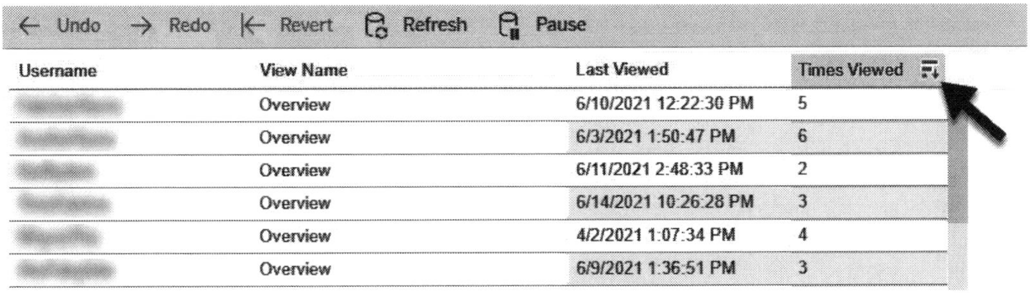

Figure 7.36 – The Who Has Seen This View? Sort By header

Lastly, clicking on the **Download** button located in the right-hand corner of your **Who Has Seen This View?** window will open a small window in the center of your screen. This will provide you with the following options when clicked on: **Image**, **Data**, **Crosstab**, **PDF**, and **PowerPoint**. The only options you will likely be interested in from this window are the **Data** and **Crosstab** options, as they provide you with a way to download the raw data as an Excel or **Comma-Separated Values** (**CSV**) file. We review each of the available options on the **Download** window, in depth, in *Chapter 8*, *Interacting with Views on Tableau Server*. An example of the **Download** window is shown in *Figure 7.37*:

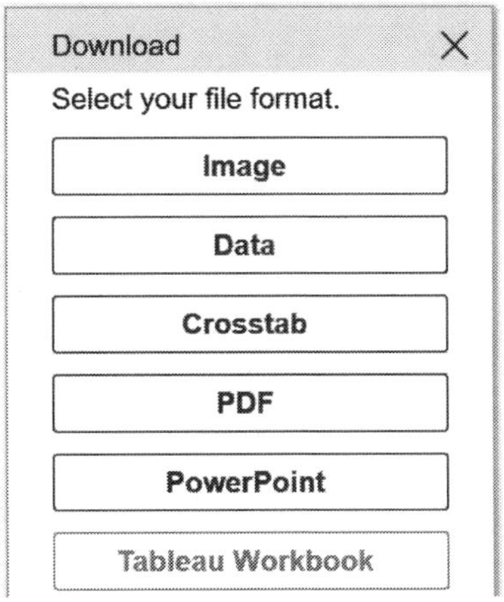

Figure 7.37 – The Who Has Seen This View? window's Download button options

In this section, you learned how to identify all the users who have seen your view. Now, let's take a look at another item from your **More actions** drop-down menu, that is, the ability to **Edit Connections**.

Examining Edit Connection

When data connections are published to Tableau Server, the connection information is stored so that the data can refresh on a schedule and users can interact with the data. A password can be embedded in the connection, or the user can be prompted to enter a password when attempting to view the data. If you need to update the data connection information, you can do so by using the **Edit Connection** option found on the **More actions** ellipsis (…).

> **Note**
>
> If you cannot see this option available, you might not have the required site role and/or be the owner of that item. Another method that you can use to edit the connection is to republish and overwrite the workbook or data source with the updated connection details.

If a workbook or data source has multiple connections, you will need to specify which connection you wish to edit. As discussed in previous chapters, you can view the individual connections using the **Connections** tab on a published data source page or by browsing the **Data Sources** tab of a workbook page and choosing **Connections** underneath the **Show As** menu.

When viewing a data source, the **Edit Connection…** option can be found on the **More actions** menu. An example showing the location of this option is presented in *Figure 7.38*:

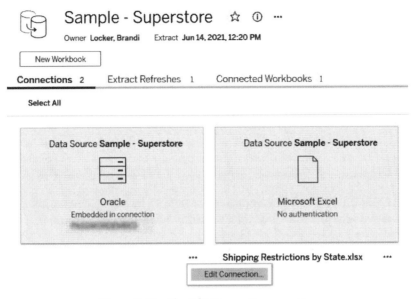

Figure 7.38 – The Edit Connection… option

Clicking on **Edit Connection…** will open the pop-up window, as shown in *Figure 7.39*:

Edit Connection

Edit the selected data connection.

Server name	
Server port	
Username	

Password ⦿ Prompt user for password if needed
         ◯ Embedded password in connection

Test Connection

Network type ⦿ Tableau Online
             ◯ Private network

Cancel   **Save**

Figure 7.39 – The Edit Connection window

Using this window, you can edit **Server name**, **Server port**, and **Username**, check whether you want to embed the password or prompt users for a password, and select **Network type**.

> **Tip**
>
> You can edit connection details for multiple data connections at a time by selecting the items using the checkboxes and the **Actions** menu. This only applies if your data connections share the same connection type.
>
> You can also edit connection details for multiple data sources at a time using the same method. However, this will only work if all of the connections within the data sources are of the same type.

Once you have completed any necessary changes, click on **Save** to keep your changes or select **Cancel** to discard them.

Now that you know how to edit data connection details, let's examine another helpful option in the **More actions** menu for data sources, that is, **Refresh Extracts**.

Examining Refresh Extracts

Refresh Extracts is an efficient way in which to run an automatic extract refresh on your data or schedule an extract refresh. This option is available on the **More actions** drop-down menu of a workbook or data source. After clicking on the **More actions** ellipsis (...) button, the **Refresh Extracts...** feature can be found near the bottom of the drop-down menu. An example of where this feature is located inside a **More actions** drop-down menu is shown in *Figure 7.40*:

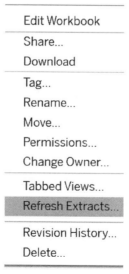

Figure 7.40 – The location of Refresh Extracts... inside a More actions workbook drop-down menu

Selecting the **Refresh Extracts...** option opens a **Refresh Extracts** window. You will be presented with two options: **Refresh Now** and **Schedule a Refresh**.

Refresh Now

The first tab and default option on the **Refresh Extracts** window is **Refresh Now**. You can view an example of this window in *Figure 7.41*:

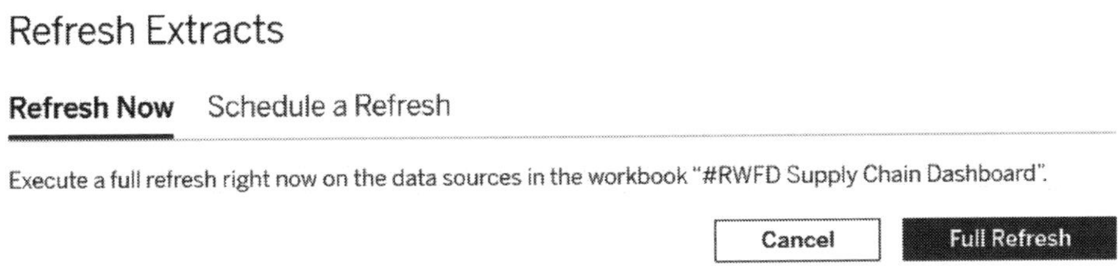

Refresh Extracts

Refresh Now   Schedule a Refresh

Execute a full refresh right now on the data sources in the workbook "#RWFD Supply Chain Dashboard".

Cancel   **Full Refresh**

Figure 7.41 – The Refresh Extracts window's Refresh Now tab

Clicking on the **Full Refresh** button in the lower-right corner of this window will run a full refresh on the data sources in the workbook and will replace all the contents within the extract.

Schedule a Refresh

The second tab on the **Refresh Extracts** window is **Schedule a Refresh**. This option allows you to select a schedule for your workbook from the available options created by your Tableau Server administrators. Clicking on the **Schedule Refresh** button in the lower-right corner of this window will create a scheduled refresh based on your choice. *Figure 7.42* presents an example of this window:

Refresh Extracts

Refresh Now   **Schedule a Refresh**

Choose a refresh schedule for workbook "#RWFD Supply Chain Dashboard".

🔍 Daily 9   ✕

Daily 9 AM

Cancel   Schedule Refresh

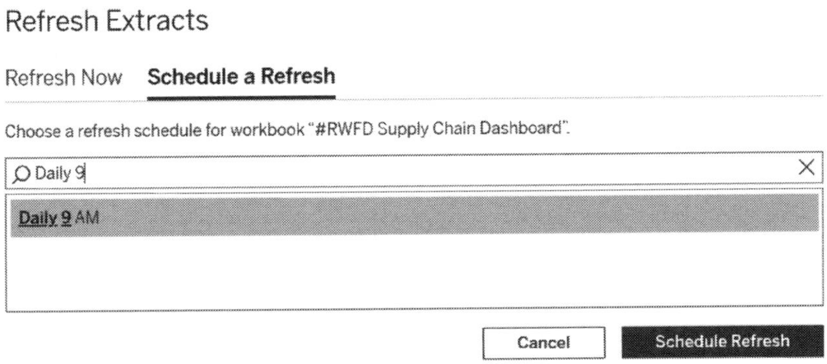

Figure 7.42 – The Refresh Extracts window's Schedule a Refresh tab

> **Tip**
> Reach out to your Tableau Server administrator if you cannot see an option for the time you would like to schedule a refresh available in your existing choices. Server administrators have the ability to create, change, and reassign schedules on Tableau Server.

In this section, you learned how to run a full refresh on your data and schedule an extract refresh. Next, let's take a look at another item from your **More actions** drop-down menu, that is, the ability to add or remove tabbed views from a workbook.

Examining Tabbed Views

If you are publishing a workbook that has multiple views (such as dashboards, worksheets, and stories), you have the option to show **tabs** during the publishing process. Tabs are buttons at the top of a view that allow users to navigate through multiple views within a single workbook. This is highlighted in *Figure 7.43*:

Figure 7.43 – Tabbed View

Dashboard images created by Chimdi Nwosu

After a workbook has been published, you can manage this preference from Tableau Server using the **Tabbed Views** option from the **More actions** ellipsis (**...**), as shown in *Figure 7.44*:

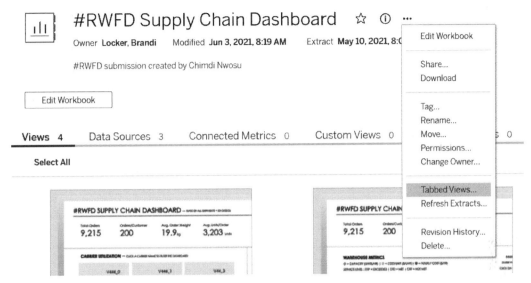

Figure 7.44 – The Tabbed Views… option

Dashboard images created by Chimdi Nwosu

Clicking on the **Tabbed Views…** option will open a pop-up window that allows you to either **Show Tabs** or **Hide Tabs**, as shown in *Figure 7.45*:

Tabbed Views

Change the tab display option for the workbook "#RWFD Supply Chain Dashboard". Show tabs to enable navigation between views in a workbook.

Figure 7.45 – The Tabbed Views pop-up window

The option that has been currently applied to the workbook will be grayed out, while the other option will be shown in blue. You can click on **Cancel** if you wish to close the pop-up window without making any changes.

Summary

As we conclude this chapter, you should now be acquainted with the **More Actions** menu, which is often represented by ellipses (...) that can be found throughout Tableau Server. You should have a better understanding of the various places where you can find this menu. Additionally, you learned how to edit views, share, and download content, and tag items so that they can be easily identified in a search or by a filter. You also learned how to rename and move content, adjust permissions rules, and change content owners. Lastly, you learned how to view an item's revision history and delete content. You also know how to discover who has seen a view, edit data source connections, refresh data extracts, and show or hide tabs on a published view.

In the next chapter, you will learn about the many features available when viewing an item on the server. These features can help you to customize the Tableau Server experience for yourself and your users.

8
Interacting with Views on Tableau Server

In this chapter, you will learn how to utilize a series of helpful options for yourself and others when exploring a published view. After completing this chapter, you will know how to interact with views, obtain the raw data behind a mark, create Custom Views, alerts, metrics and subscriptions, make web edits, and share, download, and add comments to a view on Tableau Server. Many of the things you will learn about in this chapter will help you better direct end users to their desired information and improve the utilization of content on the server.

By the end of this chapter, you will know how to leverage many of the most common options and features that can be found on a page view. To be able to do this, we will cover the following topics:

- Interacting with Views on Tableau Server

- Examining View Data

- Examining the Undo, Redo, Revert, Refresh, and Pause options

- Examining Device Layouts and Data Sources

- Examining the Favorites menu

- Examining Custom Views

- Examining Alerts

- Examining Metrics

- Examining Subscriptions

- Examining the Web Edit button

- Examining the Share button

- Examining the Download button

- Examining the Comments button

Interacting with Views on Tableau Server

In this section, we will review some of the most common ways to interact with Views on Tableau Server. The ability to quickly and easily interact with visualizations, as well as obtaining immediate insights, is one of the primary reasons why Tableau is a leading data visualization software. When looking at a view – a visualization created in Tableau – it is important to understand that unless it was purposefully designed to be a static infographic, you are likely to have a highly interactive experience available. Let's go over two of the most common ways to interact with a view to gain additional insights, filtering, and hovering. If you open a view on Tableau Server and want to know more, all you need to do to gain deeper insights or analysis is select or hover over the items on your screen.

Filtering your data is one of the easiest ways to quickly refine the information presented to you. Applying this option is as simple as clicking or dragging an available filter. The following screenshot shows an example of a view with the filterable areas identified inside the square boxes:

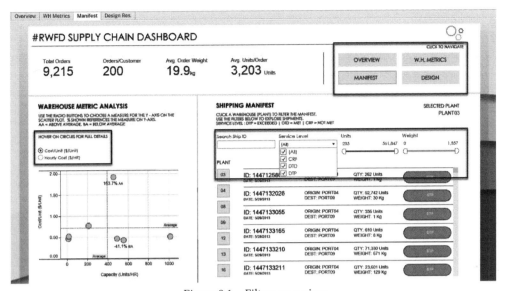

Figure 8.1 – Filters on a view

Dashboard image credit: Chimdi Nwosu

Hovering over data points in a view will often provide you with tooltips. If not removed by the developer, a tooltip is a box that appears when you hover your mouse over one or more marks in a view. The following screenshot provides an example of a tooltip after hovering over a mark:

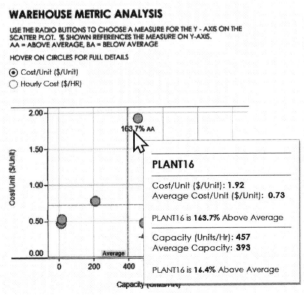

Figure 8.2 – Hovering on a view to see the tooltip

Dashboard image credit: Chimdi Nwosu

Tooltips in Tableau are used to provide additional information and details that would not otherwise fit comfortably on a view. Additionally, you may see a static image of a related view filtered to your selected mark within a tooltip. This is referred to as a **Viz in Tooltip**.

> **Note**
>
> Rest assured that interacting with a view *will not* break the view or impact the underlying data. Performing an action, such as changing a filter that alters your view results, is only a temporary change. The next time you or another user opens this same view, it will appear in its original form.

In this section, you learned how to interact with Views on Tableau Server. These capabilities allow for deeper insights and understanding of your data. Now, let's learn how to see and obtain the actual data behind a view.

Examining View Data

When looking at a view on Tableau Server, you may have the option to **view data**. This ability allows you to click on a mark and see the underlying data provided in a tabular format.

The **View Data...** function can be found by clicking a mark and looking at the top of the tooltip. It can be identified by an icon that appears as three columns and multiple rows of lines.

> **Note**
>
> If you are unable to see the View Data icon, this is because the Tableau developer who created this view decided to remove tooltips entirely, the tooltip menu command buttons option has been turned off, or you lack the necessary permissions.

The following screenshot shows an example of a tooltip with the **View Data...** icon displayed after clicking a mark:

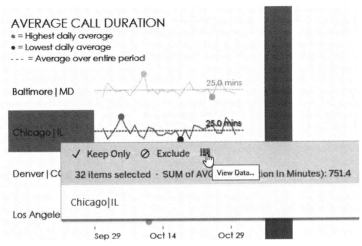

Figure 8.3 – View Data… as a mark

Dashboard image credit: Chimdi Nwosu

After clicking the **View Data…** icon in a tooltip, a new page opens. This page has two tabs: **Summary** and **Full Data**. The following screenshot shows an example of a **View Data** page with the **Full Data** tab selected:

View Data

| Summary | Full Data |

Showing first 200 rows.
Download all rows as a text file

☐ Show all columns

Call Center	Date	Reason	Sentiment	SLA met	Status	Call Timestamp (Week numbers)	Call Duration In Minutes
Chicago|IL	10/11/2020	Payments	Very Negative	Met	Within SLA	October 11, 2020	9.0
Chicago|IL	10/3/2020	Billing Question	Very Negative	Met	Within SLA	September 27, 2020	20.0
Chicago|IL	10/5/2020	Payments	Very Positive	Met	Within SLA	October 4, 2020	40.0
Chicago|IL	10/30/2020	Billing Question	Very Positive	Unmet	Below SLA	October 25, 2020	6.0
Chicago|IL	10/7/2020	Billing Question	Very Negative	Met	Above SLA	October 4, 2020	17.0
Chicago|IL	10/14/2020	Billing Question	Negative	Met	Within SLA	October 11, 2020	37.0
Chicago|IL	10/11/2020	Billing Question	Very Negative	Unmet	Below SLA	October 11, 2020	10.0
Chicago|IL	10/21/2020	Service Outage	Neutral	Met	Within SLA	October 18, 2020	34.0
Chicago|IL	10/2/2020	Payments	Negative	Met	Within SLA	September 27, 2020	7.0
Chicago|IL	10/29/2020	Billing Question	Neutral	Met	Above SLA	October 25, 2020	10.0
Chicago|IL	10/26/2020	Billing Question	Negative	Met	Within SLA	October 25, 2020	43.0
Chicago|IL	10/22/2020	Billing Question	Negative	Met	Within SLA	October 18, 2020	25.0
Chicago|IL	10/4/2020	Billing Question	Negative	Unmet	Below SLA	October 4, 2020	25.0
Chicago|IL	10/6/2020	Billing Question	Neutral	Met	Above SLA	October 4, 2020	8.0
Chicago|IL	10/5/2020	Billing Question	Neutral	Met	Within SLA	October 4, 2020	42.0
Chicago|IL	10/15/2020	Billing Question	Very Negative	Met	Within SLA	October 11, 2020	37.0
Chicago|IL	10/7/2020	Billing Question	Positive	Met	Within SLA	October 4, 2020	13.0
Chicago|IL	10/18/2020	Billing Question	Negative	Met	Within SLA	October 18, 2020	28.0
Chicago|IL	10/2/2020	Service Outage	Neutral	Unmet	Below SLA	September 27, 2020	35.0
Chicago|IL	10/29/2020	Billing Question	Very Positive	Met	Above SLA	October 25, 2020	16.0

Figure 8.4 – View Data (Full Data tab selected)

The **Summary** tab provides a simple display of only the data that represents the mark you selected, while the **Full Data** tab provides all the underlying data for the selected mark. In both tabs, you will see a link option to **Download all rows as a text file**. Clicking this link will download a **Comma-Separated Values (CSV)** file of your data.

In this section, you learned how to quickly obtain the raw data behind a mark. Now, let's learn how to undo, redo, and revert changes that have been made to a view, as well as how to refresh and pause.

Examining the Undo, Redo, Revert, Refresh, and Pause options

When viewing a dashboard or worksheet on Tableau Server, you will find a toolbar near the top left of the server window that contains options to **undo, redo, revert, refresh, and pause**, as shown in the following screenshot:

Figure 8.5 – The Undo, Redo, Revert, Refresh, and Pause options in a workbook

These buttons provide convenient shortcuts for interacting with and viewing content.

When you first open a workbook, the **Undo**, **Redo**, and **Revert** buttons will be grayed out until you begin interacting with the view. As you explore an interactive dashboard or worksheet by clicking on its filters or triggering actions, what is shown in the view will change accordingly. You can use the **Undo** button, or *Ctrl + Z* on your keyboard, to go back to previous view settings. You can use the **Redo** button, or *Ctrl + Y* on your keyboard, to reapply a setting that you have just undone. You can undo and redo as many times as you like while viewing that item. These actions will be stored by Tableau Server across all worksheets until you close the item.

The **Revert** button allows you to reset the view back to its original settings when it was published. This is a quick way to clear all filters and actions that have been selected as you browse an item.

Clicking the **Refresh** button will update the data for your view. This does not refresh the data extract, merely the data connection, which it does to ensure that the view is using the most recent data from the extract. When you manually update the data using the **Refresh** button, Tableau Server clears the cache to retrieve the latest data. This may require a long load time, depending on the size and complexity of your data source.

The last button available here is the **Pause** button. As you are viewing a published item, the server will periodically refresh the view by querying the data source. You can use the **Pause** button, as shown in the following screenshot, to temporarily stop this process so that you can interact with a view without interruption or delay. This is particularly helpful if the refresh process takes a long time to complete:

Figure 8.6 – The Pause button

Once you have paused the view from refreshing, you will see that the **Pause** button has been replaced with a **Resume** button, as shown here:

Figure 8.7 – The Resume button

Clicking the **Resume** button will refresh the data and resume the periodic server refreshes.

Now that you are familiar with the toolbar on the left-hand side of the view window, let's examine some of the options on the right-hand side, starting with **Device Layouts** and **Data Sources**.

Examining Device Layouts and Data Sources

At the top right of your server window, you will see two options next to the top toolbar that we discussed in *Chapter 3*, *Tableau Server Navigation Pane*. These two options are **Device Layouts** and **Data Sources**, as shown in the following screenshot:

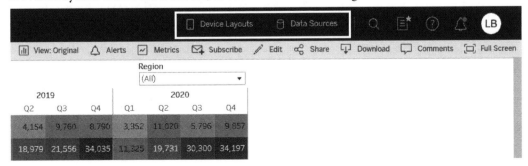

Figure 8.8 – Device Layouts and Data Sources location in a dashboard view

Let's examine each of these options.

Device Layouts

If you are familiar with building a dashboard using Tableau Desktop, then you have likely seen the **Device Preview** feature, which assists you in selecting a size for your dashboard that fits the desired device (phone, tablet, or desktop). The **Device Layouts** button in the Tableau Server environment works similarly.

Clicking **Device Layouts** will open a window similar to the following:

Figure 8.9 – Device Layouts window

This window allows you to see the view as it would be displayed on a **desktop, tablet, or phone** by clicking on the tabs located at the top of the **Device Layouts** page, above the view. If the workbook contains multiple Views, sometimes shown as tabs, then you may also see a drop-down on the top right-hand side of the window that allows you to choose which item to preview. To close this preview window and return to the normal view screen, click the **X** button in the top-right corner.

Data Sources

To the right of the **Device Layouts** button is a button labeled **Data Sources**. Clicking this button will open a pane that allows you to view the workbook's data sources, as shown here:

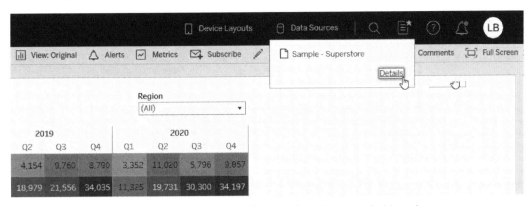

Figure 8.10 – Data Sources button when viewing a dashboard

This pane will list each data source included in the workbook and provide a link to view its **details**. Clicking this link will take you to the **Data Sources** page within the workbook. This page was discussed in *Chapter 6, Navigating Content Pages in Tableau Server*.

With that, you have learned how to utilize the **Device Layouts** and **Data Sources** buttons available at the top of the server window. Next, let's examine the additional top toolbar icon, which allows you to open your **favorites menu**.

Examining the favorites menu

When viewing workbook content or a metric, you will see an additional icon appear in the toolbar at the top right of your server window, located between the quick search icon and the help menu icon. This icon appears as a list with a star in the corner, as shown in the following screenshot:

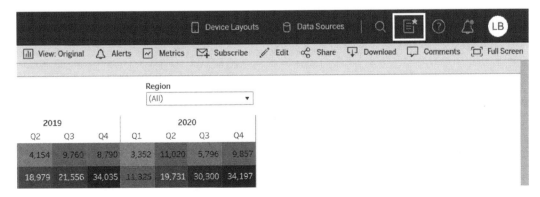

Figure 8.11 – Favorites menu icon

Clicking this button opens the **favorites menu** feature, which is a drop-down that conveniently lists all the content that you have marked as a favorite item. It also contains a search box at the top of the menu so that you can search for a specific favorited item that you have in mind. An example of this menu is shown in the following screenshot:

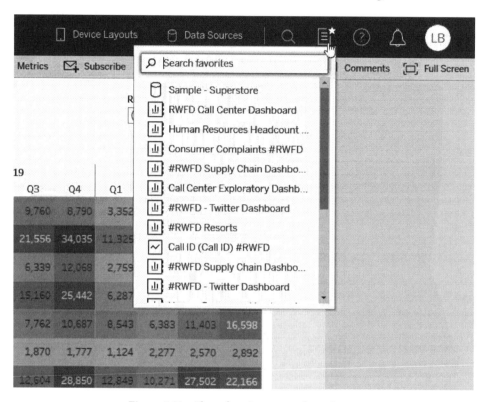

Figure 8.12 – Show favorites menu drop-down

If you utilize the search in this drop-down menu, you will only see search results that exist within this favorites list. How to add an item to your favorites list was discussed in *Chapter 3, Tableau Server Navigation Pane*.

If you need to search for content that is *not* already marked in your favorites, then you can utilize the **Quick Search** feature, which is indicated by the magnifying glass icon to the left of the **favorites menu** icon. The **Quick Search** feature was discussed in *Chapter 4, Tableau Server Top Toolbar*.

This **favorites menu** feature only appears in the top toolbar when you open an item within a workbook, such as a view, dashboard, or story, and when you open a metric. It is a shortcut that allows you to open a new item without having to return to the **Explore** window.

With that, you have learned how to use the convenient **favorites menu** feature while viewing server content to efficiently navigate to other items on the server. Next, let's examine the additional toolbar below the top toolbar icons, starting with how to create a custom view.

Examining Custom Views

If you find yourself regularly navigating to the same workbook and applying the same filters over and over again, you can take advantage of a convenient feature in Tableau Server that allows you to create a custom view to suit your own needs or preferences. A **Custom View** is a saved version of a view that retains all the filters and selections you have chosen to apply. It does not affect the original view; however, changes that have been made to the original view can affect your custom view. For example, if the original view is republished with a change in the data, your custom view will be affected. Additionally, if the original view is deleted from your Tableau Server, your custom view will no longer appear.

In this section, we will examine how to create a custom view and how to manage existing custom views.

Creating a custom view

To create a custom view, follow these steps:

1. Make any changes or selections within the view itself and then click on the toolbar button labeled **View: Original**, as shown here:

Figure 8.13 – View button

Notice in the preceding screenshot that an asterisk appears next to the **View: Original** icon, indicating that changes have been made to the view, such as applying filters.

Clicking the **View** button will open the **Custom Views** dialog, as shown in the following screenshot:

Figure 8.14 – Custom Views dialog box

2. Provide a name for the custom view in the **Name this view** box. You can also choose to make it your default view and whether it should be made visible to others.

3. Once your specifications have been set, click **Save** to create the view. The lower half of this box shows a list of your Views for that workbook and other Views if they are made visible to others.

> Tip
> The **Make visible to others** option does not automatically notify anyone of the view's existence. To share the view, use the **Share** button in the view toolbar.
> We will discuss how to share a view later in this chapter.

When you create a custom view, the workbook content page will display the view under the **Custom Views** tab. This tab will also list any Custom Views that others have created and made visible to others.

Next, we will explore how to view and manage Custom Views, starting with the **Custom Views** tab.

Viewing and managing Custom Views

Clicking on the **Custom Views** tab from a workbook's content page will show all of the Custom Views that you can see for that workbook in a list format, as shown in the following screenshot:

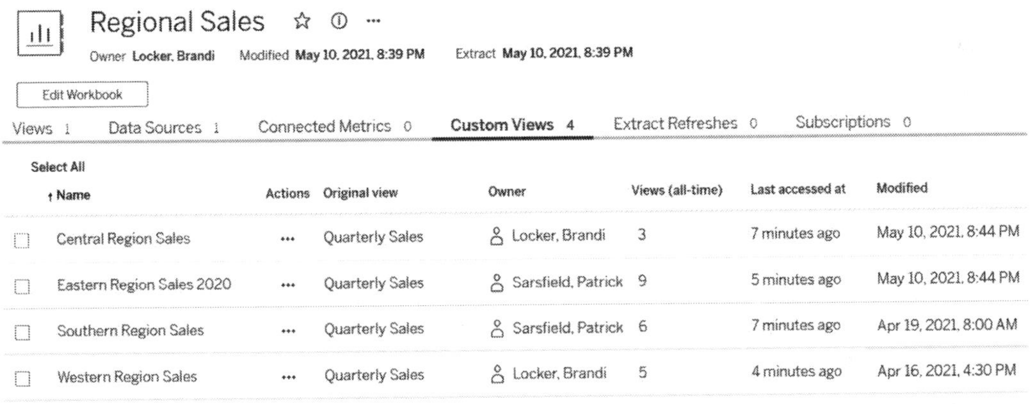
Regional Sales
Owner Locker, Brandi
Modified May 10, 2021, 8:39 PM
Extract May 10, 2021, 8:39 PM
Edit Workbook
Views 1
Data Sources 1
Connected Metrics 0
Custom Views 4
Extract Refreshes 0
Subscriptions 0
Select All
Name
Actions
Original view
Owner
Views (all-time)
Last accessed at
Modified
Central Region Sales
Quarterly Sales
Locker, Brandi
3
7 minutes ago
May 10, 2021, 8:44 PM
Eastern Region Sales 2020
Quarterly Sales
Sarsfield, Patrick
9
5 minutes ago
May 10, 2021, 8:44 PM
Southern Region Sales
Quarterly Sales
Sarsfield, Patrick
6
7 minutes ago
Apr 19, 2021, 8:00 AM
Western Region Sales
Quarterly Sales
Locker, Brandi
5
4 minutes ago
Apr 16, 2021, 4:30 PM

Figure 8.15 – Custom Views tab on a workbook page

The details on this page include the name of the custom view, an actions menu, the name of the original view, the custom view owner's name, a view count, the last access date, and the modified date. You can use the column headers to sort the Custom Views by a particular attribute. Content pages were discussed in *Chapter 6, Navigating Content Pages in Tableau Server*.

> **Note**
> Server administrators can change the owner of a custom view or delete the view. You can see all of the Custom Views for a workbook if you have *published* permissions for that workbook.

If the workbook is already open, click the **Views** button in the toolbar to see all of the Custom Views available to you. This includes Custom Views that you have created, those created by others and made visible, and the original view, as shown here:

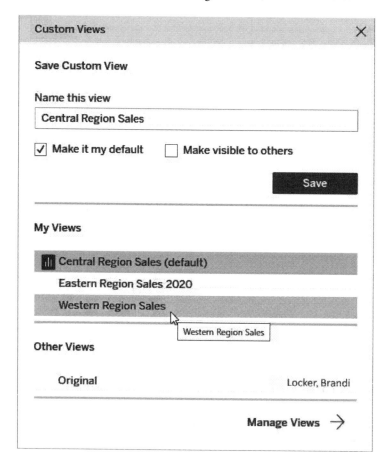

Figure 8.16 – Changing the custom view selection

You can also use this dialog box to switch between Views. The view that is selected currently will appear with a gray background. To change the view, click on your new selection to open it. In the preceding screenshot, **Central Region Sales** is currently shown, and the user is hovering over **Western Region Sales**. Clicking **Western Region Sales** will automatically open that view.

To change your *default* view, open the **Custom Views** dialog by clicking on **View** in the toolbar and selecting **Manage Views** in the lower-right corner. This button can be seen in the following screenshot:

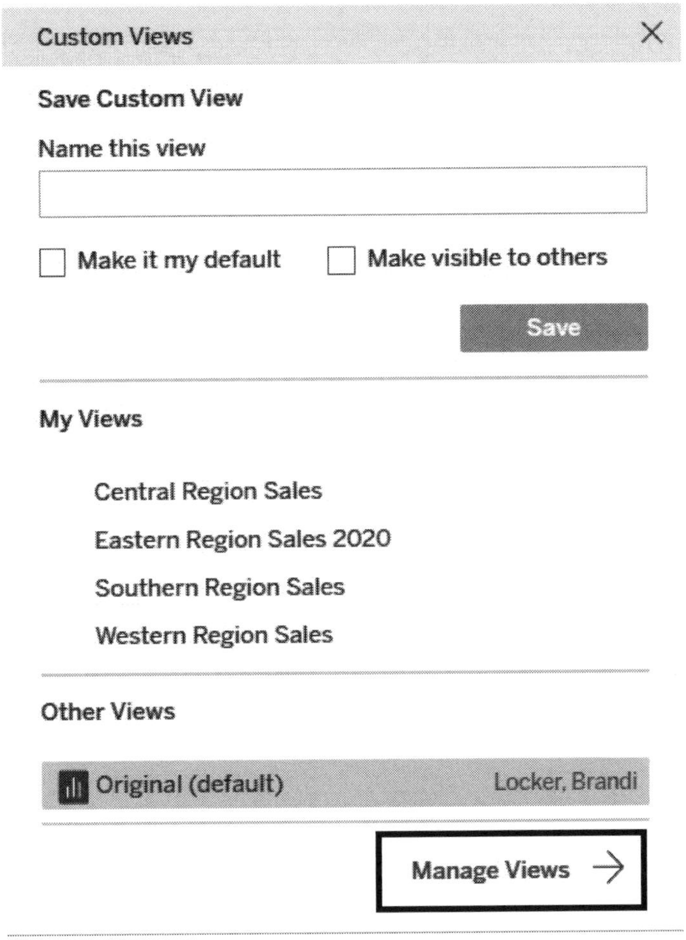

Figure 8.17 – Manage Views button

This will open a **Manage Views** section within the same dialog window. Clicking the chart icon to the left of the custom view's name allows you to choose a new default view, as shown in the following screenshot:

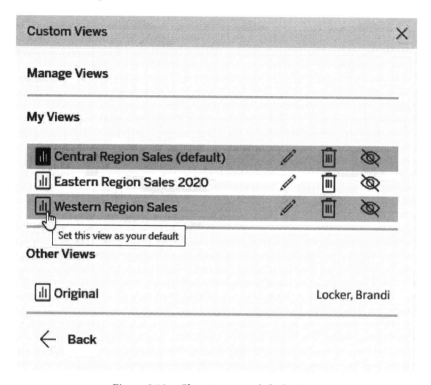

Figure 8.18 – Changing your default view

Once a new default view has been selected, the icon will change to the darker gray version, and the word **default** will appear in parentheses to the right of the view's name.

To the right of the view names, you will see three icons: a *pencil*, a *trash can*, and an *eye*. Clicking the pencil icon allows you to rename the view. Clicking the trash can allows you to delete the view. Deleting a custom view does not affect the original view, but it will delete any subscriptions that are based on the custom view. If the eye icon has a slash through it, the view is private and is only visible to you. You can click this icon to make it a public view, which will update to an eye icon without the slash. Use the **Back** button, indicated with the left-facing arrow, to return to the previous section of the **Custom Views** dialog at any time.

> **Tip**
> Even if a custom view is private, you can still share it with others by sharing the view's URL. Whoever you share it with must have permission to access the original view to be able to see your custom view. A private view just means that it will not appear in the **Other Views** list when others open the **Custom Views** dialog box.

In this section, you learned how to create a custom view, how to change your current view, and how to manage your Custom Views. This feature allows you to efficiently navigate content on the server by saving your commonly used settings. You can also use this feature to create a custom view and share it with your users to help them easily review the content they need. Next, let's examine the **Alerts** feature.

Examining alerts

An alert is an email notification that informs recipients when a data point reaches a defined threshold. You can configure alerts for yourself or other users from dashboards and worksheets. An alert cannot be made from a story. The **Alerts** button can be found on the toolbar between **View** and **Metrics**, as shown in the following screenshot:

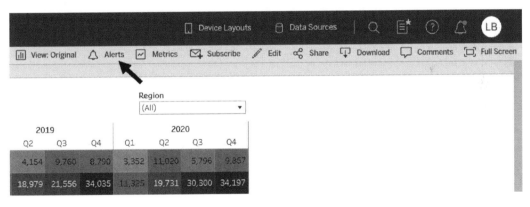

Figure 8.19 – Alerts button

First, we'll explore how to create a new alert. Then, we will examine how to manage alerts and add yourself to existing alerts.

Creating an alert

Clicking this button will open the **Alerts** side panel, to the right of your server window. This panel will indicate if there are any existing alerts for the view or will say **No alerts on this view**, as shown in the following screenshot:

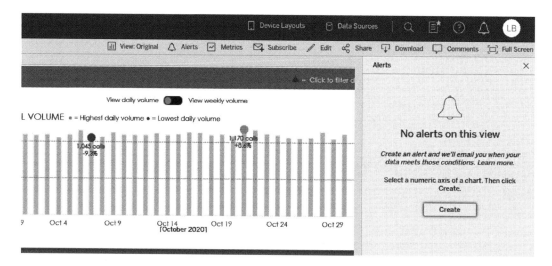

Figure 8.20 – Alerts side panel

Dashboard image credit: Chimdi Nwosu

To create an alert, follow these steps:

1. Select a continuous numeric axis from any chart. A chart must have the axis shown for you to click on it and create an alert. However, an alert cannot be created from clicking on a single data point, discrete numeric axes, numeric bins, maps, or Gantt charts.

2. After selecting the axis, click **Create** on the **Alerts** side panel. This will open the **Create Alert** pop-up window shown in the following screenshot:

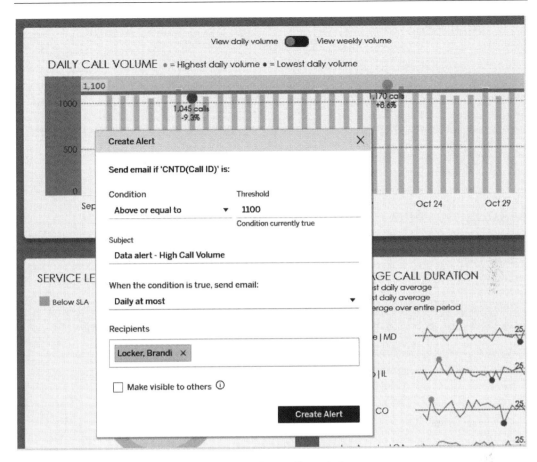

Figure 8.21 – Create Alert window
Dashboard image credit: Chimdi Nwosu

3. In this window, you can select the condition and threshold value that triggers a data-driven alert. The **Condition** drop-down allows you to select from options such as **Above or equal to**, **Above**, **Below or equal to**, **Below**, and **Equal to**. **Threshold** is a numeric value that you define based on the condition. In the view behind this window, a red line indicates where the threshold appears in the existing data.

4. The **Subject** box is where you can specify the alert email subject line. The **When the condition is true, send email** drop-down allows you to select the frequency of the alert.

5. Enter the users you would like to receive this alert email under **Recipients**. As you start typing a name in this box, suggestions will appear based on the text you are entering.

6. Checking the **Make visible to others** checkbox allows others to see your alert in the **Alerts** side panel and to add themselves to the existing alert.

7. Click **Create Alert** when you are ready to save your specifications and create the new data-driven alert.

The new alert will now appear in the **Alerts** side panel.

Managing alerts

You can review and manage existing alerts directly from the **Alerts** side panel or your content page. Next to each alert in the **Alerts** side panel is an **Actions** drop-down menu, as shown here:

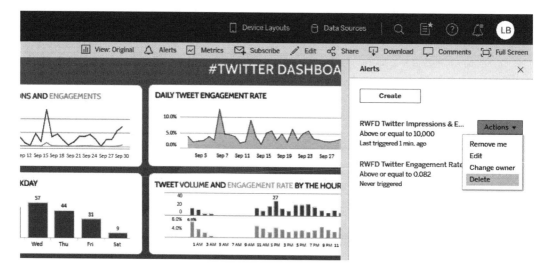

Figure 8.22 – Actions menu of the Alerts side panel

Dashboard image credit: Chimdi Nwosu

Using this menu, you can remove yourself from the alert, edit the alert, change the owner, or delete the alert if you are the creator. Clicking **Edit** will open the **Edit Alert** window shown in the following screenshot:

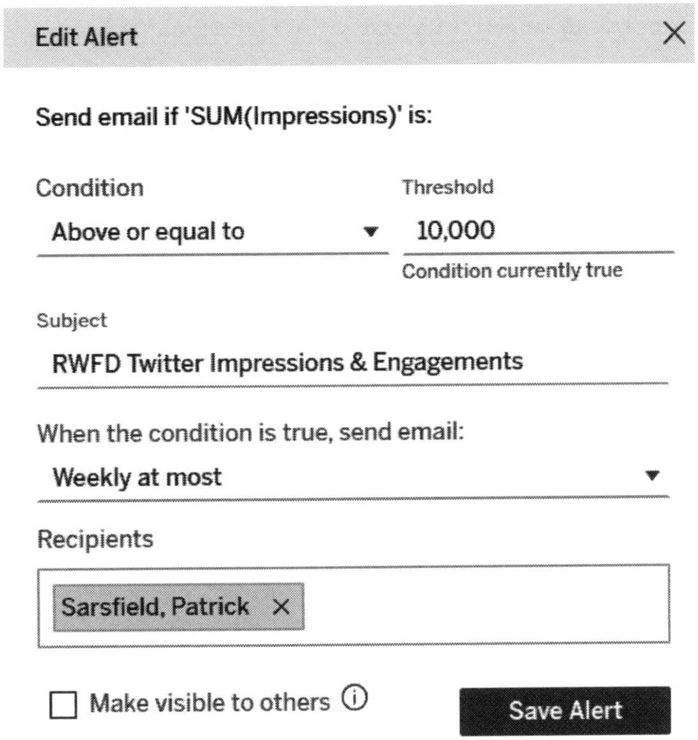

Edit Alert   ✕

Send email if 'SUM(Impressions)' is:

Condition   Threshold

Above or equal to   ▼   10,000
                                              Condition currently true

Subject

RWFD Twitter Impressions & Engagements

When the condition is true, send email:

Weekly at most   ▼

Recipients

┌───┐
│ Sarsfield, Patrick ✕   │
└───┘

☐ Make visible to others ⓘ   **Save Alert**

Figure 8.23 – Edit Alert window

This window allows you to edit the same information that was entered previously in the **Create Alert** window demonstrated in *Figure 8.21*. Here, you can adjust the **Condition**, **Threshold**, **Subject**, frequency, **Recipients**, and visibility properties of an alert. Click **Save Alert** to save your changes or the **X** button in the top-right corner of the pop-up window to close it without saving your changes.

Clicking **Change Owner** opens a window within the **Alerts** side panel that allows you to search for another user and transfer ownership of the alert to that person. **Delete** removes the alert from Tableau Server. You can only delete an alert if you are the owner. Deleting an alert does not affect the original view where it was created.

Clicking on an alert will make **Alert Overview** appear in the side panel, as shown in the following screenshot:

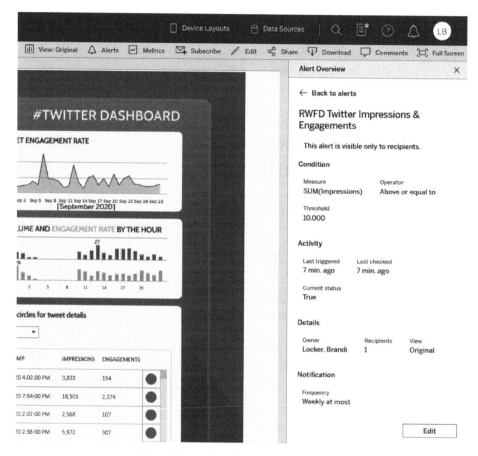

Figure 8.24 – Alert Overview inside panel

Dashboard image credit: Chimdi Nwosu

This overview will provide many of the same details shown in the **Create Alert** window, as well as additional information, such as whether the current alert status is true and when it was **last triggered or last checked**. At the bottom of the overview section is an **Edit** button. Clicking this button will open the same **Edit Alert** pop-up window that is available from the **Actions** menu.

You can also manage your alerts on your **My Contents** page, which was discussed in *Chapter 4, Tableau Server Top Toolbar*. To do this, click your profile icon in the top-right corner of the server window and select **My Content** from the drop-down menu.

Your content page has an **Alerts** tab that contains details about all your alerts, as shown in the following screenshot:

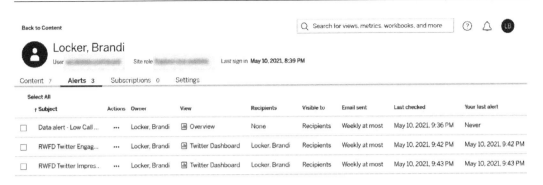

Figure 8.25 – Alerts page within the My Content page

This page allows you to see the alert's **subject, owner, view, and recipients**; who the alert is **visible to**; when an email has been sent; when it was **last checked**; and **your last alert** in a **list view**. Notice that some of these fields are hyperlinks that enable you to navigate directly to the view, or the owner or recipient's Tableau Server profile, from your **Alerts** page. You can click on the column headers to sort your alerts as desired. This page also contains an **Actions** menu, indicated by an ellipsis button (**…**), in each row of the **Actions** column. Clicking the ellipsis will open a drop-down menu that allows you to add or remove yourself from the alert, edit the alert, change the owner, or delete the alert.

Clicking the **Edit Alert** option will take you to the view with the **Edit Alert** pop-up window open, where you can make the necessary changes, as shown previously in *Figure 8.23*. Click **Save Alert** to save any changes, or you can click the **X** button in the top-right corner of the window to close the edit window without saving.

On the **Alerts** page, the **Recipients** column may indicate a name, followed by a plus sign and a number, as shown in the following screenshot:

View	Recipients	Visible to
📊 Twitter Dashboard	Locker, Brandi +1	Recipients
📊 Overview	Locker, Brandi	Recipients

Figure 8.26 – Recipients column on the Alerts page

As you may have guessed, this indicates that there are multiple recipients on that particular alert. You can also click on that plus sign and number indicator to browse or search through who the additional recipients are in a pop-up window.

Adding yourself to an alert

You can add yourself as a recipient to an existing alert directly from the view by clicking the **Alerts** button in the toolbar. This will open the **Alerts** side panel on the right-hand side of the server window. In this panel, you can see alerts that you've created, whether or not you are a recipient, and alerts that have been created by other users, if they chose to make the alert(s) visible to others. If you are not a recipient of an alert, you will see a button that says **Add Me....** Clicking this button will add you to the recipient list for that alert.

If you are the owner of an alert but are not a recipient, you can add yourself to the recipient list from your **Alerts** page within **My Content**. To do this, click the ellipsis (**…**) next to the corresponding alert within the **Actions** column, as shown in the following screenshot:

Figure 8.27 – Using the Actions menu to add yourself to an existing alert

From this menu, select **Add me** to be added as a recipient. Note that **Add me** appears grayed out if you are already a recipient.

If you are already a recipient of that alert, you will have the option to remove yourself from the alert by clicking **Remove Me....** When you click **Remove Me...** from the **Actions** menu on your **Alerts** page, a pop-up window will appear so that you can confirm your removal by clicking **Remove Me**. Alternatively, you can click **Cancel** to avoid making changes.

In this section, you learned how to create and manage data-driven alerts. This feature can be used to automatically notify you and your users of when your data reaches a defined threshold. Next, we'll look at how to utilize metrics to enable you to monitor and evaluate important data measurements.

Examining metrics

Tableau **metrics** are created from an existing view and provide quick, at-a-glance data values. They are helpful for monitoring **Key Performance Indicators** (**KPIs**) for an organization without requiring developers or analysts to build a separate KPI view. Metrics allow users who are unfamiliar with Tableau Desktop, the **Web Edit** feature, or those who just don't want to go through the process of building an entire dashboard to almost instantaneously create an easy-to-understand, clean view connected to the original data source that allows them and others to monitor the performance of an important metric. The feature allows you to create metrics for all the important numbers that are frequently monitored from all the different reports, and then have them all available in a single location. Metrics are also optimized for both mobile and desktop use. They update automatically and display the most recent value. An example of some metrics is shown in the following screenshot:

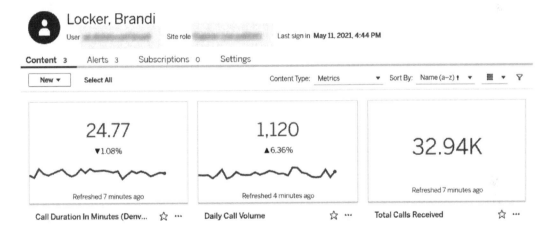

Figure 8.28 – Metrics

A metric is created from an aggregate measure and may also include a date dimension. If a metric includes a date dimension in its definition, it will display a timeline. The data granularity will match whatever was in the original view. If there is no date dimension, a single number will be shown without a timeline. The preceding screenshot illustrates metrics with a timeline and a metric without a timeline.

> **Note**
>
> A **measure** is a quantitative value, meaning it can be measured and aggregated, such as the speed of a car. A **dimension** is a qualitative value that provides detail to your data, such as customer names, sales categories, or geographical data.

Remember, the quick insights metrics provide can be beneficial, regardless of whether a date dimension is available or not.

> **Note**
>
> It is important to remember that filters that have been applied to the view before the metric was created will also apply to the metric itself.

We will explore how to view, interact with, and create metrics in this section.

Viewing metrics

You can view metrics that are connected to a view while you have it open by clicking on the **Metrics** button in the toolbar, as shown in the following screenshot:

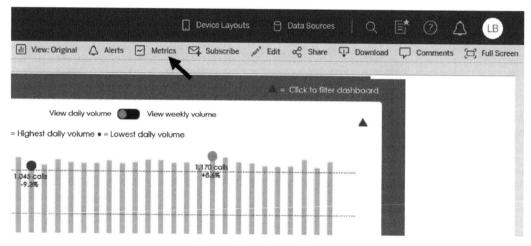

Figure 8.29 – Metrics button

Dashboard image credit: Chimdi Nwosu

Clicking this button will open a side panel to the right of the server window. If there are no metrics currently available for the view, this will be indicated with a prompt to *select a mark to create a metric*. If there are existing metrics available, you will see a preview of them in the side panel, much like those shown in the following screenshot:

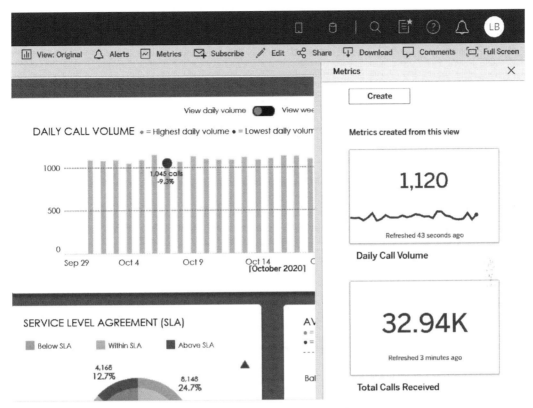

Figure 8.30 – Metrics side panel

Dashboard image credit: Chimdi Nwosu

If there are multiple metrics available in this panel, they will be ordered by creation date, from newest to oldest.

> **Note**
>
> The **Create** button on the **Metrics** side panel will only appear for individuals with a Creator or Explorer (can publish) site role. However, all site roles can see **metrics** connected to a view.

If you click on one of these metrics, a new browser tab or window will open with a detailed metric page. This page was discussed in depth in *Chapter 6, Navigating Content Pages in Tableau Server.*

You can also see metrics that are connected to an entire workbook by clicking on the **Connected Metrics** tab of a workbook's content page, as shown in the following screenshot:

Figure 8.31 – Connected Metrics
Dashboard image credit: Chimdi Nwosu

Metrics are unique in that they do not require you to open them to see the values. Whether you are in **Grid View** or **List View**, you can see a preview of the metric's current value. You can use the **Sort By** menu to customize how the metrics on the page are displayed. Clicking on a metric will also open the same detailed metric page we discussed previously. An example of this page is shown in the following screenshot:

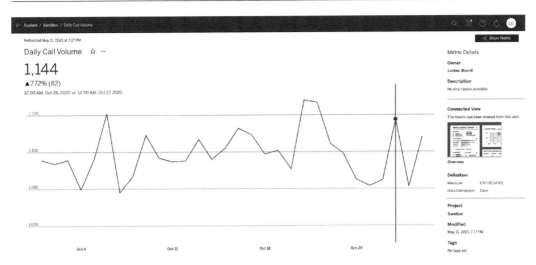

Figure 8.32 – Metric page

Dashboard image credit: Chimdi Nwosu

This page allows you to explore details about the metric and see the timeline of the metric's values, if applicable. As you hover over the data points, the numbers and labels at the top of the view will update with the appropriate values.

You can see all of the metrics that are available to you on your server's site by clicking on **Explore** from the navigation pane and filtering the **Content Type** menu at the top of the page to **Metrics**. Similarly, you can see metrics within specific projects by utilizing the same **Content Type** menu after navigating to the desired location.

To see all of the metrics that you own, navigate to your content by clicking on your profile icon in the top-right corner of the server window and selecting **My Content**. The **Content** tab will open by default, and you can use the **Content Type** menu to filter the page to show **Metrics**.

Tip

If there are metrics that you need to monitor regularly, you can mark them as a favorite or save them in a unique project location. Metrics do not have to be located in the same project as the original view.

You can manage metrics that you own by using the **Actions** menu, which you learned about in the previous chapter. Some commonly available actions include **Share**, **Rename**, **Move**, **Edit Description**, and **Delete**. Metrics are independent of the view that they are created from. You can manage a metric similar to how you manage a workbook.

Creating metrics

If you navigate to a workbook that has no metrics established and click on the **Metrics** button in the toolbar, you will see the empty **Metrics** side panel open on the right-hand side of the server window, as shown in the following screenshot:

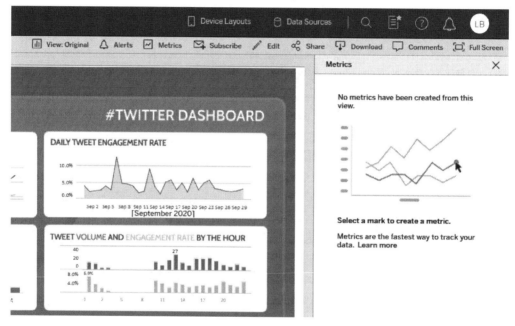

Figure 8.33 – Metrics pane with no metrics

Dashboard image credit: Chimdi Nwosu

To create a metric, follow these steps:

1. Select a mark, or a data point, in the view. As stated previously, any filters that you have applied to the view up to this moment will automatically be applied to the metric that you create. Your new metric will be defined by the measure of the selected mark and the date dimension, if applicable.

    With the **Metrics** side panel open, you will see a preview of the metric after you click on a mark in the view, as demonstrated in the following screenshot. If there are metrics that have already been created in the side panel, you can add a new one by clicking on a mark or data point and selecting **Create** from the **Metrics** side panel:

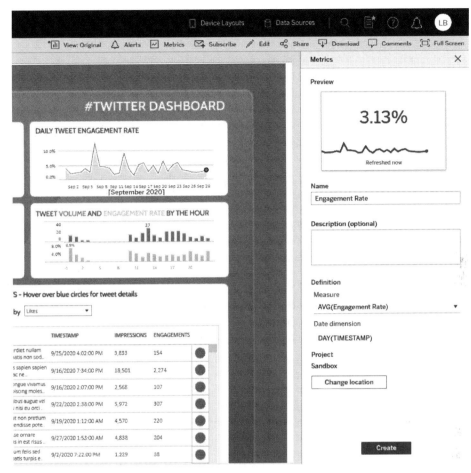

Figure 8.34 – Creating a metric preview

Dashboard image credit: Chimdi Nwosu

2. Using the preview in the **Metrics** side panel, you can edit its name and add a helpful description, if desired.

> **Tip**
> The description box is a great place to note any filters that you applied to the view before creating the metric.

3. The **Definition** section of this panel indicates which specific **measure and date dimension** apply to the mark that you selected. You may have the option to select a different measure from a drop-down menu if the selected mark is associated with multiple measures.

> **Note**
>
> The metric preview always shows the most recent value, regardless of which mark you clicked on in the view. If the view has a date dimension and you click on a historical value, the metric preview will show the current value.

4. The **Project** will default to the same project that the view is located in, but you can change this by clicking on the **Change location** button. Clicking this button will open a pop-up window that allows you to browse through the projects available to you on your server site. Click the project that you would like to save the metric to, and then click **Choose Project** or click **Cancel** to close the **Choose Project** window without saving changes.

5. Once you have made the necessary changes, click **Create** to save the metric. After you click **Create**, you will see a green **Success** banner with a link that reads **Go to Metric** at the top of the server window.

Metrics automatically update by checking the original connected view for new data, without having to schedule a separate refresh for it to do so. The refresh frequency of a metric will be based on the extract refresh schedule of the original view. If the original view has a live connection, the metric will refresh every 60 minutes. The last refresh time will be indicated on the metric itself. If no changes have been made to the data, the metric value will remain the same.

Metrics in the same project must have unique names. You can overwrite an existing metric by creating a new metric and giving it the same name as the original. When you click **Create** in the **Metrics** side panel, a dialog box will appear that notifies you if you are about to overwrite an existing metric. In this box, you can click **Cancel** to return and edit the metric, or you can click **Overwrite** to confirm your changes. Overwriting a metric is useful because it allows you to make a change without affecting the metric permissions or removing it from other users' favorites lists.

Troubleshooting metrics

There are some cases where you cannot create a metric. If this occurs, you will receive an error message with information about why metrics are not supported for the selected mark.

> **Note**
>
> This section is summarized via a useful resource on the Tableau Help pages. For further assistance with troubleshooting metrics, please refer to `https://help.tableau.com/current/server/en-us/metrics_create.htm`.

Some of these causes include the following:

- Your access may be limited due to settings such as row-level security or user filters. You must have access to the full data in the chart to create a metric.

- The connected workbook's data source password is no longer valid or is not embedded.

- The data in the chart may not be at the necessary level of granularity. You will be unable to create a metric if the data in the chart is not aggregated or if there are multiple values per cell of data, which can occur from data blending.

The chart uses a date dimension that is not supported by metrics. This can occur if the date dimension does not use the standard Gregorian calendar, a custom date dimension is aggregated at the level of *month/day/year* or *month/year*, or if the chart contains both date values and date parts.

Sometimes, you may receive an email indicating that your metric refresh has failed. This occurs when a metric is unable to access the underlying data or the connected view. Some causes of a refresh failure may be that permissions changed for the connected view, the view was deleted or modified, the password is invalid or no longer embedded, or there was a temporary connectivity issue.

To quickly check whether the connected view still exists, you can either navigate to the view itself using one of the methods discussed previously, or you can open the metric to view the **Metric Details** area. If you no longer see the view, you can contact your Tableau Server administrator to confirm whether the view was deleted or whether the permissions were changed.

If you are still able to see the connected view, you will need to open it to identify which of the other possible scenarios may be causing the metric refresh failure.

If you are prompted for a password when attempting to open the view, then either the workbook owner or your administrator needs to update the data source credentials or embed the password:

- If you cannot view the full data for the chart, the workbook owner or your administrator should check your permissions for the view.

- If it appears that the chart you created the metric from has changed, the necessary measure or date dimension may no longer be present. If this occurs, you should contact the workbook owner to discuss restoring the original view. The workbook owner or an administrator will be able to review the workbook's revision history and restore previous versions.

You may also receive an email notifying you that the metric refresh has been suspended. This occurs after multiple refresh failures. When this happens, a metric will continue to display historical data, but Tableau will no longer attempt to refresh the metric by checking for new data.

After identifying the cause of the refresh failure using the methods described previously, you can resume the refresh by navigating to the affected metric and clicking **Resume refresh** from the warning message. Once you do this, Tableau will attempt to refresh the metric. You will be notified if the attempt was successful, and the refresh will resume its normal schedule. If the attempt fails, your metric refresh will remain suspended. If this occurs, you can try to overwrite the metric or delete it.

Tip

If you are unsuccessful at troubleshooting a metric refresh failure, it is a good idea to contact the workbook owner to verify whether there were any changes to the data, the view, or permissions. The workbook owner is usually the most familiar with the content. If the owner is unable to assist, you may need to contact your administrator.

Metrics are a convenient way to track important data points and to empower the data consumer with a simple solution that does not require the developer team to build additional Views. You now understand where to find metrics, how to create them, and how to troubleshoot common problems.

In the next section, you will learn how to utilize subscriptions to further customize the Tableau Server experience for yourself and your users.

Examining subscriptions

A subscription to a view in Tableau Server means that you will automatically receive regularly scheduled emails containing an image or **Portable Document Format** (**PDF**) of a view or workbook. So long as your Tableau Server administrators enabled the subscriptions function for your site, you should see the **Subscriptions** button on the toolbar in the top-right corner of your page. This button can be identified by the letter icon with a plus sign and the word **Subscribe** next to it, as shown in the following screenshot:

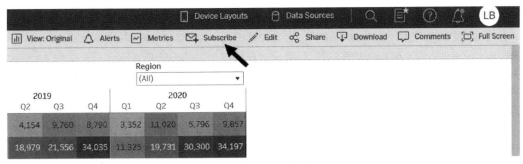

Figure 8.35 – Subscribe button

This feature is extremely useful for keeping yourself or others informed of the latest view or workbook without the need to sign into Tableau Server.

First, we'll explore how to create a subscription. Then, we will review how to update or unsubscribe from a subscription.

Creating a subscription

To create a subscription, follow these steps:

1. Click the **Subscribe** button shown in the previous screenshot to open the **Subscribe** window shown here:

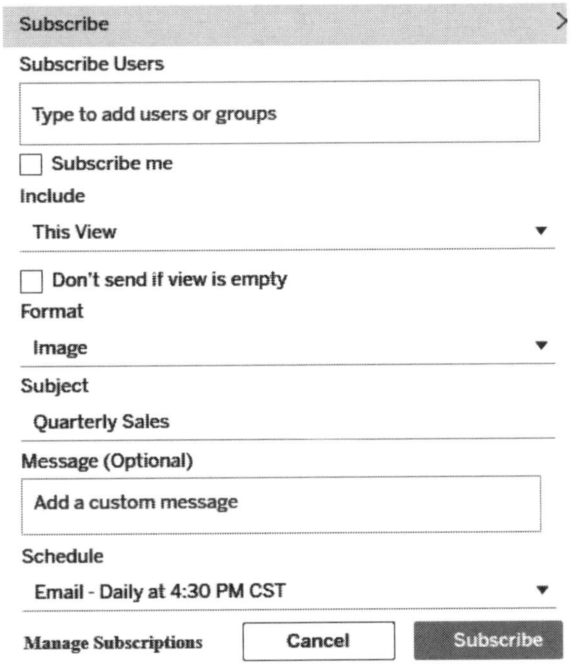

Figure 8.36 – Subscribe window

2.   The first option that appears at the top of the **Subscribe** window is the **Subscribe Users** box. Type in the name of a person or group to begin a subscription. Names will auto-populate as you enter text. Clicking the **Subscribe Me** checkbox will automatically add you to the list of subscribed users.

> **Note**
>
> You can only add other users to a subscription if you are the content owner or have the appropriate site role.

3.   The next option is the **Include** drop-down menu. This provides you with the ability to select whether your subscription email includes **this view or your entire workbook**. The menu defaults to the **This View** option, which includes only the current view in your subscription email.

4.   Next, you need to choose the **Format** property so that you can choose how you want to receive your email snapshot. You will be provided with a menu with three choices to choose from: **Image, PDF,** or **Image and PDF**. If you select **Image**, then you will receive the image of your selected view or workbook in **Portable Graphics Format** (PNG) format. Choosing the **Image** option provides a subscriber with the ability to navigate directly to the view or workbook in Tableau Server by clicking the emailed image they have received. The **PDF** option provides a link to the view or workbook; however, it is contained within the body of the message. If you choose the **PDF** option, you will be asked to make two additional selections: **Paper Size** and **Orientation**. Deciding which of the 15 **Paper Size** options to select is largely dependent on the size of the paper you want to print this image to.

> **Tip**
>
> If you want to receive a **PDF** of your view, but aren't sure which **paper size** to choose, try selecting **Unspecified** from the **Paper Size** drop-down menu. This option expands to fit the entire view on a page.

There are two **Orientation** menu options available: **Portrait** and **Landscape**. Put simply, the **Portrait** option vertically orients your view on a page, while the **Landscape** option horizontally orients your view on a page.

5. Your next tasks are to add a **subject**, which refers to the email subscription subject line, and an optional customized email **message**. When subscribing others to a view or workbook, remember to be clear and direct. Write an informative subject line, something such as "First Class Shipping Scorecard." While there is no character limit in the optional message box, whatever you write should be both brief and pertinent. These recommendations are good general practices for most business email communications, and they are good considerations for neurodiverse friends and co-workers.

> **Tip**
> You can combine your knowledge from this chapter by creating subscriptions for Custom Views. We discussed how to create a **Custom View** earlier in this chapter.

6. Choose the **Schedule** subscription by using the drop-down menu to select when you or others should receive the subscription email. The subscription schedule options in your drop-down are determined by your Tableau Server administrators.

7. To create your subscription, click the green **Subscribe** button in the bottom-right corner of your window.

After following these steps, you should see a green **Success** banner at the top of your window, indicating that the subscription was successfully created.

Changing or unsubscribing from a subscription

There are a couple of ways to edit or unsubscribe from an existing subscription. First, you can click the **Manage my subscriptions** link at the bottom of a subscription email, as shown in the following screenshot. Selecting this link will transport you to **My Content** and open your **Subscriptions** tab:

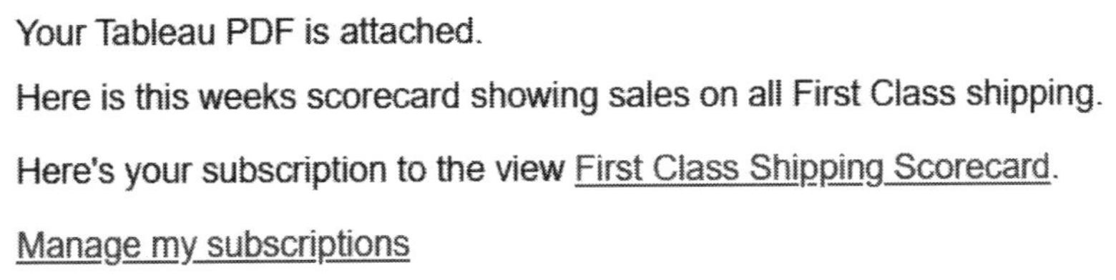

Your Tableau PDF is attached.

Here is this weeks scorecard showing sales on all First Class shipping.

Here's your subscription to the view First Class Shipping Scorecard.

Manage my subscriptions

Figure 8.37 – Subscription email showing Manage my subscriptions

Alternatively, you could navigate to this same location manually. This can be accomplished by clicking on your user icon, which is located in the top-right corner of your Tableau Server page, selecting **My Content** from the drop-down menu, and clicking the **Subscriptions** tab. The following screenshot shows a subscription under the **Subscriptions** tab:

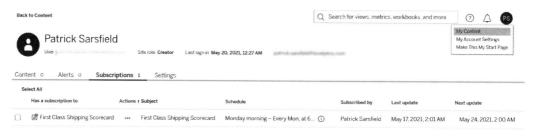

Figure 8.38 – Getting to Subscriptions

Next, use the checkbox to select the subscription option you'd like to change, then click the **Actions** drop-down menu, and then click **Unsubscribe...**, or select the subscription option you'd like to change. Alternatively, you can click the **Actions** ellipsis (**...**) for the view you want to change or unsubscribe from.

Clicking either the **Actions** drop-down menu or the **Actions** ellipsis (**...**) once you have selected the subscription you want to change will provide you with a list of options. You can change your subscription's frequency, subject, empty view mode, format, or unsubscribe from the subscription. An example of the **Actions** drop-down menu is shown in the following screenshot:

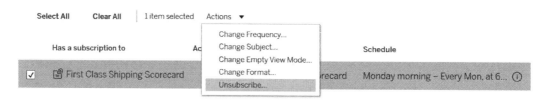

Figure 8.39 – Actions drop-down menu

This menu allows you to select multiple subscriptions at once to make changes.

An example of the **Actions** ellipsis (...) menu is shown in the following screenshot:

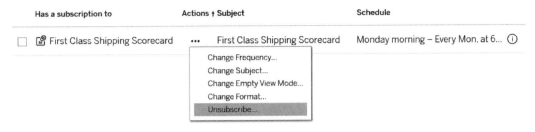

Figure 8.40 – Actions ellipsis (...)

Using the ellipsis (...) menu is a quick way to make changes to a single subscription without having to select it, which you do by clicking the checkbox and then navigating to the other drop-down menu.

> **Note**
>
> Deleting a custom view will also eliminate any subscriptions that were created based on that custom view.

In this section, you learned how to create, change, and unsubscribe from a subscription. Proper utilization of this feature can help keep even the busiest business partners well informed using automated reoccurring emails containing their desired content. Next, we'll look at how to utilize Tableau Server's web editing feature, which will enable you to make changes to Views and create workbooks right from your browser.

Examining the Web Edit button

Web Edit and Web Authoring are terms used to describe a user's ability to perform edits or create workbooks in Tableau Server without leaving their web browser. We will refer to any web-based editing or publishing as web editing for the remainder of this section. This ability to edit or build upon existing workbooks in Tableau is available to individuals with the proper server permissions. If available, the web editing feature can be found in a view. This option is located on the toolbar, in the top-right corner of your page, and can be identified by the pencil icon with the word **Edit** next to it, as shown in the following screenshot:

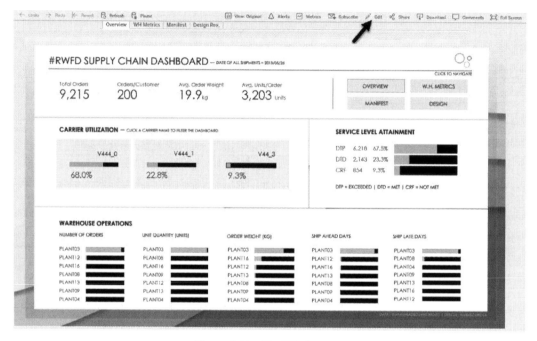

Figure 8.41 – The Edit button

Dashboard image credit: Chimdi Nwosu

> **Note**
>
> We previously discussed different ways to use the **Web Authoring** feature to create a new workbook directly through Tableau Server in *Chapter 3, Tableau Server Navigation Pane*, and *Chapter 5, Filtering and Sorting Content*.

Server permissions for web editing

In Tableau, a **site** refers to an assortment of content, users, and groups that are separate from any other content, users, and groups within the same Tableau Server. For each site, a user is assigned a site role. A **site role** controls the extent of a user's abilities on a site. Your site role can vary depending on the site because this role is assigned to each site and is constrained by your license.

Your permissions to access content on a site are determined by your site role. To have web editing capabilities, you'll need to have the appropriate one. The following is a list of user site roles and their web editing capabilities:

- **Creators**, **site administrator creators, and server administrators** can create and publish new data sources.

- **Explorers** or **site administrator explorers** can publish, but they are limited to the data that has already been published to the site.

- **Explorers** can have access to web edits but cannot save or publish their edits.

- **Viewers** cannot make web edits.

Access to the web editing feature also requires you to have the required permission settings. **Permissions** determine your capabilities to interact with content. Your capabilities are your ability to do things such as view content, delete content, make web edits, and more. Your permissions for content on a site are restricted to only what you've been permitted access to based on your site role. We discussed assigning permissions in depth in *Chapter 7, What is in the More Actions (…) Menu*. A site administrator determines **Web Edit** abilities and other permissions for users and groups at the site level, as shown in the following screenshot:

Figure 8.42 – Permissions grid showing Web Edit

If you want to learn more about site roles, licenses, and permissions, they were discussed in *Chapter 1, What is Tableau Server?*.

> **Tip**
> If you're feeling a little overwhelmed with trying to understand whether your site role, license, and permissions grant you web editing abilities, just remember that all you need to know is that if the **Edit** button is appearing in the toolbar of your view, then you have access to this feature.

Web Edit basic layout

After clicking the **Edit** button on a content page, you will be taken to Tableau's online web editing environment. This feature is similar to Tableau Desktop and should look very familiar if you have used it previously:

Figure 8.43 – Web Edit workspace layout

You can use the preceding screenshot as a visual reference for the following brief overview of a basic **Web Edit** workspace's layout:

1. **Workbook name:** This area displays the name of the workbook.

2. **Menu bar:** This consists of a row of drop-down menu options such as **File**, **Data**, **Worksheet**, **Dashboard**, **Analysis**, **Map**, **Format**, and **Help**.

3. **Toolbar icons:** This toolbar is used to quickly access popular commands and features.

4. **Show Me**: Clicking this option allows you to create a view from the fields you have selected on the **Data** pane and fields already being used in your view.

5. **Sidebar**: This is available when, in a worksheet, the sidebar area contains tabs for both the **Data** and **Analytics** panes.

6. **Cards and shelves**: Placing fields on a card or shelf will add that data to your view.

7. **View**: This is the canvas where you build your data visualizations.

8. **Sheet tabs**: Each tab represents a sheet in your workbook. A sheet can be a worksheet, dashboard, or story.

> **Tip**
> If you find yourself frequently using the web editing feature because you enjoy developing content to answer questions, identify issues, and find new insights, and you do not possess a Tableau Desktop license, this is an indication that you are a good candidate for one.

After editing an existing view or building a new one on Tableau Server, you may want to save your work. The options you have available will depend on your license and established permissions. You may have the ability to save the changes you have made in the current workbook, but you may need to save your work to an entirely new workbook on Tableau Server.

Tableau Server web editing versus Tableau Desktop

The web editing feature that exists within the Tableau Server environment has many of the same functionalities as Tableau Desktop. However, if you want to have full report development capabilities, you'll need to use Tableau Desktop. In this section, we'll review the major components that are missing when web editing and compare Tableau Server's web editor to Tableau Desktop.

The following list includes some of the important elements available in Tableau Desktop that are missing in Tableau Server's 2020.3 and 2020.4 web editor:

- Formatting a distribution or reference band.
- Adding, editing, removing, or formatting a forecast.
- Editing or formatting totals.
- Adding a parameter or set action to a dashboard.
- Seeing the **Description** field on the data pane.
- The ability to copy/paste fields on the data pane.

- Formatting alignments, shading, borders, and cells.

- Formatting legends.

- Replacing or duplicating a data source in a data connection.

- The right-click menu action is not available for all the items on a page.

Andrew Pick has created an extraordinarily helpful visualization on Tableau Public that provides a detailed breakdown of the features available on Tableau Desktop versus Tableau web editor. This dashboard can be filtered by your server version and can be viewed at `https://public.tableau.com/profile/andrew.pick#!/vizhome/ TableauDesktopvTableauWebEditing/DesktopvsWebEdit`.

> **Note**
>
> Keyboard shortcuts for web editing can differ from those on Tableau Desktop. Here is a link to a list of keyboard shortcuts for Tableau Desktop, Tableau Server, and Tableau Online: `https://help.tableau.com/ current/pro/desktop/en-us/shortcut.htm`.

In this section, you learned about web editing in Tableau Server. If you have permission to use this feature on a piece of content, it can be very useful in answering many of the questions that may arise. This feature has its limitations compared to Tableau Desktop, but it can provide you with the ability to make quick edits, perform ad hoc analysis, or create entirely new workbooks without ever leaving your browser. Now, let's look at the next item on your toolbar, the **Share** button.

Examining the Share button

The **Share** button is an effortless way to share content with others. You can share Views, workbooks, data sources, and flows. In this section, we will look at sharing a view, though the general concept for sharing any type of content is the same. You can find the **Share** button on the top right-hand side of your page's toolbar. This button can be identified by an icon with three circles connected by a line and the word **Share** next to it. The following screenshot provides an example of the **Share** button's location on a page's toolbar:

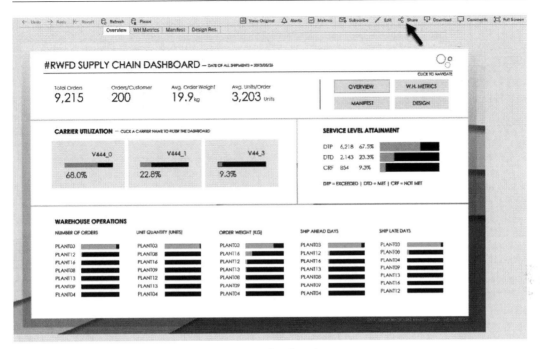

Figure 8.44 – The Share button

Dashboard image credit: Chimdi Nwosu

Clicking the **Share** button will open the **Share View** window, as shown in the following screenshot:

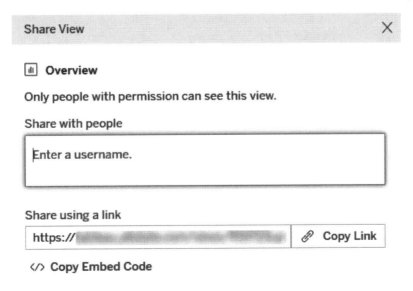

Figure 8.45 – Share View

At the top of the **Share View** page, you will see the name of the view you are looking to share. In this example, the view is titled **Overview**. Next, you will be notified that only people who have permission will be able to see this view when shared. There are three ways to share a view, as follows:

- **Share with people**
- **Share using a link**
- **Copy Embed Code**

We'll begin by looking at the first option – sharing content with people.

Share with people

You have the option to share content on Tableau Server directly with people. To do this, simply type in the names of one or more individuals under the **Share with people** box. Names will auto-populate as you enter text. Your window will update to show an image similar to the one presented here after typing in the name of a person who you would like to share a view with:

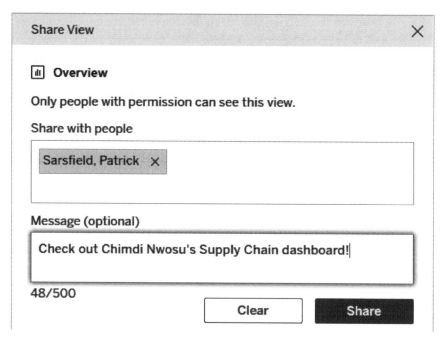

Figure 8.46 – Share with people

After entering a name in the **Share with people** box, you'll notice that the bottom part of the window has changed to offer a **Message** box. You have the option to add a message that's up to 500 characters in length. Selecting the **Share** button will add this piece of content to the **Shared with Me** page of the people you have chosen, and it will email a hyperlinked image of the view, along with any message you have entered. For more information on this page, you can reference *Chapter 3*, *Tableau Server Navigation Pane*, where we examined the entire **Shared with Me** page.

The next option we'll discuss for sharing a view is copying and sharing a link.

Share using a link

You also have the option to copy and share the link that's been generated for a piece of content. This option allows you to share the link to a piece of content with whomever you choose, without generating an email to specific people or adding the content to their **Shared with Me** page, unlike the previous option to **Share with people**. To make this selection, simply click the **Copy Link** button, shown in the following screenshot, and paste the link wherever you decide to share it:

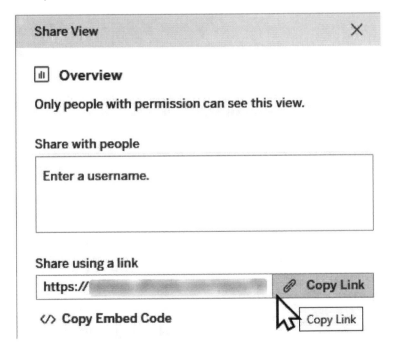

Figure 8.47 – Share using a link

Let's examine the final way to share a view – copying an embed code.

Copy Embed Code

Finally, you have the option to copy the embed code to share a view on a web page. To select this option, simply click the words **Copy Embed Code** located in the bottom-left corner of the window. The following screenshot shows this option and its location:

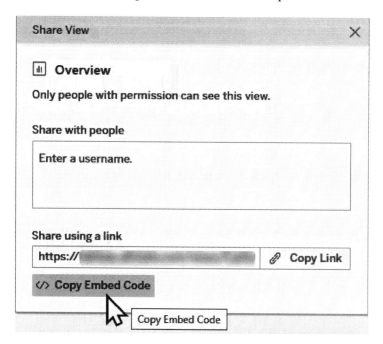

Figure 8.48 – Copy Embed Code

Clicking **Copy Embed Code** will allow you to copy and paste the embedded code for a view to a web page. This content should appear the same on the web page as it does in Tableau Server.

In this section, you learned about sharing content. You now know the three options available for sharing a piece of content and how and when to use each option. Now, let's look at the next item on your toolbar – the **Download** button.

Examining the Download button

The **Download** button is a quick way to download different forms of content from a view. You can download content in six different forms: **Image**, **Data**, **Crosstab**, **PDF**, **PowerPoint**, or **Tableau Workbook**. You can find the **Download** button on the top right-hand side of your page's toolbar. This button can be identified by an icon of a square with an arrow inside it, pointing down, and the word **Download** next to it. The following screenshot shows where you can find the **Download** button on your page's toolbar:

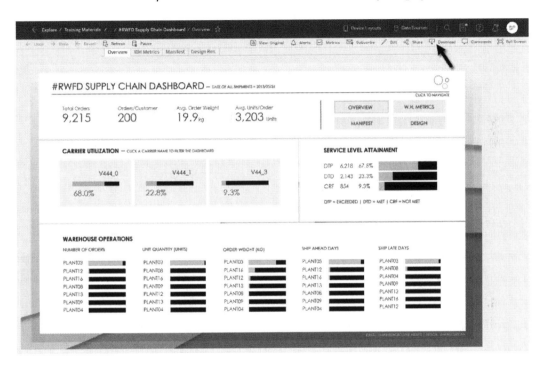

Figure 8.49 – The Download button

Dashboard image credit: Chimdi Nwosu

Clicking the **Download** button will open the **Download** window, as shown in the following screenshot:

Figure 8.50 – Download window

It's important to remember that some options, such as downloading data, may require you to click on a mark in the dashboard before appearing, and that not all download file formats may be available to you. If you see a file format that is grayed out on your **Download** window, then you have not been granted permissions by site administrators and/or content owners. The **Download** window presents you with six potential download options:

- **Image**: Clicking this option will download a **Portable Graphics Format (PNG)** image of whatever is currently being displayed on your screen. This means that any selections, filters, or parameters that have been made will be reflected in the image you download.

- **Data**: When downloading data from a dashboard, which can contain many sheets, you need to click on the sheet containing the data you want and then click the **Download** button. The **Data** option will appear grayed out until a sheet is selected. Clicking this option will open a new page in your browser. This page will contain two tabs called **Summary** and **Full Data**, as shown in the following screenshot. The **Summary** tab provides you with only the data that was selected. On the other hand, the **Full Data** tab provides you with all the underlying data in a view. Both options provide you with a link titled **Download all rows as a text file**. Clicking this link will download a **CSV** file of your data. If this page looks familiar, it's because we saw this same page appear in the *Examining View Data* section, earlier in this chapter:

View Data

| Summary | Full Data |

Showing first 12 rows.
Download all rows as a text file

| | | Summary | |
Region	Category	YEAR(Order Date)	SUM(Sales)
East	Technology	2014	$45,479
East	Technology	2017	$87,138
East	Office Supplies	2014	$35,969
East	Office Supplies	2017	$65,091
East	Furniture	2014	$47,233
East	Furniture	2017	$60,854
East	Technology	2017	$87,138
East	Office Supplies	2017	$65,091
East	Furniture	2017	$60,854
East	Technology	2014	$45,479
East	Office Supplies	2014	$35,969
East	Furniture	2014	$47,233

Showing first 12 rows.
Download all rows as a text file

Figure 8.51 – View Data – Summary tab

> **Note**
>
> If you suspect that the **View Data** columns' order has changed, you may be correct. Beginning with Tableau Desktop version 2020.2, an enhanced data model from the traditional method of a join connection was introduced. Tableau Desktop now offers *relationships*. A relationship is like a flexible automatic join that does not require tables to be merged. Just remember that this change could have resulted in the order of the columns in your **View Data** window and exported **CSV** file being different.

- **Crosstab**: Clicking this option will open a window titled **Download Crosstab**, as shown in the following screenshot. If you are on a dashboard, you will be given the option to select which sheet you would like to download. You will also be given two format options to download your data: Excel or **CSV**. When you select **Download**, any selections, filters, or parameters that you have made will be reflected in the resulting pivot table:

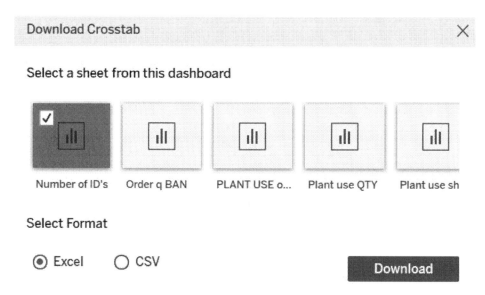

Figure 8.52 – Download Crosstab window

- **PDF**: Clicking this option will open a window titled **Download PDF**, as shown in the following screenshot. This type of file format can be viewed, printed, and electronically shared and provides a digital image that appears like a printed document. The **Download PDF** window contains four drop-down menus. The **Include** menu provides you with the ability to select this view, specific sheets from a dashboard, or specific sheets from a workbook. The **Scaling** menu provides you with the ability to control your image's appearance on the PDF. Finally, you also have menus for selecting **Paper Size** and **Orientation**. Just remember, whatever web browser you are using in the view will not be included in the PDF image:

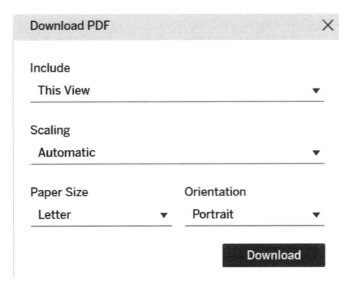

Figure 8.53 – Download PDF window

- **PowerPoint**: Clicking this option will open a window titled **Download PowerPoint**, as shown in the following screenshot. The initial window contains a drop-down menu titled **Include**, which gives you the ability to download selected sheets as this view, specific sheets from a dashboard, or specific sheets from a workbook as images on slides in PowerPoint. Remember, whatever selections, filters, or parameters you have made and are currently being displayed on your screen will be reflected in your PowerPoint images. The downloaded PowerPoint file will contain a title slide with a hyperlink of your workbook name and the file-generated date:

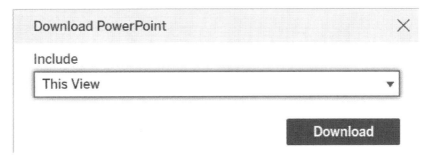

Figure 8.54 – Download PowerPoint window

- **Tableau Workbook**: Clicking this option will open a window titled **Download Tableau Workbook**, as shown in the following screenshot. Under the **Version** menu, your default option is the workbook's current version of Tableau. However, you can select different versions of Tableau that you may want to download the workbook as. Just remember, if you select an older version of Tableau, you may lose some of the more recent functionalities:

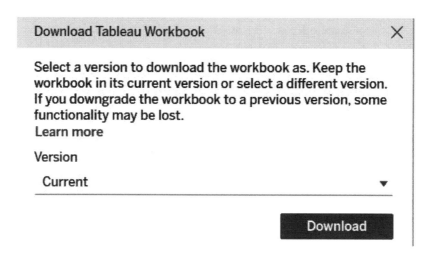

Figure 8.55 – Download Tableau Workbook window

In this section, you learned about downloading content. You now know the six options available for downloading a piece of content and how to use them. Now, let's look at the next item on your toolbar – the **Comments** button.

Examining the Comments button

The **Comments** button is a great way to share and discuss data insights with other Tableau Server users. Clicking the **Comments** button on the top right-hand side of your page's toolbar will open a **Comments** pane on the right-hand side of your page. This button can be identified by an icon that appears as a speech bubble, pointing down, and the word **Comments** next to it. The following screenshot shows where to locate the **Comments** button on your page's toolbar, as well as the **Comments** pane that opens after this button is clicked:

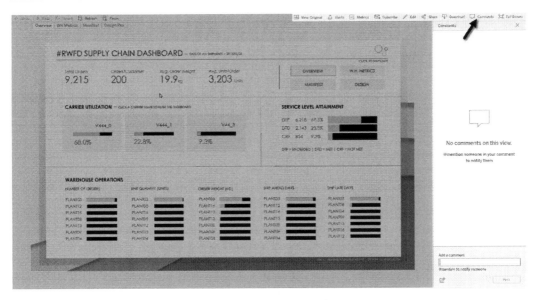

Figure 8.56 – The Comments button and Comments pane

Dashboard image credit: Chimdi Nwosu

At the bottom of the **Comments** pane is a box titled **Add a comment**. This is where you can add your comments about the view and include an **@mention** if you want a specific user to be notified about a comment. The following screenshot shows a **Comments** pane with comments:

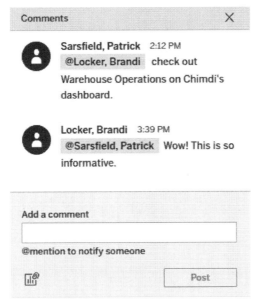

Figure 8.57 – The Comments pane with comments

When you **@mention** a user in a comment, an email notification is automatically sent to that user. This email advises the person that they were mentioned in a comment and provides the comment itself, along with a link to the view on Tableau Server.

> **Tip**
>
> If you are having difficulty finding somebody by their name, try searching for them using their username. For example, instead of searching for @Angus MacGyver, try his username; that is, @amac.

If you want to add an image that identifies what you are commenting on, click the snapshot icon located in the bottom-left corner of the **Comments** pane. If you hover over the icon, it advises you that clicking this icon will **Add a snapshot of the view to your comment**. The following screenshot shows this feature's location:

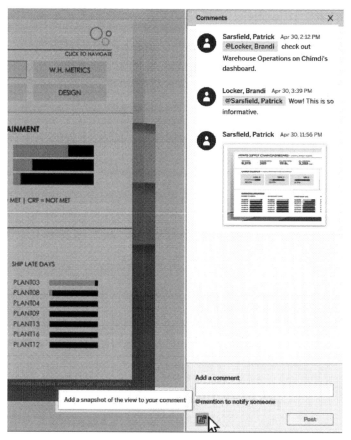

Figure 8.58 – The Comments pane – Add a snapshot

Dashboard image credit: Chimdi Nwosu

Snapshot images are interactive. If you have added a snapshot that contains filters, parameters, or selections, clicking that image will apply the same filters, parameters, or selections at the time the snapshot was taken of your view. This allows you to visually pass on the same analysis you observed to other users, in addition to your comments. This functionality is similar to creating Custom Views, which we discussed earlier in this chapter.

Finally, if or when you want to remove a comment, simply click the **X** button that appears in the right-hand corner when you hover over a comment. If you can't delete a comment, this means you do not have the appropriate site role to make this change.

In this section, you learned about adding comments to a view. You now know how to include comments, notify users of those comments, add interactive images, and remove comments.

Summary

In this chapter, you learned how to interact with and utilize many of the commonly available options on a view in Tableau Server.

We reviewed some basic ways to interact with a view. You also learned a quick way to obtain the raw data from a selected mark. We then discussed the **Undo, Redo, Revert, Refresh, and Pause** button options. The *Examining Device Layouts and Data Sources* section taught you how a view would appear on different devices and how to identify the data sources used to construct a view. Then, we learned about Custom Views and how to modify a view to your needs and then save your selections for future use. In addition, you should feel confident in setting up and receiving alerts, metrics, and subscriptions. The web editing feature is something you can use to make changes to existing workbooks or create new ones directly on Tableau Server. Lastly, you should possess a firm understanding of how and when to utilize the **Share, Download, and Comments** buttons.

This concludes *Section 3, Managing Content on Tableau Server*. In the next chapter, we will look at server best practices, which will teach you our recommendations for optimizing content and improving efficiency in Tableau Server.

Section 4: Final Thoughts

In this section, you will learn recommended best practices for optimizing your content to improve the efficiency and performance of workbooks and data sources on Tableau Server. You will also receive suggestions and resources for further learning and development.

This section comprises the following chapters:

- *Chapter 9, Tableau Server Best Practices*
- *Chapter 10, Conclusion*

9
Tableau Server Best Practices

In this chapter, you will learn about best practices when publishing content to Tableau Server and refreshing data, and ways you can optimize the performance of your data and workbooks. Understanding these principles will help reduce the space used on the server, improve the refresh speed of your data, and increase the efficiency and performance of your published content. Following these guidelines will help you in discussions with your company's Tableau Server administrators and improve the user experience of those interacting with your published content.

> **Note**
>
> This chapter assumes some familiarity with developing calculations and data visualizations in Tableau Desktop. Additionally, this chapter is not meant to be an exhaustive list of all best practices but contains some of the most useful advice that the authors have learned through research and personal experience.

As you read through this chapter, it is important to remember that each Tableau Server environment and each organization's data culture is unique. What works very well for one team may not be equally effective for another. It is recommended that you use this chapter as a starting point for further independent learning. We also recommend that you try the best practices presented in this chapter when you can, but also be willing to explore the reasoning behind the suggestions and adjust them to fit the needs of you and your organization accordingly.

When you complete this chapter, you will have an understanding of best practices for the following:

- Examining row-level security

- Leveraging naming conventions

- Utilizing published data sources

- Refreshing your data

- Improving performance

Examining row-level security

After publishing a workbook to Tableau Server, all the users who are granted access to that workbook can view all the data within those views. But what if you want different users to have different access to the data being provided? That is where **Row-Level Security (RLS)** comes in. In Tableau, RLS allows the dashboard developer to restrict what data a certain user can see when interacting with a workbook or data source. This is accomplished by applying a filter that defines security policies that stipulates which "rows" of data a user can see when they sign in to Tableau Server. RLS helps provide better control over the data a person can see based on the restrictions placed on their username when they log in to Tableau Server.

Let's imagine RLS in practice. Pretend you work for a large U.S. insurance company. The company divides the country into four regions in which it provides insurance coverage: North, East, South, and West. The company wants to share the report you created in Tableau Desktop with all its regional sales leaders on Tableau Server, however, it wants to restrict access to the data that a regional leader can see to only the sales that occurred within their specific region. This would be a good use case for RLS so that when a regional leader views a workbook or data source in Tableau Server, they only see the rows of data they are permitted to.

Adding RLS helps protect your company's data privacy when you have information you don't want exposed to certain users. There are two main approaches to RLS:

- Manually creating a user filter

- Creating a calculation using a security field

Let's take a high-level look at each option.

Manually creating a user filter

Creating a user filter to safeguard your workbook or data source is the quickest and easiest way to implement and learn about RLS. This process allows you to manually map which user or user group can see which values of a dimension.

This process of manually creating a user filter can be enough to accomplish your RLS goals if the following applies:

- You are not looking to make it scalable because you are only applying user filters to a limited number of workbooks.

- The set of users or groups managed by the user filter are relatively small in size.

- The set of users or groups managed by the user filter does not frequently change.

- You are using a data source that is either a live connection or an extract data source that uses tables stored as multiple tables.

To manually create a user filter, you need to take the following steps:

1. Open a workbook that needs RLS applied in Tableau Desktop.

2. Select the worksheet you want to apply a user filter to.

3. Click the **Server** drop-down menu from the top toolbar. Then click **Create User Filter**. *Figure 9.1* shows an example of this process:

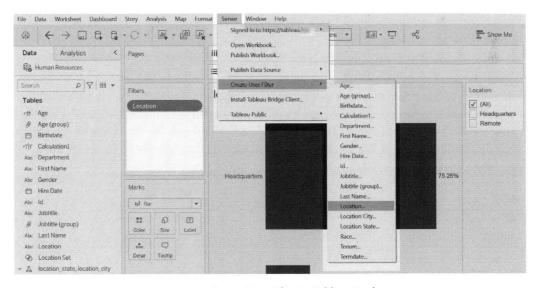

Figure 9.1 – Create User Filter in Tableau Desktop

Workbook created by Mark Bradbourne

4. Choose the field you want to apply a user filter to. Selecting the field you want to apply a user filter to will open a **User Filter** pop-up window. *Figure 9.2* presents an example of this window:

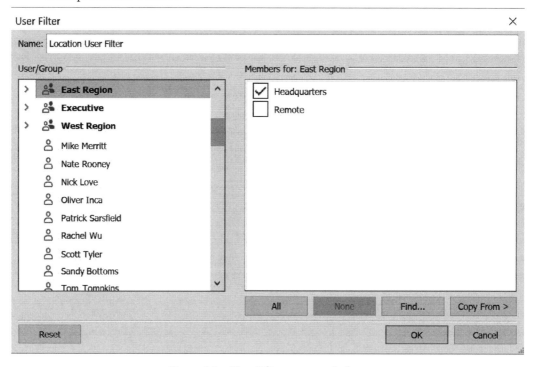

Figure 9.2 – User Filter pop-up window

5. On the left panel of your **User Filter** pop-up window, select a user or group from the list under **User/Group**.

6. On the right panel of your **User Filter** pop-up window, you see the members of the field you picked to apply your user filter to earlier. Select the members of that field that you want the selected users or groups to be able to view when they access this view on Tableau Server. Repeat this process as many times as you need for an additional user or group.

7. Select **OK** when you are finished creating your user filters or select **Cancel** to close this window without saving your selected user filters.

8. If you click **OK**, the user filter you created will appear as a set in the left sidebar data pane.

9. To finish, drag and drop your user filter onto the **Filters** shelf. After you do this, you will notice that the filter automatically turns gray, indicating that it has become a context filter. *Figure 9.3* presents an example of this filter:

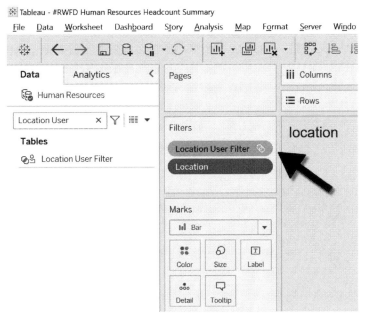

Figure 9.3 – Add User Filter to the Filters shelf

Workbook created by Mark Bradbourne

If your workbook is not connected to a published data source, you can preview how the user filter you created will work in a published view by using the **Filter as User** menu. This filter allows you to see the workbook as another user or group would see it. To see a preview of how the RLS filter will work, click the drop-down arrow to the right of your name in the bottom right-hand corner of your workbook. Select a user or group from the list of options in the **Filter as User** menu. *Figure 9.4* provides an example of where this filter is located:

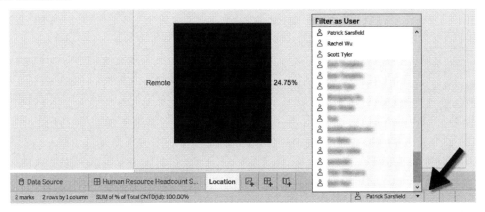

Figure 9.4 – Filter as User

Workbook created by Mark Bradbourne

This should help provide you with a good understanding of the basics behind manually creating an RLS user filter in Tableau Desktop to help protect your enterprise's data security by better controlling the information that is visible to your company's Tableau Server users. Remember, this approach to RLS is hardcoded. This is the major drawback to this approach. It means that if you want to make any entitlement changes, you will need to go back into Tableau Desktop and take time to manually make the necessary updates per workbook. Next, you'll learn how to apply RLS by creating a dynamic filter using a calculation.

Creating a calculation using a security field

To create a calculation using a security field, you first need to determine which user groups can see what information. Using our previous insurance company example, perhaps you want executive-level management to be able to see all insurance sales but want to restrict regional sales leaders to only seeing sales within their region. You will need to find an existing user group or have a new one created in Tableau Server. Contact your server administrator to determine your organization's preferred method to create a new user group. Also, remember, users can be assigned to multiple groups.

To implement RLS via a calculation that uses a security field, you need to take the following steps:

1. Open a workbook that needs RLS applied in Tableau Desktop.

2. Open a worksheet and create a calculated field. One way to do this is by clicking the **Analysis** drop-down menu from the top toolbar. Then click **Create Calculated Field…**. *Figure 9.5* shows an example of this process:

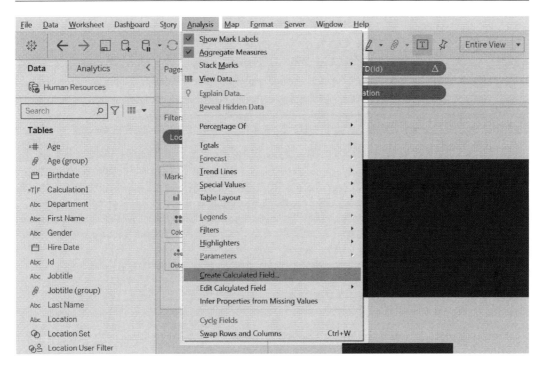

Figure 9.5 – Create Calculated Field…

Workbook created by Mark Bradbourne

3. Enter a user function in the open calculated field window. You can use either the
    ISMEMBEROF() or USERNAME() function. In *Figure 9.6*, you can see an example
    of this process:

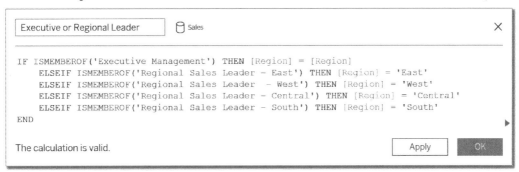

Figure 9.6 – Create a user function

> **Tip**
>
> We recommend using the `ISMEMBEROF()` function over the `USERNAME()` function. This is because the `USERNAME()` function may require you to go back into Tableau Desktop to update your calculation when a user changes roles, whereas with `ISMEMBEROF()`, when a person's role changes, you simply need to update the group on Tableau Server.

4. Drag and drop the calculation you just created on the **Filters** shelf and set the filter to **True**. For our example, this sets the filter so that only **Executive Management** can see all the data in the view, while **Regional Sales Leaders** can only see their region. *Figure 9.7* provides an example of how this will look on your Tableau Desktop worksheet:

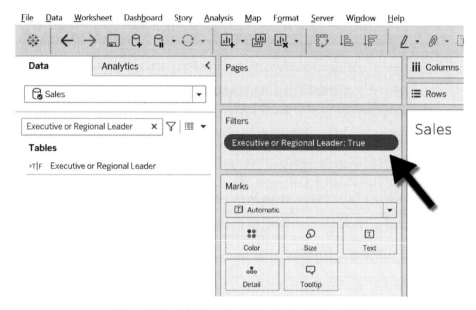

Figure 9.7 – Add the calculation to the Filters shelf

Just as with manually creating a user filter, you can test how the security field calculation you have added to the filters shelf will work in a published view by using the **Filter as User** menu. To see a preview of how your filter will work, click the drop-down arrow to the right of your name in the bottom right-hand corner of your workbook. *Figure 9.8* provides an example of where this filter is located:

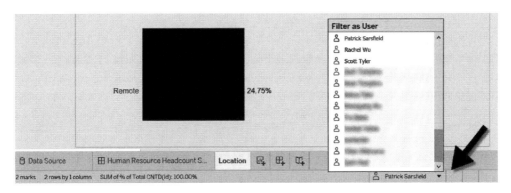

Figure 9.8 – Filter as User

Workbook created by Mark Bradbourne

Select a user or group from the list of options to test out how your security field calculation will work. Remember, if your workbook is connected to a published data source, you won't be able to use this option.

Adding a security field calculation as a data source filter

You could choose to publish your workbook after the last step. However, if you don't want to repeat this process for each workbook you create, you can apply the calculation you created as a data source filter and use the data source for other workbooks.

To add a security field calculation as a data source filter, take the following steps:

1. Click the **Data Source** tab located in the bottom-left corner on Tableau Desktop.

2. On the **Data Source** page, look in the top-right corner and click the word **Add**, under the word **Filters**. *Figure 9.9* identifies the location of the **Add** filter button on the **Data Source** page:

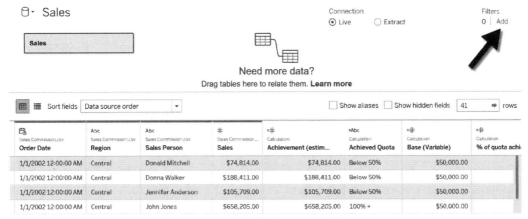

Figure 9.9 – Add a data source filter

3. In the open **Edit Data Source Filters** pop-up window, click **Add**. This will open the **Add Filter** window. Select the security field calculation you created and set the filter to **True**. *Figure 9.10* provides an example of the **Edit Data Source Filters** window:

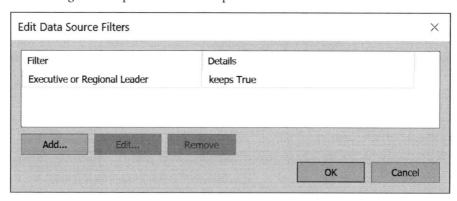

Figure 9.10 – Edit Data Source Filters

4. Click **OK**.

5. Finally, you can publish the data source or workbook to Tableau Server after the data source filter has been applied.

One advantage of applying your security field calculation to the data source filter of a published data source is that you can use the data source for multiple workbooks. An additional benefit of applying your security field calculation to the data source filter is that it helps to reduce the amount of data in the data source, which improves the performance of your dashboard.

In this section, you have learned how to create a manual user filter and a dynamic security field calculation. Also, you learned the benefits of each process. Understanding how to implement RLS will help protect your enterprise's data security by better controlling the information that is visible to your company's Tableau Server users. Next, we'll examine how to develop and implement good naming conventions.

Leveraging naming conventions

It seems like nobody thinks much about good naming conventions until after it's an issue. We've all looked for content or a file that we knew was located on Tableau Server or a shared drive but were unable to find it, at least not without a lot of work and some serious self-doubt. In fact, you were probably looking right at what you wanted and failed to recognize it because the name it was given meant absolutely nothing to you. However, if the name had been clear and easy to understand, it would have popped right out to you as your eyes hovered over it.

This is because names are most helpful when they make sense to as many users as possible. A well-thought-out naming convention helps reduce the effort required for your users to read, understand, and find content. A name should help frame your work in a way that describes it and connects it to other related content. To maximize the end user experience on Tableau Server, we recommend taking a few moments to think deeply about the names you assign to the content you publish.

The following lists contain a few simple suggestions for what makes a good or a bad naming convention. On Tableau Server, these recommendations can apply but are not limited to projects, workbooks, views, metrics, and data sources.

General rules to make good naming conventions

The following list contains some general rules for creating good names:

- *Descriptive* – Try to make sure the names you use are clear and meaningful to you and others in your company.

- *Intuitive* – A good naming convention should have the ability to be understood quickly and easily. The cognitive load (mental effort) placed on a user to understand a name when they read it should be as minimal as possible.

- *Consistent* – Utilizing the same naming conventions to describe connected or related content will help users more easily find and identify what they need. It will also help you stay more organized.

- *Short* – Less is more. Keep names as concise as possible.

Things to try to limit or avoid

The following list contains some things to avoid or limit the use of when creating a name:

- *Acronyms* – Showing only the first letter of a word instead of the entire word is often the opposite of a good naming convention. Your goal should be to clearly communicate with your audience in an unambiguous way. While the intention of an acronym is to save time by increasing the speed at which your audience interprets something, acronyms can actually take longer to understand and unintentionally alienate members of your audience. If used, please do so with purpose and sparingly.

- *Nicknames* – Don't use a name if it would have little meaning to the majority of your audience. A nickname used lovingly for a metric on your small team would likely be a poor name to select for a dashboard that will be consumed at a company level.

- *Long or Verbose Names* – Keep your names as simple as possible, but no simpler. Your goal should be to present a clear understanding of what you want to express, not to impress people with your vocabulary.

> **Tip**
>
> Naming conventions can be a divisive topic within companies, with members of different groups or areas of an organization unable to agree on the right approach. Remember that **tags** are available if you cannot use a good naming convention due to office politics, mandatory legacy reporting names, or some other reason outside of your control. Tags are a way to help users more easily find your content when searching a site, while placating higher-ups by still providing the exact title(s) they request. A well-named tag can be used to classify content by a project, topic, or any other useful attributes that can help you and others find content in a search. We examine tags in depth in *Chapter 7, What is in the More Actions (...) Menu.*

In this section, you have learned about the importance of names, some general rules for good names, and what to limit or avoid. This should help individuals who had not previously thought much about this topic and serve as a refreshing confirmation for those who have. Next, we'll provide some recommendations for how to utilize published data sources efficiently.

Utilizing published data sources

In *Chapter 1, What is Tableau Server?*, you learned that a **published data source** is a data source that has been created and published to Tableau Server. Once on the server, a single published data source can be used by multiple workbooks. Published data sources are useful when your organization has important metrics that will be used in multiple reports or visualizations housed in different workbooks. If each workbook has its own data source, it not only takes up more room on Tableau Server and consumes more server resources when each extract refreshes, but it can also cause data variances if the workbooks are not refreshed at the same time. For example, if one workbook refreshes on Monday and another refreshes on Wednesday, but both workbooks visualize the same business metric, then end users are likely to be confused and contact you with questions when they notice differences in the data presented by the two workbooks. To avoid this, you can create one published data source that each workbook connects to so that the data across each workbook is consistent and only needs to be refreshed once to automatically update all connected workbooks.

Published data sources encourage data to be shared by establishing a single source of data that is readily available on Tableau Server and is already formatted for multiple users to connect to and explore. They also allow users that have access to Web Edit to connect to the data from Tableau Server, even if they don't yet have a Tableau Desktop license. Permissions to access the data can be set at the project level or for each data source (depending on the project settings) to manage data security.

Formatting data prior to publishing

When you intend to publish a data source to Tableau Server, we recommend finalizing all of the data formatting and cleaning prior to publishing. There are some limitations to what you can adjust in your workbook when connecting to a published data source, such as data field types, aliases, calculations, and connection details, so it is best to do this ahead of time.

Data types

Before publishing a data source to Tableau Server, you will want to check all of the data field types in your data and ensure that they are set to the correct type that will be required for analysis in Tableau Desktop. **Data types** in Tableau include Number (decimal), Number (whole), Date & Time, Date, String, Boolean, and various Geographic types. This is recommended because once the data source is published to Tableau Server, users connecting to the data will be unable to edit the data type themselves as they normally would when connecting to data using their own live connection or data extract.

For example, data often needs to be analyzed by date. However, if all of the fields included in the published data source are formatted as strings, also known as text values, then you and other users will be unable to take advantage of the basic Tableau features, such as date aggregations, that make it easy to visualize data by year, month, day, and so on, and will also be unable to use any of the date functions available in calculations, such as DATETRUNC or DATEDIFF functions. To work around this, users would have to either duplicate the field and edit that duplicated field's data type or would have to create a calculation that transforms the text into a date format. Not only is this inconvenient for you and other users, but it also increases the likelihood of mistakes being made in calculations and uses more computational resources within Tableau, which could decrease the overall workbook performance.

Ideally, your original data source, whether it is an Excel file or a data table in Oracle, should already be formatted to the appropriate field types (integer, string, and so on) before you establish a connection in Tableau. Making sure this is done in your original database reduces the amount of work that Tableau needs to do. However, Tableau is very good at automatically determining the appropriate data field types. Certain data connectors, such as Google Sheets or Microsoft Excel, allow you to use the **Data Interpreter** tool found on the left side of the **Data Source** page within Tableau Desktop, indicated in *Figure 9.11*:

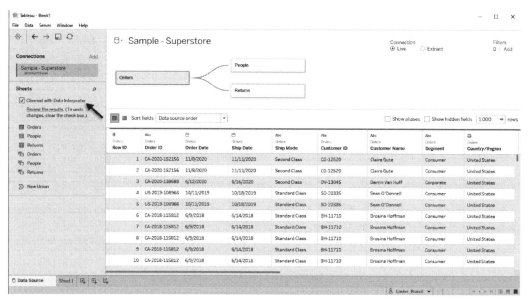

Figure 9.11 – Tableau Desktop Data Interpreter

This tool can clean up things like empty cells or extra header rows without changing the underlying data.

If you have no influence on how your original data source is formatted, or if Tableau does not assign the correct data type, you can adjust the type manually on the **Data Source** page or within the **Data** pane found in Tableau Desktop.

The **Data Source** page contains a preview of your dataset and indicates the individual field types with an icon above each field header. You can click this icon to open a drop-down menu that allows you to select another type to assign to that field, as shown in *Figure 9.12*.

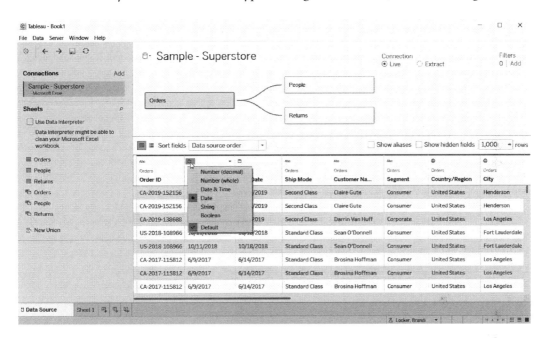

Figure 9.12 – Change the field type from the Data Source page

The **Data** pane can be found from any worksheet within Tableau Desktop or Tableau Server Web Edit. Each data field is listed in the **Data** pane on the left side of the window, and each field has the corresponding type icon to the left of its name. Clicking this icon will open the same menu that allows you to choose another data type, indicated in *Figure 9.13*.

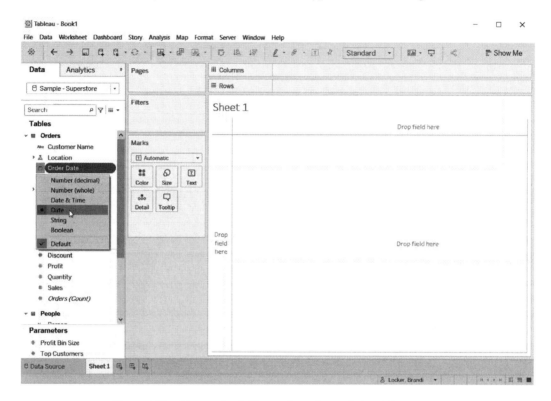

Figure 9.13 – Change the field type from the worksheet's Data pane

It can be easy to forget to check the data types in your data source, but it is usually well worth the time up-front to confirm that everything is in the correct format before starting your analysis.

Aliases

Another thing to do before publishing your data source is to establish any **aliases** that you need. Aliases are alternate names for the members of a dimension, which will dictate how their labels appear when that dimension is used in a view. For example, you may have a field called **Region** that contains the members NE, NW, SE, and SW. It would probably be clearer and more useful to end users to see the regions written out: Northeast, Northwest, Southeast, and Southwest. You can do this by creating aliases in the Region dimension. Once a data source has been published to Tableau Server, uses connecting to it will be unable to create an alias or to edit existing aliases in their workbooks without duplicating the field. You can read more about aliases at `https://help.tableau.com/current/pro/desktop/en-us/datafields_fieldproperties_aliases_exlediting.htm`.

Calculations

It is also helpful to understand whether you should create a calculation prior to publishing a data source to Tableau Server or after publishing. When a calculation is created prior to publishing the data source, users connecting to the published connection will be unable to edit the calculation. This can be a helpful way to ensure a consistent formula is used for a certain business metric throughout multiple workbooks. It can also be useful if there are changes to how the value should be calculated. If it is included in the published data source, you will only have to edit the calculation in one location rather than editing it in each connected workbook. Another benefit to this is that it can be calculated by Tableau in the data extract, which can improve workbook performance.

However, we have also witnessed this feature causing many developers frustration. If you know that departments in your company are constantly adapting their business strategies or changing processes, then creating one-size-fits-all metric calculations may not be beneficial. There are many occasions where you or other users may benefit from having the flexibility of editing a calculation instead of using an established field in the data. To help you determine whether or not to include a calculation in the published data source, it may be useful to discuss with your team or other developers to get their experience at your organization, as well as discussing how a data source could be utilized in the future with **Subject Matter Experts** (**SMEs**) and knowledgeable end users who are more involved in business operations. If there is no need for granular customization, your data source could benefit from including these calculations in the data source prior to publishing to Tableau Server.

> **Note**
>
> We do not recommend including *every* calculation in a published data source. For the most part, you will need to fine-tune your data source before the real work in data visualization can begin, and you will want to be as flexible as possible without limiting yourself during the creative and analytic process. The recommendations in this section are meant to be applied to calculations that define critical measures within your company and may benefit from the added data governance.

Connection details

One important detail about published data sources is that you can only edit the data connection information, including any joins or relationships, in the workbook containing the original data source, meaning the workbook that contains the live connection or the data extract prior to when the data source was published. You cannot edit the data connection detail in workbooks that connect to the published data source.

You also cannot use published data sources in joins or relationships. If you have a published data source that needs to be combined with a secondary source, you will have to use data blending. You can read more about data blending at `https://help. tableau.com/current/pro/desktop/en-us/multiple_connections.htm`.

While it may seem frustrating to be unable to edit these items within a published data source, this is actually an intentional feature. A published data source is generally meant to be considered a single source of truth. Preventing changes to the data is one way to ensure data integrity.

Naming and describing data sources

You learned about the importance of following quality naming practices earlier in the chapter, in the *Leveraging naming conventions* section. This becomes particularly important when dealing with published data sources, because you cannot rename data sources on Tableau Server as you would another content type, such as a workbook.

The only way to change the name of a published data source is to republish the data with the updated name as a new data source on Tableau Server and then repoint any connected workbooks to that new data source. If your original data source has more than a couple of workbooks connected to it, and you need to change the data source name, you are in for a long day. We've made this mistake and it can be unpleasant.

We recommend choosing a descriptive name that clearly identifies the data content, without naming specific details that may change. For example, if you name a data source "Monthly Sales," but later on the data needs to be changed to weekly, then the name "Monthly Sales" will no longer be applicable. To be accurate, you would then need to republish the data source as "Weekly Sales" and repoint any workbook that was connected to the original published data source to the new weekly published data source. To avoid this, you can omit any details that are subject to change from the name. You can always include details like "weekly" or "monthly" in the description of a data source.

We recommend using the **Description** feature when publishing data sources to Tableau Server. They allow you to indicate details about the data source to other users. Descriptions can be added during the publishing process, as shown in *Figure 9.14*.

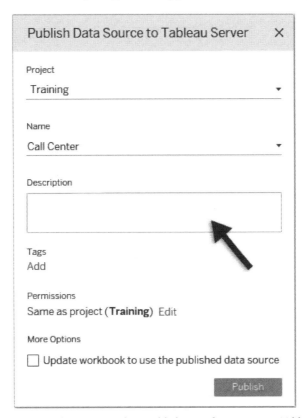

Figure 9.14 – Add a description when publishing a data source to Tableau Server

If you own the data source or have the necessary permissions, descriptions can also be added after the data source has already been published to Tableau Server by clicking on the info icon on a data source page, shown in *Figure 9.15*, to open the **Data source details** window.

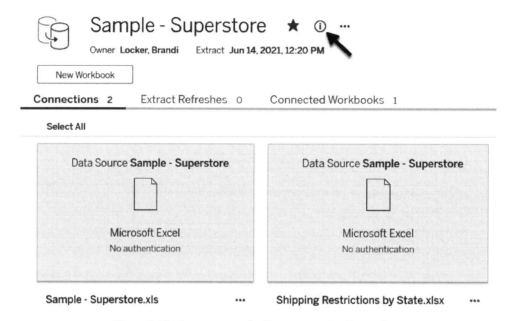

Figure 9.15 – Icon to open the Data source details window

In this window, click **Edit** in the **About** section to add a description, as illustrated in *Figure 9.16*, and click **Save**.

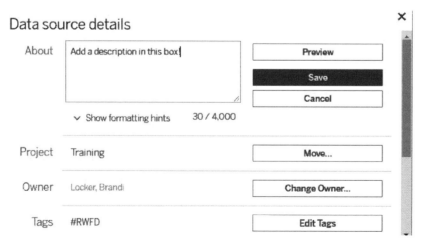

Figure 9.16 – Add a description from Tableau Server

Descriptions appear under the data source owner's name on Tableau Server. This is an ideal place to provide details that you are not able to indicate in the data source name, such as any filters applied to the data, when the data refreshes, or what database was used to create the data source. Data source filters are a particularly helpful detail to make other users aware of in a description, since they can be easily overlooked within Tableau Desktop.

Published data sources can be an excellent way to ensure data consistency and integrity and to share curated information with other users. In the next section, you will learn a few tips for choosing which data connection type is best for your circumstance and some considerations for refreshing your data.

Refreshing your data

As you learned in *Chapter 1*, *What is Tableau Server?*, an **extract** is a subset of your data that has been optimized for Tableau using the Tableau Data Engine. When you go to publish a workbook to Tableau Server, data extracts and live connections will be embedded in the workbook. Unlike published data sources, **embedded data sources** can only be used in the workbook in which they are published.

Choosing a data connection type

If you choose to embed a data extract in your workbook, and you publish it to Tableau Server, you can create extract refresh schedules so that the data will refresh automatically according to the selected date and time. You can even create multiple refresh schedules for a single workbook or data source, such as every month on the first day of the month and every Wednesday.

> **Note**
> You can create a data extract in a workbook and then publish only the data source to Tableau Server to create a published data source. Just like any data extract, you can set up an extract refresh schedule for the data source once it has been published to Tableau Server.

Extracts are particularly useful for large datasets or slow connections because they increase performance and reduce the load on your organization's databases. If you are using an extract, you can even continue your analysis in Tableau Desktop in the event that your organization experiences a temporary server outage. You may find that you use extracts the majority of the time and rarely have a reason to use a live connection. Depending on your organization and the resources available to your development team, you may even be directed to avoid live connections altogether.

When deciding between a live data connection or a data extract, we generally recommend using a data extract, unless you have a very specific need to query live data. If you believe that you need to use a live connection, it would be wise to consult your Tableau Server administrators and any data governance teams at your organization first.

> **Note**
> You must create a data extract before publishing a workbook to Tableau Public.

When deciding between an embedded extract or a published data source, you will have to consider the unique circumstances of your assignment or workbook and your organization's data practices. Embedded extracts may be the most efficient option for a single workbook, but if the data source could potentially be used in numerous workbooks, then you should consider using or creating a published data source. This is because if you have the same data embedded in multiple workbooks, the overall cost in terms of storage on Tableau Server and query load from the original databases may be too great relative to the payoff in individual workbook performance. As always, when in doubt, consult your Tableau Server administrator.

Choosing a refresh schedule

Choosing when to refresh your data extract does not have to be complicated, but there are a few things to consider that could make the decision easier for you and the outcome better for your organization:

- When the data in your original database refreshes
- What the peak demand times are for your Tableau Server environment
- How the priority number will affect the timing of the refresh time

We will briefly review each of these considerations.

Considering when the data in your original database refreshes

It is important to understand when the data in your original database refreshes so that you have the most recent and relevant data available before your data extract refreshes.

For example, if you schedule a Tableau extract refresh for every Monday at 8:00 a.m. but your Oracle database does not refresh its data until Monday at 10:00 a.m., then your Tableau extract will not have the most recent information, because it was not available in the original database when the extract ran. Understanding when your underlying database updates and selecting an appropriate extract refresh time accordingly may save you a headache and may even prevent a question from an end user wondering why your dashboard is out of date.

> **Tip**
> Even if you know when the underlying database should be updated, we find it helpful to allow a few hours of buffer time between the database update time and your extract refresh scheduled time. This way, if there is a delay in your organization's database refresh process, it has a chance to resolve itself prior to when your extract refresh begins.

Considering what the peak demand times are for your Tableau Server environment

We recommend selecting an extract refresh time that occurs when the server is less busy. For example, if the majority of your organization's data teams and Tableau developers work from 9:00 a.m. to 5:00 p.m., then the server will probably be quite busy during those hours. Instead of scheduling your data extract to refresh every Monday at 9:00 a.m., you could request it to be refreshed every Sunday at 10:00 p.m. or every Monday at 3:00 a.m. As long as the underlying database has been updated prior to the time you select, your data extract should reflect the most current data available in the database. Selecting a non-peak refresh time can help with the refresh speed and can potentially avoid connection or timeout failures that can occur with a busy server.

Considering how the priority number will affect the refresh time

In *Chapter 6, Navigating Content Pages in Tableau Server*, you learned that each extract refresh gets assigned a priority number, ranging from 1 to 100. The lower the number, the higher the priority. It is important to understand that the time you select your extract to be refreshed is the time that your extract goes into a queue of other server jobs, such as data extracts. Put simply, jobs currently in process will run first, followed by manually initiated jobs (when **Run Now** is selected from the **Actions** menu), followed by the highest priority jobs (starting with the lowest priority number). Because **Run Now** essentially jumps the line, it is important to be aware of its potential downstream impact and to be courteous of other Tableau Server users who have jobs in the queue. If you don't have this option available, it's possible that your organization may have chosen to disable this feature for this very reason.

> **Note**
> Tableau provides a detailed breakdown of the Tableau Server job prioritization at `https://help.tableau.com/current/server/en-us/task_prioritization.htm`.

This means that an extract that is scheduled to refresh at 2:00 p.m. may not be completed right at 2:00 p.m. The speed with which your organization's instance of Tableau Server runs jobs is dependent on many factors that are too advanced to explore in this book. Experience at your organization will give you an idea of what is normal for you to expect, and it may be helpful to discuss with your Tableau Server administrator or other teammates.

Refreshing your data is generally a straightforward task. We hope that these recommendations help you to be able to "set it and forget it" and avoid revisiting your refresh schedule selection over and over or using a non-optimal connection type.

In the next section, you will learn more about creating efficient data sources and workbooks by improving their performance.

Improving performance

When end users are interacting with content on Tableau Server, such as a dashboard, it is important to consider the user experience, much like you would when building a website. This means considering how clearly the information is presented, how easy the tool is to navigate, and how quickly the information can load with each click.

According to UX Planet (`https://uxplanet.org/how-page-speed-affects-web-user-experience-83b6d6b1d7d7`), 0.1 to 1 second is the ideal load time for a web page, and 10 seconds is the longest a user is willing to wait before performing other tasks or leaving the website. Other sources suggest that you only have 1-2 seconds before a large portion of the audience abandons the page. Although your business partners or end users may have more patience waiting for a dashboard to load because of their need for the specific data than the average person browsing the internet, it is still important to keep user experience in mind when developing content for Tableau Server. If users get frustrated using your dashboards or waiting for them to load, they will be less likely to use them and more likely to seek alternative reporting.

There is an overwhelming number of ways you can seek to improve workbook and data source performance. In this section, we will discuss tips we have personally found to be helpful and then will introduce you to a detailed resource for further learning.

Analyzing performance in Tableau Desktop

An often overlooked feature available in Tableau Desktop is **Performance Recording**. This tool records various performance events as you interact with your workbook, including query execution, data source connections, layout computations, and more.

Once you complete a performance recording, a temporary workbook will open that contains the performance results. You can use the performance results to determine what is slowing down your workbook and optimize performance. The results workbook contains two primary dashboards. The first dashboard shown in *Figure 9.17* is a **Performance Summary** dashboard that is meant to provide an overview.

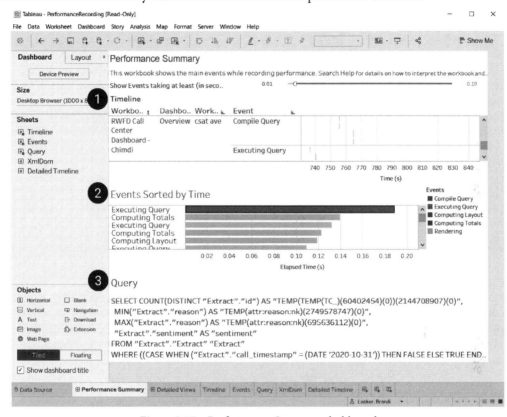

Figure 9.17 – Performance Summary dashboard

The **Performance Summary** dashboard contains the following views:

1. The **Timeline** view provides a chronological account of events that occurred during the recording, with results shown by **Workbook**, **Dashboard**, **Worksheet**, and **Event** columns. The chart indicates the duration of each event relative to the other events.

2. The **Events Sorted by Time** view shows the duration of each event, sorted in order of longest duration to shortest duration. This chart is color-coded by event type.

3. The **Query** view is blank until you click on an **Executing Query** event in either the **Timeline** or **Events** view. This view will display the query text. If using a published data source, the query text is shown in XML. If using an embedded data source, the query text is shown in SQL.

The second dashboard is called **Detailed Views**. This dashboard is only available when the performance recording workbook is opened in Tableau Desktop and is intended to assist advanced users during the workbook design process. Because this book is intended for beginners using Tableau Server, we will not discuss the **Detailed Views** dashboard in depth.

> **Note**
>
> Keep in mind that if a workbook is slow in Tableau Desktop, it will be slow on Tableau Server. We recommend using the performance recording feature to help you troubleshoot slow workbooks. You can learn how to run a performance recording and read more about analyzing the results at `https://help.tableau.com/current/pro/desktop/en-us/perf_record_create_desktop.htm`.

Optimizing the data source

The first step to analyzing and visualizing data is to establish a dataset and connect to it. Therefore, it would be beneficial to ensure that your data is optimized and that you do everything within your power to create an efficient data source and/or workbook.

Using tall data

In order to optimize data for Tableau, one of the most important things to understand is how to structure the data. Tableau prefers data that is stored in rows and columns, such as a spreadsheet. The key is that a tall format with fewer columns and more rows works best with Tableau instead of a wider format with many columns and fewer rows.

An example of a wide dataset is shown in *Figure 9.18*. Wide datasets are common in spreadsheets and are usually designed for people to read. This is not optimal for Tableau.

	A	B	C	D	E	F	
1	Date	Apples	Bananas	Grapes	Kiwis	Oranges	
2	1/1/2021	38	23	27	38	32	
3	1/2/2021	40	35	26	41	27	
4	1/3/2021	27	22	25	28	27	
5	1/4/2021	29	33	17	35	20	
6	1/5/2021	39	19	23	24	31	
7	1/6/2021	19	39	30	31	20	
8	1/7/2021	16	18	29	43	44	
9	1/8/2021	39	18	30	15	22	
10	1/9/2021	31	41	44	19	26	
11	1/10/2021	23	36	20	33	18	
12							
13							
14							
15							

Fruit Sales (lbs)

Figure 9.18 – Example of wide spreadsheet data

An example of a tall dataset optimized for Tableau is shown in *Figure 9.19*.

	A	B	C	
1	Date	Fruit	Sold (lbs)	
2	1/1/2021	Apples	38	
3	1/1/2021	Bananas	23	
4	1/1/2021	Grapes	27	
5	1/1/2021	Kiwis	38	
6	1/1/2021	Oranges	32	
7	1/2/2021	Apples	40	
8	1/2/2021	Bananas	35	
9	1/2/2021	Grapes	26	
10	1/2/2021	Kiwis	41	
11	1/2/2021	Oranges	27	
12	1/3/2021	Apples	27	
13	1/3/2021	Bananas	22	
14	1/3/2021	Grapes	25	
15	1/3/2021	Kiwis	28	
16	1/3/2021	Oranges	27	
17	1/4/2021	Apples	29	
18	1/4/2021	Bananas	33	
19	1/4/2021	Grapes	17	
20	1/4/2021	Kiwis	35	
21	1/4/2021	Oranges	20	
22	1/5/2021	Apples	39	

Fruit Sales (lbs)

Figure 9.19 – Example of tall spreadsheet data

If you are using a Microsoft Excel, text file, Google Sheets, or `.pdf` data source, and have no control over how the data is structured, you can use the pivot feature in Tableau Desktop to format the data in a columnar format. *Figure 9.20* shows how this example data looks in Tableau Desktop originally, in a wide format, and how to correct this. To pivot the data, select the columns that need adjusting and click the small arrow that appears in the top-right corner of a column. The arrow will appear when you hover over one of the selected columns. From the menu that opens, click **Pivot**.

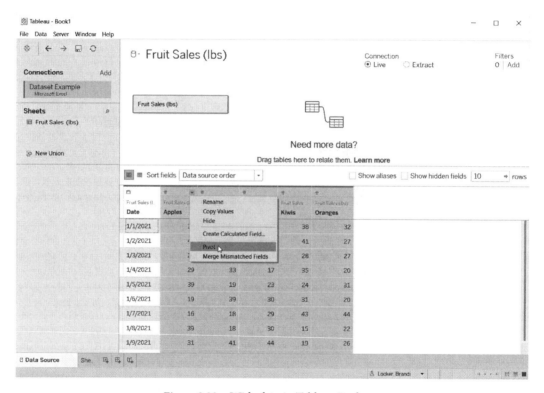

Figure 9.20 – Wide data in Tableau Desktop

Figure 9.21 shows how this same data looks after a pivot has been applied.

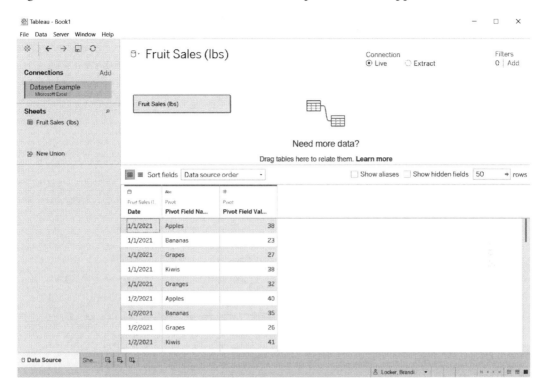

Figure 9.21 – Pivoted data

If you are using another data source type that is not compatible with this pivot feature, you can read about how to use custom SQL to pivot your data at `https://help.tableau.com/current/pro/desktop/en-us/pivot.htm#Pivot`.

Using efficient queries

Tableau is designed so that you can connect to data and analyze it without having to know how to write advanced SQL queries. You can use Tableau to connect to multiple data tables and combine them using joins, unions, and relationships. Tableau actually generates its own **VizQL** behind the scenes to query data for you.

However, sometimes there is a need to use the **Custom SQL** feature within Tableau. If you have the ability to write your own SQL, it is helpful to understand how to write an efficient query.

One easy way to optimize the query is to simply not bring in unnecessary data. It can be tempting to query all of the available fields from a data table or to bring in additional fields "just in case" you may need them later. However, doing this can result in a complex query that may even have extra table joins to bring in that additional data. If you do not need a particular field to use in your analysis, then it is best to not add it to the query. You can always add it to the query later on if you discover that a field is missing.

> **Note**
>
> It also helps to keep in mind that because Tableau is still running VizQL in the background, using custom SQL generates a double-query as you use Tableau. It is optimal to avoid using custom SQL and instead connect directly to data tables.

Cleaning your extracts

Another simple way to enhance the performance of a data extract in Tableau is to hide any unused fields. When you first connect to the data for analysis, you may not yet know what fields you need to create your visualizations. However, after you have completed the development of your Tableau workbook, hiding unused fields allows you to reduce the size of the data extract, which should boost performance.

> **Note**
>
> You may or may not wish to do this with a published data source. A refined data source will refresh more quickly, but you may prefer to leave all of the original fields in the data so that other users can explore what is available. Alternatively, a simplified and curated data source is a great way to manage data integrity throughout your organization. The needs of your organization will be key to making this decision.

To hide unused fields, find the **Data** pane on the left side of the Tableau Desktop window and click on the small, downward arrow in the top-right corner of the **Data** pane. From the drop-down menu shown in *Figure 9.22*, click on the **Hide All Unused Fields** option.

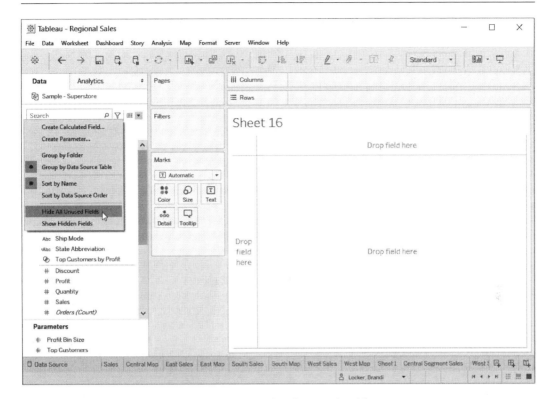

Figure 9.22 – Hide All Unused Fields

Clicking this option will hide any field that is not used in the workbook. You can also click on the option directly below it, **Show Hidden Fields**, to unhide any fields.

After the extra fields are hidden, you are ready to refresh the data extract and publish the workbook to Tableau Server.

Optimizing workbook and dashboard designs

You learned a few tips to help optimize data source performance earlier in this chapter. It is equally important to learn how to optimize the workbook and data visualizations using that data.

More marks mean more time

It shouldn't really surprise us that the more complicated something is, the longer it takes to process. When you add measures and dimensions to a worksheet, you are adding marks to the view. A mark is how Tableau displays data. Adding more marks to a view requires more processing power and uses more memory to render all the marks. Put simply, the more "stuff" on a worksheet, the longer it takes to load and the more resources it consumes.

You can check the number of marks used in your worksheet by looking at the lower-left corner of the Tableau Desktop window. *Figure 9.23* indicates where to see how many marks are used. In this view, there are seven marks – one for each day's average room rate at a resort.

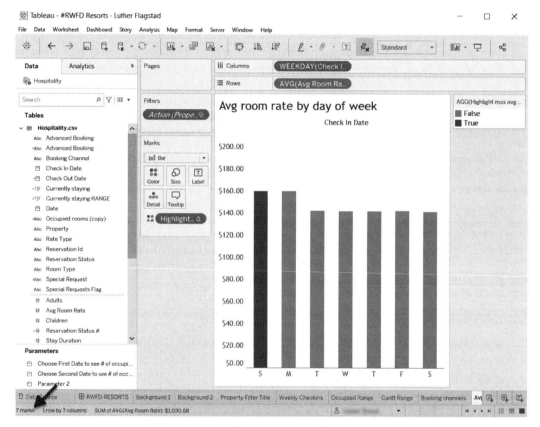

Figure 9.23 – Marks counter in Tableau Desktop

Workbook and view created by Luther Flagstad

There is no right or wrong answer for how many marks are considered too many marks. The number of marks will be influenced by factors such as your data and the granularity of the view.

Because a higher number of marks requires more processing power and memory, we recommend using crosstabs, or tabular views, sparingly. It can be easy to default to creating a view that mimics a spreadsheet, particularly if that is what your organization has primarily used to visualize data in the past. You may even experience pressure from users and leaders within your organization to create these tabular views.

However, crosstabs traditionally require a higher number of marks to be shown on the view. They also add visual clutter for the user and can make analyzing the data a slower, less effective process. Tableau's strength is in aggregating data and enabling you to visualize information for quick insights. We recommend that you take advantage of some of its key features, such as action filters, to connect related views that allow the user to explore the data in an interactive way.

Cleaning workbooks after development

Once you finish creating a dashboard, it is tempting to publish the workbook as is and share it with others. However, the development process can be messy. Spending a few extra minutes to clean up a workbook can help performance and can help prevent any confusion from teammates who may need to use or edit your workbook in the future.

In the previous section, you learned about hiding unused fields in your workbook. This is one way to clean up the file. Another way is to delete unused worksheets, calculations, groups, sets, or parameters. While it may seem trivial, these items all use resources and make the file size larger. Removing unused details from your workbook reduces the amount of information that Tableau has to process and load.

Another recommendation is to give worksheets meaningful names. When you add a new sheet in Tableau, the default name will be Sheet 1, Sheet 2, Sheet 3, and so on. When you are designing multiple dashboards within a single workbook, you could end up having 20, 50, 70, or even 100 or more worksheets within your workbook. Failing to take the time to give these worksheets meaningful names early in the process will make things very frustrating later when you are searching for a specific worksheet. You don't want to be trying to remember whether the worksheet you are looking for is Sheet 45, Sheet 72, or something in between. It would be best to name each sheet according to its content, such as "Sales by State bar chart." This may seem like an obvious tip, but we've seen the pitfalls of failing to rename worksheets many times.

Along with renaming worksheets comes renaming calculations. You may remember what "Calculation6" does as you are working through your analysis and it is fresh in your mind, but you do not want to be digging through all of the calculations to refresh your memory in 6 months when a user has a question about a number on your dashboard. Trust us – save yourself the trouble later and give your calculations a useful name now.

We also recommend organizing your worksheets. Not only does this include deleting unneeded worksheets and giving worksheets meaningful names, but it also includes arranging them in a helpful way. For example, when you have multiple dashboards, one potential sorting method is to group worksheets that belong to the same dashboard together. You could even add color-coding to help differentiate worksheets in a visual way. Dashboards could be placed at the beginning of the list of sheets, at the end, or grouped with the corresponding worksheets.

You can move sheets around by dragging and dropping sheets to rearrange their order. This method works regardless of whether you are viewing the worksheets using tabs, the filmstrip, or the sheet sorter view shown in *Figure 9.24*. This screenshot illustrates a workbook that contains a single dashboard with its worksheets organized in order of their appearance on the dashboard from top to bottom, approximately.

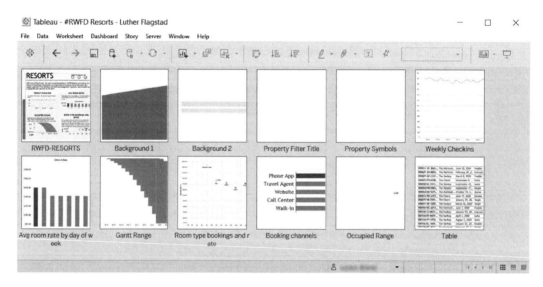

Figure 9.24 – Sheet sorter view to arrange worksheets

Workbook created by Luther Flagstad

For an extra clean look, you can hide the worksheets that are used in a dashboard by right-clicking on a dashboard tab and selecting **Hide All Sheets**. This can reduce some of the visual clutter in a workbook and help you find other workbook components faster.

Anyone who has had to take over the work of a fellow Tableau developer can probably remember the frustration that comes with inheriting someone else's work. We all approach problem-solving differently and have a unique creative process. It can be hard to look at someone else's work and pick up where that person left off. We've even struggled when revisiting our own work after a long period of time has passed. Following the tips presented in this section will make things easier for you in the future, and for your teammates.

For a more intensive look into how to improve your Tableau workbook performance, you will benefit greatly from reading the *Designing Efficient Workbooks* whitepaper found at `https://www.tableau.com/learn/whitepapers/designing-efficient-workbooks`. This invaluable resource will give you more insight into how Tableau functions and is full of tips to help you improve your Tableau data sources and workbooks.

Tableau also has a convenient checklist full of additional resources to help you learn more about improving performance and optimizing your work. You can find the checklist at `https://help.tableau.com/current/pro/desktop/en-us/perf_checklist.htm`.

Summary

In this chapter, you learned how to implement RLS to manage who can access specific data within a data source or workbook. You also learned our recommendations to create meaningful naming conventions, to select the appropriate data connection type for each situation, and to understand some of the considerations when selecting a data extract refresh schedule. Finally, you learned some of our recommendations for improving the performance of your data sources and workbooks and have a few suggested resources for further learning.

In the next and final chapter, you will find additional resources to continue learning about data visualization and Tableau.

10
Conclusion

Tableau Server is an extremely powerful and valuable tool. When leveraged properly, it can help you increase the utilization of the content on your server, seamlessly manage everyday tasks behind the scenes, manage the security of your data, and can help organize content and share analytic insights throughout your organization.

Tableau Public provides a way for anyone to practice and improve their data visualization skills and get involved with the Tableau community. Doing so will not only sharpen your skillset for your benefit and career potential, but it will also benefit your organization when you apply the data visualization skills you have learned to your daily work.

In this chapter, we will review what you have learned throughout this book and provide suggested resources that will help you further your skills in data visualization, Tableau Desktop, and Tableau Server.

In this chapter, we will cover the following topics:

- What you have learned
- Why and how to get involved with the Tableau community
- Where to find data for personal projects
- Additional resources
- Thank you

What you have learned

We hope this book has helped reveal many of the major benefits of Tableau Server to regular everyday users. Understanding how to leverage this platform will help you communicate information through data and drive better analytical insights. If this book has helped you get up and running with Tableau Server, increased end user engagement with content, and reduced redundant tasks, then it has accomplished its goals.

In this book, you explored Tableau Server's structure and learned how to get started by getting connected, publishing content, and navigating the software interface. You also explored how to interact with the Tableau Server interface to efficiently locate, sort, filter, manage, and customize content. Later, you discovered how to leverage valuable features that enable you and your audience to share, download, edit, and interact with content on Tableau Server. You even learned how to automate repetitive tasks by utilizing features such as alerts, subscriptions, and data-extract-refresh schedules.

It is our sincere hope that the knowledge in this book will aid you in your career and that it continue to serve as a useful reference guide. We would like to leave you with some additional information and resources to help you if you would like to continue your Tableau journey.

Why and how to get involved with the Tableau community

One of the most important things that sets Tableau apart is its community. We have personally never used another piece of software that has as robust of a community as Tableau. The Tableau community is made up of Tableau users who are eager to learn more and support others. They range from complete novices to recognized experts and have a variety of skillsets. They are passionate about data analytics, visualizing information, networking, and building relationships. They help and encourage each other, challenge one another, share ideas and information, and inspire one another to help elevate the graphicacy and data literacy of those involved. These data-literate individuals help propagate this new knowledge throughout their respective organizations and groups.

Why get involved?

It can be intimidating to try and enter a new community, particularly if you are new to using the software or are not confident in your skillset yet. However, this is exactly why it is so beneficial to get involved. The Tableau community is key in helping you develop your technical and professional skills by providing a place to get inspiration for new ideas, feedback on your work, learn about the possibilities of what can be created in Tableau, and find help when you get stuck.

Connecting with the Tableau community means learning from the best. Every year, Tableau recognizes exemplary leaders within the community that have demonstrated mastery of the software and who regularly collaborate with and teach others. These select few are honored with the title of **Tableau Zen Master**.

Tableau also recognizes ambassadors every year. **Tableau Ambassadors** embody the spirit of the Tableau community by fostering a positive environment and a safe place for everyone to learn, share ideas, and have meaningful conversations. They promote new ideas, recent community members, and elevate the overall community experience.

Throughout the year, the Tableau Public team partners with Tableau Public Ambassadors to select and spotlight talented members of the community. These members are called **Featured Authors**. These individuals are showcased on the Tableau Public website, on the **Authors** page. This is a great way to learn about and connect with other community members.

Choosing to get involved with the community means that you get the chance to network with some of the brightest Tableau users and creators. It also means that you have a place to turn to when you are discouraged or need help and a place to connect with and encourage others. The Tableau community would not be what it is without the dedication and generosity of others, so as you learn from them, be sure to provide credit to those that have helped and inspired you. We also encourage you to give back to the community when you can by sharing your knowledge and experiences.

How to get involved

If you are ready to start your journey into the Tableau community, you may be wondering how to even begin. Without a little guidance, figuring out how to join the community can be a daunting task. We hope to make this easier for you by outlining the most popular resources and sharing our experiences with each of them.

It is important to keep in mind that it may take a while to feel "plugged in" with the community. It takes time to build relationships with others, and like many things, the more time and effort you invest, the greater your results will be. Those who regularly engage with others, encourage others, and participate in conversations, challenges, or events, are more likely to feel connected. We encourage you to be bold and reach out to others for help or advice when you need it.

The wonderful thing about the Tableau community is that you have control over the level of involvement that you are willing to commit to. If connecting with others feels like too much for you at this time, then rest assured that you can still benefit from the community resources mentioned in this chapter. There are blogs, how-to videos, webinars, and more to help you improve your technical skills in Tableau.

There are many ways you can get connected with the Tableau Community, but first things first: create a Tableau Public profile if you haven't already and download the software to get started. Keep reading to learn how.

Tableau Public

In *Chapter 2, How to Connect and Publish to Tableau Server*, we dedicated two full sections to Tableau Public. We discussed what Tableau Public is and how to create a Tableau Public profile. This section will focus on more of the benefits of creating a Tableau Public profile.

Let's quickly review what Tableau Public is. Tableau Public is a free platform that allows you to create an online public portfolio to showcase and store your data visualizations. Creating a Tableau Public profile is a great way to gain inspiration, discover what is possible in dashboard design, demystify how something was created, and network with other community members.

Use the following link to sign up and create a Tableau Public profile:

`https://public.tableau.com`.

An easy way to find inspiration is to follow other authors on Tableau Public. The following screenshot shows the **Follow** button, which you can click to track another Tableau author once you have created your profile:

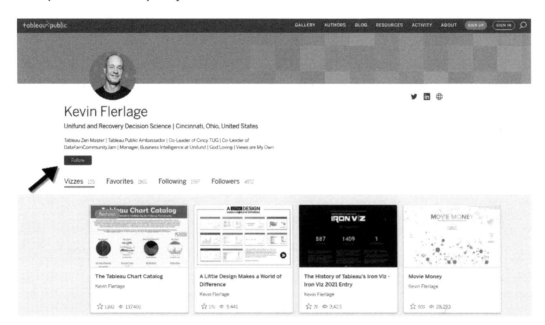

Figure 10.1 – Follow button on Tableau Public

Tableau Public profile of Kevin Flerlage

The **Activity** tab on Tableau Public will alert you to what the authors in your network have recently **favorited** and **published**. The following screenshot shows the **Activity** page on Tableau Public:

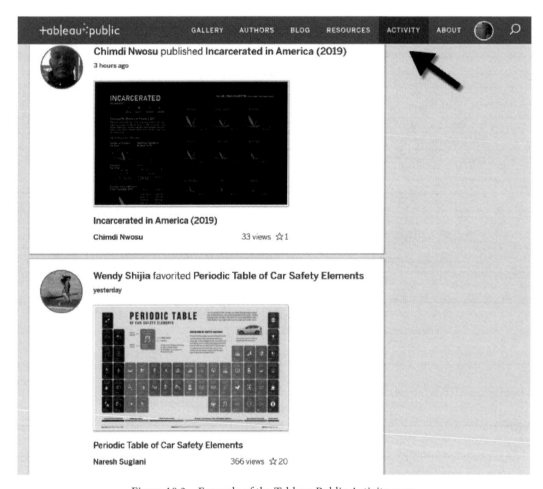

Figure 10.2 – Example of the Tableau Public Activity page

Once you see a Viz that you love, consider marking it as a favorite on Tableau Public. This will allow you to quickly find it for future reference, inspiration, or to see how something was accomplished. The following screenshot shows the star icon you can click to add a Viz to your **Favorites** under your Tableau Public profile:

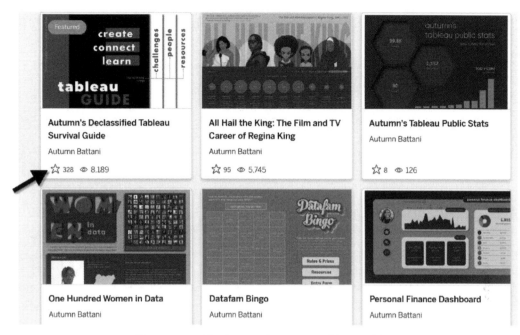

Figure 10.3 – The Favorite button on Tableau Public

Tableau Public Dashboards created by Autumn Battani

Another great learning feature of Tableau Public is the ability to demystify most visualizations on Tableau Public by using either the **Make a copy** or **Download** icon. This helps reverse engineer how something was created on a dashboard by dissecting it in your browser using web authoring on Tableau Public or as a downloaded workbook. It is a common courtesy among Tableau Public authors to allow other community members to see how a dashboard was created. The following screenshot shows the location of the **Make a copy** icon on the Tableau Public dashboard page:

Figure 10.4 – Make a copy icon on the Tableau Public dashboard

The following screenshot shows the location of the **Download** icon on the Tableau Public dashboard page:

Figure 10.5 – The Download button on the Tableau Public dashboard

There are many other benefits of Tableau Public, but let's review a few more great reasons to create a profile. Signing up for **Viz of the Day** will provide you with an email notification of an amazing example of a recent work created by a community member. The **Authors** page will show you a list of the most recent Tableau Public Featured Authors. This is a group of talented data Viz individuals who have been selected by Tableau Public Ambassadors and the Tableau Public team that you should consider following. Lastly, under the **Resources** page, there are how-to videos and sample data for you to explore.

If you don't have access to Tableau Desktop yet, Tableau Public allows you to download a free Desktop version or create visualizations directly from your web browser through Tableau Public's web authoring feature. These options will give you access to the software's capabilities, only with fewer data source connection options.

Use the following link to download a free Desktop version of Tableau Public:

`https://public.tableau.com/en-us/s/download`.

If you find that you enjoy using Tableau at work and want to improve your skills or learn more, consider signing up and starting a Tableau Public profile of your own.

Tableau Community Hub

There was a time when the Tableau community was shared primarily by word-of-mouth, social media, or maybe you would discover a new community initiative by attending a webinar. Now, Tableau has created a thorough resource for you, known as the **Community Hub**, as shown in the following screenshot:

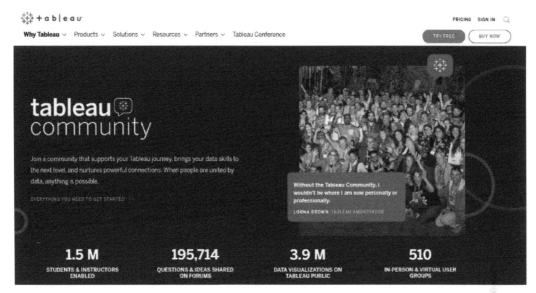

Figure 10.6 – The Tableau Community Hub website

The Community Hub is a centralized location on the Tableau website that features some of the most commonly used and helpful community resources and content. It is curated and organized by Tableau to help you filter through the massive amounts of information out there. It is an amazing resource to bookmark for yourself and to share with those who are new to Tableau and trying to improve their skills.

The Community Hub highlights the latest blogs and events, showcases community member profiles, and provides links to community programs and community data initiatives. In this section, we will discuss many of these resources and the opportunities available to you, starting with the data initiatives.

You can find the Community Hub at `https://www.tableau.com/community`. To learn more about the Community Hub, we suggest reading this Tableau blog post introducing the Community Hub, written by *Stephanie Richardson*: `https://www.tableau.com/about/blog/2021/2/announcing-tableau-community-hub`.

At the bottom of the Community Hub website, you will find a link to the *Tableau Community Code of Conduct*. The Code of Conduct gives you an idea of what is expected from everyone who chooses to participate in the community. It is centered around kindness, respect, and giving appropriate credit to others. These are important principles to embrace to keep the community a safe and positive space for everyone.

Community projects

Tableau community projects are created and led by members of the Tableau community, who host data challenges or opportunities for community members to practice and improve their knowledge of Tableau and data visualization in general. The community projects generally center around a theme, such as a social cause or challenge type, and are available regularly throughout the year. Community projects are an excellent way to test your knowledge and challenge yourself to learn new concepts.

This section will provide a list of community projects currently available and details surrounding their theme or topic, frequency, website, Twitter hashtag, and a brief synopsis of the project.

Makeover Monday

- *Theme/Topic*: Subject matter varies from week to week
- *Frequency*: Weekly
- *Website*: `https://www.makeovermonday.co.uk/`
- *Twitter Hashtag*: **#MakeoverMonday**

Synopsis: A link to a visualization in need of improvement and its dataset is provided each week. The challenge of the initiative is to develop a better version of the original visualization using the dataset provided. You can receive feedback from the Makeover Monday leaders and other participants. Additionally, previous Makeover Monday challenges are a good source for clean datasets on a diverse array of topics.

Iron Quest

- *Theme/Topic*: Subject matter varies from month to month
- *Frequency*: Monthly
- *Website*: `https://sarahlovesdata.co.uk/tag/ironquest/`
- *Twitter Hashtag*: **#IronQuest**

Synopsis: A new project theme is selected each month, and you are responsible for finding your own datasets to showcase your analytics, design, and storytelling abilities. Some past themes have included food and drink, sea creatures, crime data, maps, and designing for mobile phones. This community initiative was created with a similar format to the Tableau Iron Viz feeder competitions and, as a result, serves as a great way to prepare for it.

Project Health Viz

- *Theme/Topic*: Healthcare
- *Frequency*: Monthly
- *Website*: `https://vizzendata.com/projecthealthviz`
- *Twitter Hashtag*: **#projecthealthviz**

Synopsis: A new dataset themed around a healthcare topic is provided each month. Some previous healthcare datasets include global emissions, alcohol use, prostate cancer, and the causes of child mortality. A monthly blog by the initiative leaders reviewing the submissions is posted the following month.

Real World Fake Data

- *Theme/Topic*: Business
- *Frequency*: Monthly
- *Website*: `http://sonsofhierarchies.com/real-world-fake-data/`
- *Twitter Hashtag*: **#RWFD**

Synopsis: This is a community initiative that provides business datasets with phony data. The goal of this project is to create and share good examples of business dashboards for different industries on Tableau Public. If you need ideas when creating a business dashboard for work, try searching for **#RWFD** on Tableau Public for inspiration. Lastly, most of the dashboard examples featured in this book were from authors who participated in this initiative and were gracious enough to allow us to share their amazing work.

Sports Viz Sunday

- *Theme/Topic*: Sports
- *Frequency*: Monthly
- *Website*: `https://www.sportsvizsunday.com/`
- *Twitter Hashtag*: **#SportsVizSunday**

Synopsis: A sports-themed dataset is provided by the Sports Viz Sunday team each month. Prior sports datasets included Formula 1 racing data, Kentucky Derby results since 1875, PGA and LPGA prize money, and every shot taken in the NBA since the 1997/1998 season. A weekly roundup blog post is written by a member of the Sports Viz Sunday team highlighting the week's submissions.

Storytelling with Data

- *Theme/Topic*: Subject matter varies from month to month
- *Frequency*: Monthly
- *Website*: `https://community.storytellingwithdata.com/`
- *Twitter Hashtag*: **#SWDchallenge**

Synopsis: You are given a new data challenge that's created by the **Story Telling with Data** (**SWD**) team each month. The data visualization challenges are tool-agnostic, meaning that you can create your visualization in any tool. Challenges are posted on the SWD website and you can receive feedback from both the SWD team and community if you submit a visualization.

The Sustainable Development Goals (SDG) Viz Project data

- *Theme/Topic*: Sustainable Development Goals
- *Frequency*: Monthly
- *Website*: `https://thesdgvizproject.com/`
- *Twitter Hashtag*: **#TheSDGVizProject**

Synopsis: The goal is to use social media and data visualization to help promote and raise awareness of Sustainable Development Goals. A dataset that helps promote these project initiatives is provided by the SDG team each month. Previous challenges include datasets on affordable clean energy, climate action, gender equality, and clean water and sanitation. A monthly blog post is written by the SDG team highlighting that month's submissions and what was learned.

Viz for Social Good

- *Theme/Topic*: Non-profit organizations
- *Frequency*: As projects with non-profit organizations become available
- *Website*: `https://www.vizforsocialgood.com`
- *Twitter Hashtag*: **#VizforSocialGood**

Synopsis: This project uses datasets provided by non-profit organizations. This challenge aims to help non-profits visualize their data so that they can promote their cause on their website, social media, press releases, and more. Previous projects include work for Bridges to Prosperity, Academics Without Borders, and UNICEF.

Workout Wednesday

- *Theme/Topic*: Challenges vary from week to week

- *Frequency*: Weekly

- *Website*: `http://www.workout-wednesday.com/`

- *Twitter Hashtag*: **#WOW2021**

Synopsis: You are provided with a new data analytics-related problem to solve every Wednesday. These weekly challenges are a great way to learn new skills and features in Tableau and Power BI. The challenge levels range from intermediate to advanced.

Twitter #datafam

Joining Twitter may be one of the easiest and most impactful decisions you can make to enhance your Tableau skills. The Tableau community on Twitter is an amazing way to connect with other data professionals, find inspiration, constantly learn new things, and, most importantly, enter a global community that is overwhelmingly positive and supportive.

If you don't already have a Twitter account, don't worry. It's easy to set up, and we recommend that you create an account that is specifically focused on networking within the data visualization community.

Use the following link to set up a Twitter account:

`https://twitter.com/i/flow/signup.`

The following are a few recommendations you should consider after creating a Twitter account for Tableau/data visualization:

- Make it clear that your Twitter account is for Tableau by indicating that you are interested in Tableau and/or data visualization in your profile description.

- Find and follow some inspirational or informative Tableau Zen Masters.

  List of Tableau Zen Masters on Twitter:

  `https://twitter.com/tableau/lists/tableau-zen-masters`

- Find and follow some inspirational or informative Tableau Ambassadors.

  List of Tableau Ambassadors on Twitter: `https://twitter.com/tableau/lists/tableau-ambassadors`

- Retweet interesting/valuable posts from individuals that you follow.

- Participate in community initiatives (for example, Sports Viz Sunday, Makeover Monday, Real World Fake Data) and tweet your results (don't forget to use community initiative hashtags).

Don't get discouraged or upset if you don't become a viral data viz sensation overnight. If you remain consistent, you will slowly cultivate a group of followers who enjoy what you share or create and want you to succeed. Just keep engaging with people, sharing useful content, participating in initiatives, and adding value where you can, and good things will happen.

LinkedIn

Like Twitter, there is a Tableau community presence available on LinkedIn. Since the primary purpose of LinkedIn is professional networking, it is an excellent place to share your work on Tableau Public.

Your Tableau Public can be a place to store not only your fun, creative work but also a way to showcase your professional skills. By including a link to your Tableau Public profile on your LinkedIn profile, you are providing others with the opportunity to see what you can do with data. Sharing your work on LinkedIn is not only a way to draw attention to your work and connect with other community members – it can also open potential job opportunities for you as you grow in your career.

While we find the Tableau community on Twitter to be more robust and connected, we recommend utilizing both Twitter and LinkedIn simultaneously. When you publish a dashboard to Tableau Public, share it on both social media platforms! This gives you the most exposure and allows you to share your work with the largest audience. Doing this helps you get more connected with the Tableau community and helps you market your professional skills to potential employers.

When sharing content on LinkedIn, remember that you can include hashtags with each post. Hashtags help your post appear in other users' searches and give your post more exposure. Many of the hashtags that you may use on Twitter will also be effective on LinkedIn, such as **#Tableau**, **#TableauPublic**, and **#DataFam**.

It is also important to remember to credit any work or authors that inspired you or helped you when posting your work to LinkedIn. Doing this shows that you respect the community, are a team player, and may even help introduce someone else to a valuable resource for their learning.

Tableau User Groups

A **Tableau User Group (TUG)** is a group of users that come together to network and develop their Tableau skills. Attending a TUG is a great way to meet like-minded individuals and to learn and share new skills.

Groups are hosted by Tableau and led by members of the Tableau community. Many groups meet in person, but there are also virtual TUGs and hybrid groups that have both in-person and virtual events. Many companies have chosen to mimic these events and have created their own internal company TUGs. Most TUGs are based on geographic areas, but there are also groups for specific industries and initiatives, such as the Non-Profit Tableau User Group and the Veterans Advocacy Tableau User Group.

To find a TUG, you can use the Community Hub website or go directly to the **User Group** page at `https://www.tableau.com/community/user-groups`. This page, shown in the following screenshot, shows upcoming events and contains a weekly blog. You can also click on **Join a User Group** to find a list of all available groups. If you see an opportunity in the TUG offerings, you can even apply to **Start a User Group** from the same web page:

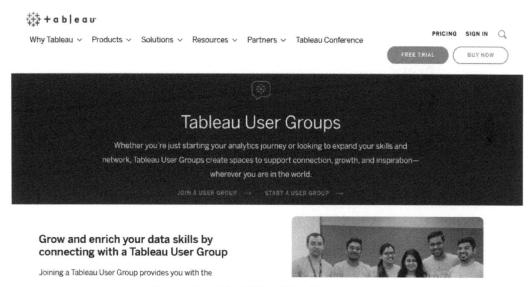

Figure 10.7 – The Tableau User Groups website

Virtual User Group events are recorded and published on the *Tableau Software* YouTube channel at `https://www.youtube.com/c/tableausoftware`. If you miss a session or want to watch a session again, you can always go to this channel, click on **Videos**, and search for the name of the user group that you are looking for. The video search feature is shown in the following screenshot:

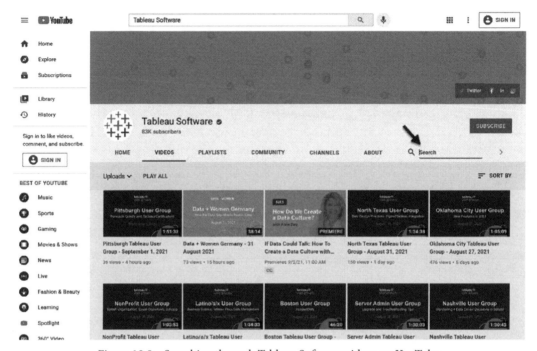

Figure 10.8 – Searching through Tableau Software videos on YouTube

There is also a link to the Virtual Tableau User Group playlist on the **User Group** page mentioned previously.

Getting involved with a TUG is one of the easiest ways for you to gain knowledge, network with others, and get involved with the Tableau community – either locally or virtually.

Tableau Conference

Tableau Conference is one of the world's leading data analytics conferences. It gathers thousands of members of the Tableau community to engage, present, share, discuss, interact, question, and learn from each other.

The first Tableau Conference occurred in 2008 at the Edgewater Hotel in Seattle, WA, and around 200 people attended it. By comparison, the Tableau Conference in 2019 was held at the Mandalay Bay Convention Center in Las Vegas, NV, and had around 20,000 people in attendance. That's a 9,900% increase in attendance in a little over a decade!

Tableau Conference is typically an in-person event that gathers thousands of Tableau users for 4 days of sessions, hands-on learning, meet-ups, certifications, keynotes, networking, and fun! The conference is organized so that you can select and attend sessions that are the most relevant to your skill level, industry, and role. This makes Tableau Conference valuable to both seasoned Tableau veterans and individuals who are completely new to the software.

Even a global pandemic couldn't stop the Tableau community from gathering, albeit online. In 2020, Tableau Conference went virtual due to COVID-19 and was held as a 100% free event that had more than 145,000 data enthusiasts register to attend.

Don't worry if you can't attend Tableau Conference – many of the sessions and keynotes are made available online. However, if you can attend, this conference is worth the trip. It packs more knowledge and fun into 4 days than most people receive in years of using the software.

Use the following link to learn more about Tableau Conference: `https://www.tableau.com/events/conference`.

Tableau Community Forums

Tableau Community Forums is an amazing place to ask Tableau-related questions and receive answers from experts. If you have a question or run into a problem while working with Tableau and enter your question into your favorite search engine, you will often find the answer to your question on a forum post. It's important to remember that the individuals helping you solve your Tableau-related problems through the forums are other community members who are just looking to help. Additionally, these forums can be a good way for people who are introverted to connect with other community members.

Use the following link to begin exploring Tableau Community Forums:

`https://community.tableau.com/s/explore-forums`.

The forums are a great place to search for answers to your questions, but if you can't find an answer, you can pose a question yourself. To add your question to a Tableau Community Forum, simply select the topic that your question relates to and click the **Ask A Question** button. An example of the resulting **Post To** pop-up window is shown in the following screenshot:

Figure 10.9 – Asking a question on the Tableau Community forums

> **Note**
> Don't worry if you have a question that touches on more than one topic – you can include additional topics before you submit your post. This option is located at the bottom of the **Post To** window, under **ADD TOPIC**.

Lastly, if you find benefit from these forums, consider giving back when you are comfortable by answering the questions of other community members in areas where you feel you can help or add value.

Where to find data for personal projects

One of the most challenging aspects of getting started when building a Tableau Public portfolio is finding data to use in your analysis. The good news is that there is a wealth of data out there – you just have to know where to look.

The following are some of our favorite places to find data sources:

- **Community data initiatives**: Initiatives such as #RWFD, as discussed in the previous section.

- `data.world`: Create a free community account to access 100,000+ open datasets.

- `kaggle.com`: Create a free account to access open datasets in a variety of formats.

- **Wikipedia**: Use this site to compile data sources or find tables of existing data. Note that tables of data copied from a web browser and pasted into a spreadsheet may contain hidden characters and present formatting and cleanup challenges.

- `catalog.data.gov`: An extensive catalog of open data available in multiple formats from the US government.

- `data.census.gov`: A collection of US Census data.

- `data.worldbank.org`: A robust catalog of open data for worldwide developmental measures.

- **Your data**: You can create data sources from data that's been collected with sleep trackers, step trackers, food and beverage trackers, and more. You can also catalog your data by taking inventory of various media (books, movies, and so on) or access your data using software such as Spotify or Twitter.

This is not by any means a comprehensive list of the data resources available to you, but it can get you started. We encourage you to be creative and explore other possibilities. For even more suggestions, be sure to check out this helpful blog written by *Jacob Olsufka*: `https://www.tableau.com/about/blog/2019/2/public-data-sets-102221`.

Additional resources

It would be impossible to list every helpful resource available as more content is created every day. This is another reason to get involved with the Tableau community. By getting plugged in, you will be made aware of new content and resources.

The following lists include some of our favorite and most recommended resources. We hope they serve you well.

Blogs

- Adam Mico: `https://adammico.medium.com`
- Data Muggle: `https://juditbekker.com`
- Playfair Data: `https://playfairdata.com/blog`
- Sons of Hierarchies: `http://sonsofhierarchies.com`
- The Flerlage Twins: `https://www.flerlagetwins.com`
- VizArtPandey: `https://vizartpandey.com`

Books

- *Avoiding Data Pitfalls* by Ben Jones
- *The Big Book of Dashboards* by Jeffrey Shaffer, Steve Wexler, Andy Cotgreave
- *The Big Picture* by Steve Wexler
- *How Charts Lie* by Alberto Cairo
- *Learning Tableau 2020* by Joshua N. Milligan
- *Practical Tableau* by Ryan Sleeper
- *Steal Like an Artist* by Austin Kleon
- *Storytelling with Data* by Cole Nussbaumer Knaflic

Podcasts

- Data + Love: `https://datapluslove.buzzsprout.com/`
- Data Viz Today: `https://dataviztoday.com/`
- Storytelling with Data: `https://www.storytellingwithdata.com/podcast`
- The Tableau World Podcast: `https://tableauwannabepodcast.libsyn.com/`

YouTube channels

- Andy Kriebel: `https://www.youtube.com/c/AndyKriebel`
- Sqlbelle: `https://www.youtube.com/c/sqlbelle`
- Tableau Software: `https://www.youtube.com/c/tableausoftware`
- Tableau Tim: `https://www.youtube.com/user/tfngwena`

Webinars

- Chart Chat: `https://www.datarevelations.com/chart-chat/`
- VizConnect: `https://community.tableau.com/s/vizconnect`

Thank you

We appreciate you reading this far. We hope that this book has helped you gain confidence in maximizing Tableau Server. Lastly, we hope this book has sparked an interest or fanned an existing flame regarding data analytics and data visualization.

Packt.com

Subscribe to our online digital library for full access to over 7,000 books and videos, as well as industry leading tools to help you plan your personal development and advance your career. For more information, please visit our website.

Why subscribe?

- Spend less time learning and more time coding with practical eBooks and Videos from over 4,000 industry professionals

- Improve your learning with Skill Plans built especially for you

- Get a free eBook or video every month

- Fully searchable for easy access to vital information

- Copy and paste, print, and bookmark content

Did you know that Packt offers eBook versions of every book published, with PDF and ePub files available? You can upgrade to the eBook version at packt.com and as a print book customer, you are entitled to a discount on the eBook copy. Get in touch with us at customercare@packtpub.com for more details.

At www.packt.com, you can also read a collection of free technical articles, sign up for a range of free newsletters, and receive exclusive discounts and offers on Packt books and eBooks.

Other Books You May Enjoy

If you enjoyed this book, you may be interested in these other books by Packt:

Tableau Prep Cookbook

Hendrik Kleine

ISBN: 978-1-80056-376-6

- Perform data cleaning and preparation techniques for advanced data analysis
- Understand how to combine multiple disparate datasets
- Prepare data for different Business Intelligence (BI) tools
- Apply Tableau Prep's calculation language to create powerful calculations
- Use Tableau Prep for ad hoc data analysis and data science flows
- Deploy Tableau Prep flows to Tableau Server and Tableau Online

Mastering Tableau 2021- Third Edition

Marleen Meier, David Baldwin

ISBN: 978-1-80056-164-9

- Get up to speed with various Tableau components
- Master data preparation techniques using Tableau Prep Builder
- Discover how to use Tableau to create a PowerPoint-like presentation
- Understand different Tableau visualization techniques and dashboard designs
- Interact with the Tableau server to understand its architecture and functionalities
- Study advanced visualizations and dashboard creation techniques
- Brush up on powerful self-service analytics, time series analytics, and geo-spatial analytics

Packt is searching for authors like you

If you're interested in becoming an author for Packt, please visit `authors.packtpub.com` and apply today. We have worked with thousands of developers and tech professionals, just like you, to help them share their insight with the global tech community. You can make a general application, apply for a specific hot topic that we are recruiting an author for, or submit your own idea.

Share Your Thoughts

Now you've finished *Maximizing Tableau Server*, we'd love to hear your thoughts! Scan the QR code below to go straight to the Amazon review page for this book and share your feedback or leave a review on the site that you purchased it from.

`https://packt.link/r/1801071136`

Your review is important to us and the tech community and will help us make sure we're delivering excellent quality content.

Index

T